BEATING
THE STREET

The Best-selling Author of *One Up on Wall Street*
Shows You How to Pick Winning Stocks and
Develop a Strategy for Mutual Funds

PETER LYNCH
with John Rothchild

A Fireside Book
Published by SIMON & SCHUSTER
New York   London   Toronto   Sydney   Tokyo   Singapore

FIRESIDE
Rockefeller Center
1230 Avenue of the Americas
New York, New York 10020

FIRESIDE and colophon are registered trademarks
of Simon & Schuster Inc.

Designed by Irving Perkins Associates
Manufactured in the United States of America

10 9 8 7 6 5 4 3 2 1   (pbk.)

Library of Congress Cataloging-in-Publication Data is available.

ISBN 0-671-75915-9
89163-4 (pbk.)

ACKNOWLEDGMENTS

To John Rothchild for his amazing talent, hard work, and good humor, which enabled *One Up on Wall Street* and *Beating the Street* to occur.

To Peggy Malaspina, who challenged every assumption and played a crucial role in shaping the ideas in both of these books; and to her research staff, who worked overtime assembling data and checking facts: Davida Sherman and Andrew Wolf, backed up by Michael Graber, Christine Coyne, Lyn Hadden, and Erik Masci.

To employees at Fidelity, particularly my associate Evelyn Flynn, but also Bob Hill and the staff of the Fidelity Chart Room, Guy Cerundolo, Bob Beckwitt, Lauren Allansmith, Phil Thayer, and Jacques Perold.

For searching out the facts, no one beats the dedicated staff of Fidelity's Fixed Income and Equity Research Information Centers, especially Shawn Bastien, Karen O'Toole, and Sheila Collins. Jeff Todd and Christopher Green in the Management Information and Analysis Group provided many of the charts and performance calculations.

Also thanks to editor Bob Bender, his assistant Johanna Li, copy supervisor Gypsy da Silva, and copy editor Steve Messina at Simon & Schuster.

This book would not have happened without the efforts of Doe Coover, a Boston literary agent who marshaled the proposal through its various stages.

John Rothchild thanks his agent, Elizabeth Darhansoff. He was assisted in Miami by Bruce Lemle, who plays a mean game of duplicate bridge.

DEDICATION

To my wife, Carolyn, and our daughters, Mary, Annie, and Beth. To my brothers, Eugene Lynch and Thomas Lynch, and my cousin Thomas Leahy.

CONTENTS

4 Contents

PREFACE

I turned off my Quotron at the Fidelity Magellan Fund on May 31, 1990. This was exactly 13 years from the day I took the job. Jimmy Carter was president back then, and he admitted to having lust in his heart. I had lust in my heart as well—lust for stocks. In the end, I figure I'd purchased more than 15,000 of them for investors in Magellan—and many more than once. No wonder I'd gotten a reputation for never having met a share I didn't like.

My departure was sudden, but it wasn't something I dreamed up overnight. The task of keeping track of so many companies had begun to take its toll by mid-decade, as the Dow hit 2000 and I hit 43. As much as I enjoyed managing a portfolio the size of the GNP of Ecuador, I missed being home to watch the children grow up. They change fast. They almost had to introduce themselves to me every weekend. I was spending more time with Fannie Mae, Freddie Mac, and Sallie Mae than I spent with them.

When you start to confuse Freddie Mac, Sallie Mae, and Fannie Mae with members of your family, and you remember 2,000 stock symbols but forget the children's birthdays, there's a good chance you've become too wrapped up in your work.

In 1989, with the Great Correction of 1987 already behind us and the stock market sailing along smoothly, I was celebrating my 46th birthday with my wife, Carolyn, and my daughters, Mary, Annie, and Beth. In the middle of the party, I had a revelation. I remembered that my father had died when he was 46 years old. You start to feel mortal when you realize you've already outlived your parents. You start to recognize that you're only going to exist for a little while, whereas you're going to be dead for a long time. You start wishing you'd seen more school plays and ski meets and afternoon soccer games. You remind yourself that nobody on his deathbed ever said: "I wish I'd spent more time at the office."

I tried to convince myself that my children required less of my attention than they had when they were younger. In my heart, I knew the reverse was true. During the Terrible Twos they rush around and bang into things, and parents have to patch them up, but patching up a toddler takes less time and effort than helping adolescents with Spanish homework or the math that we've forgotten, or driving them for the umpteenth time to the tennis court or the shopping mall, or reassuring them after they've taken the latest hard knocks from being teenagers.

On weekends, to have any hope of keeping up with teenagers and their thoughts, parents must listen to their music and make a perfunctory stab at remembering the names of rock groups, and accompany them to movies that otherwise no adult would ever want to see. I did all this, but infrequently. Saturdays, I was sitting at my desk facing a Himalaya of paperwork. On the rare occasions I took the kids to the movies or the pizza parlors, I looked for an investment angle. It was they who introduced me to Pizza Time Theater, a stock I wish I hadn't bought, and Chi-Chi's, a stock I wish I had.

By 1990, Mary, Annie, and Beth had reached the ages of 15, 11, and 7, respectively. Mary was away at boarding school and came home only on the odd weekend. In the fall she played in seven soccer games, and I'd gotten to see just one. That was also the year the Lynch family Christmas cards went out three months late. We kept scrapbooks of our children's accomplishments, stuffed with piles of memorabilia that hadn't yet been pasted in.

The nights I didn't stay late at the office, I could be found attending a meeting of one of a number of charitable and civic organizations on whose boards I'd volunteered to serve. Often, these organizations put me on their investment committees. Picking stocks for worthy causes was the best of all possible worlds, but the demands of my pro bono activities had continued to grow, right along with the demands of the Magellan Fund, and of course my daughters, whose homework assignments were getting more difficult, and who had to be driven to more and more lessons and activities every day.

Meanwhile, I was seeing Sallie Mae in my dreams, and my wife, Carolyn, and I had our most romantic encounters as we met coming in and out of the driveway. At my annual medical checkup, I confessed to the doctor that the only exercise I got was flossing my teeth. I was aware that I hadn't read a book in the last 18 months. In two years, I'd seen three operas, *The Flying Dutchman, La Bo-*

hème, and *Faust,* but not a single football game. This leads me to Peter's Principle #1:

When the operas outnumber the football games three to zero, you know there is something wrong with your life.

By mid-1990, it finally dawned on me that the job had to go. I remembered that my fund's namesake, Ferdinand Magellan, also retired early to a remote island in the Pacific, although what happened to him afterward (torn to shreds by angry natives) was enough to give me pause. Hoping to avoid a similar fate at the hands of angry shareholders, I met with Ned Johnson, my boss at Fidelity, along with Gary Burkhead, the director of operations, to discuss a smooth exit.

Our powwow was straightforward and amicable. Ned Johnson suggested I stay on as a group leader for all the Fidelity equity funds. He offered to give me a smaller fund to operate, one, say, with $100 million in assets as opposed to the $12 billion with which I'd had to cope. But even with a couple of digits knocked off, it seemed to me that a new fund would require the same amount of work as the old one, and I'd be back to spending Saturdays at the office. I declined Ned's gracious invitation.

Unbeknownst to most people, I'd also been running a $1 billion employees' pension fund for several major corporations, including Kodak, Ford, and Eaton, with Kodak having the largest stake. This pension fund had a better record than Magellan because I was able to invest the money without as many restrictions. For instance, a pension fund was allowed to put more than 5 percent of its assets into a single stock, whereas a mutual fund could not.

The people at Kodak, Ford, and Eaton wanted me to continue to manage their pension money whether I left Magellan or not, but I declined their gracious invitation as well. From outside Fidelity, I'd gotten numerous offers to start a Lynch Fund, the closed-end variety listed on the New York Stock Exchange. The would-be promoters said they could sell billions of dollars' worth of Lynch Fund shares on a quick "road show" to a few cities.

The attraction of a closed-end fund, from the manager's point of view, is that the fund will never lose its customer base, no matter how badly the manager performs. That's because closed-end funds are traded on the stock exchanges, just like Merck or Polaroid or any other stock. For every seller of a closed-end fund there has to be a buyer, so the number of shares always stays the same.

This isn't true of an open-ended fund such as Magellan. In an open-ended fund, when a shareholder wants to get out, the fund must pay that person the value of his or her shares in cash, and the size of the fund is reduced by that amount. An unpopular open-ended fund can shrink very fast as its customers flee to other competing funds or to the money markets. This is why the manager of an open-ended fund doesn't sleep as soundly as the manager of the closed-end kind.

A $2 billion Lynch Fund listed on the NYSE would have continued to be a $2 billion enterprise forever (unless I made a series of horrendous investment boo-boos and lost the money that way). I would have continued to receive the 75 basis points ($15 million) as my annual fee, year in and year out.

It was a tempting proposition, monetarily. I could have hired a bunch of assistants to pick stocks, reduced my office hours to a leisurely minimum, played golf, spent more time with my wife and my children plus gotten to see the Red Sox, the Celtics, and *La Bohème*. Whether I beat the market or lagged the market, I'd still have collected the same hefty paycheck.

There were only two problems with this arrangement. The first was that my tolerance for lagging the market is far exceeded by a desire to outperform it. The second was that I've always believed fund managers should pick their own stocks. Once again, I'd be back where I started, stuck in the office of the Lynch Fund on Saturdays, lost in the piles of annual reports, a man with a thicker bankroll but just as time poor as ever.

I've always been skeptical of millionaires who congratulate themselves for walking away from a chance to enrich themselves further. Turning one's back on a fat future paycheck is a luxury that few people can afford. But if you're lucky enough to have been rewarded in life to the degree that I have, there comes a point at which you have to decide whether to become a slave to your net worth by devoting the rest of your life to increasing it or to let what you've accumulated begin to serve you.

There's a Tolstoy story that involves an ambitious farmer. A genie of some sort offers him all the land that he can encircle on foot in a day. After running at full speed for several hours, he acquires several square miles of valuable property, more soil than he could till in a lifetime, more than enough to make him and his family rich for generations. The poor fellow is drenched with sweat and gasping for breath. He thinks about stopping—for what's the point of going any further?—but he can't help himself. He races ahead to maximize his opportunity, until finally he drops dead of exhaustion.

This was the ending I hoped to avoid.

PREFACE TO THE TRADE PAPERBACK EDITION

The publication of this paperback edition gives me a chance to respond to the feedback I got from the hardcover edition, both from the press and from callers on late-night radio call-in shows.

There are points I thought that I made quite forcefully in the hardcover edition but that the reviewers have never mentioned. There are other points that caught the reviewers' fancy that I never intended to make at all. This is why I'm delighted to have this new preface, where I can correct what I think are three important misconceptions.

At the top of my list is the one that puts Lynch on a pedestal as the Babe Ruth of Investing, talking down to the Little Leaguers and giving them the false hope that they can perform like Big League professionals. The Babe Ruth comparison, although flattering, is wrong on two counts. First, I've struck out or grounded out far too often to be compared to the Sultan of Swat. Second, I don't think the Little Leaguers, a.k.a. small investors or average investors or the general public, should even try to imitate the Big League professionals.

What I've tried to get across is that the average investor isn't in the same ballpark with the Wall Street mutual-fund or pension-fund managers. The individual is free of a lot of the rules that make life difficult for the professionals. As an average investor, you don't have to own more than a handful of stocks and you can do the research in your spare time. If no company appeals to you at the moment, you can stay in cash and wait for a better opportunity. You don't have to compete with the neighbors, the way professionals do, by publishing your quarterly results in the local shopper.

Proof that average investors can do quite well for themselves, free of the burdens that weigh down the professionals, comes from the NAIC, the organization that represents 10,000 local investment clubs, which are made up of ordinary men and women. According to the NAIC, 69.4 percent of the local clubs managed to outperform the S&P 500 in 1992. More than half these clubs have beaten the S&P in four of the past five years. It appears that the investment clubs are getting more adept at picking stocks, by taking full advantage of their amateur status.

If you have done well as a stockpicker, it's probably because you have also exploited your natural advantage of being an amateur. You have researched your own investments and bought shares in great companies that Wall Street may have overlooked. The remarkable record of local mutual savings banks and S&Ls is powerful evidence that neighborhood investing pays off.

Misconception #2 is that Lynch thinks everybody should be out there with hand-held calculators, reading balance sheets, investigating companies, and buying stocks. In fact, millions of Americans should refrain from buying stocks. These are people who have no interest in investigating companies and cringe at the sight of a balance sheet, and who thumb through annual reports only for the pictures. The worst thing you can do is to invest in companies you know nothing about.

Unfortunately, buying stocks on ignorance is still a popular American pastime. Let's return to the sports analogy. When people discover they are no good at baseball or hockey, they put away their bats and their skates and they take up amateur golf or stamp collecting or gardening. But when people discover they are no good at picking stocks, they are likely to continue to do it anyway.

People who are no good at picking stocks are the very ones who say that they are "playing the market," as if it is a game. When you "play the market" you're looking for instant gratification, without having to do any work. You're seeking the excitement that comes from owning one stock one week, and another the next, or from buying futures and options.

Playing the market is an incredibly damaging pastime. Players of the market may spend weeks studying their frequent flier miles, or poring over travel guides in order to carefully map out a trip, but they'll turn around and invest $10,000 in a company they know nothing about. Even people who are serious about their vacations get caught up in playing the market. The whole process is sloppy and ill-conceived.

This is a group I'd like to address, the chronic losers with a history of playing their hunches. They buy IBM at $100 a share because they sense it's overdue for a comeback or they buy a biotech stock or a riverboat casino stock because they've heard it's "hot."

Whatever they can salvage from these losses they sink into deutschemark futures or call options on the S&P 500 because they have a feeling that the S&P 500 is going up this month. In the end they're more convinced than ever that Wall Street is a game, but that's because they've made it one.

Misconception #3 is that Lynch has it in for mutual funds. Why would I bite the hand that fed me so well? Equity mutual funds are the perfect solution for people who want to own stocks without doing their own research. Investors in equity funds have prospered handsomely in the past, and there's no reason to doubt they will continue to prosper in the future. There's no rule that says you can't own individual stocks *and* mutual funds. There's no rule that you can't own several mutual funds. Even in an equity fund that fails to beat the market average the long-term results are likely to be satisfying. The short-term results are less predictable, which is why you shouldn't buy equity mutual funds unless you know you can leave the money there for several years and tolerate the ups and downs.

I'm cheered by the evidence that individual investors are learning not to get scared out of their stocks or their equity mutual funds during market corrections, as occurred in October 1987. There was a scary period in 1989 when the Dow Jones Industrial Average dropped 200 points and another big drop of 500 points in 1990, and in both cases the general public was a net buyer of stocks in the aftermath. So perhaps the message about corrections being as routine as snowstorms, and not the end of the world, is beginning to sink in.

One message that hasn't sunk in, apparently, is that in the long run owning stocks is more rewarding than owning bonds and CDs. Recently, I was dismayed to discover that in the retirement accounts that thousands of people have opened at my own firm, Fidelity, only a small percentage of the money is invested in pure equity funds. Most of it has gone into money-market funds, or bond funds, or the equity income funds. Yet history shows that over a long period of time assets will grow much faster when they are 100 percent invested in stocks. The retirement account is the perfect place for stocks, because the money can sit there and grow for 10 to 30 years.

INTRODUCTION

Escape from Bondage

A retired fund manager is qualified to give only investment advice, not spiritual advice, but what inspires me to retake the pulpit is that a majority in the congregation continue to favor bonds. Obviously, they must have slept through the last sermon, *One Up on Wall Street,* in which I tried to prove once and for all that putting money into stocks is far more profitable than putting it into bonds, certificates of deposit, or money-market accounts. Otherwise, why are 90 percent of the nation's investment dollars still parked in these inferior spots?

Throughout the 1980s, which was the second-best decade for stocks in modern history (only the 1950s were slightly more bountiful), the percentage of household assets invested in stocks declined! This percentage, in fact, has been declining steadily—from nearly 40 percent in the 1960s to 25 percent in 1980 to 17 percent in 1990. As the Dow Jones average and the other stock indexes quadrupled in value, a mass of investors was switching out of stocks. Even assets invested in equity mutual funds shrunk from around 70 percent in 1980 to 43 percent in 1990.

This calamity for the future of individual and national wealth cannot go unchallenged. Let me begin, then, where I left off the last time: if you hope to have more money tomorrow than you have today, you've got to put a chunk of your assets into stocks. Maybe we're going into a bear market and for the next two years or three years or even five years you'll wish you'd never heard of stocks. But the 20th century has been full of bear markets, not to mention recessions, and in spite of that the results are indisputable: sooner or later, a portfolio of stocks or stock mutual funds will turn out to be a lot more valuable than a portfolio of bonds or CDs or money-market funds. There, I've said it again.

The most persuasive bit of proof I've discovered since I argued this point before can be found in the *Ibbotson SBBI Yearbook, 1993*, chapter 1, page 17, under the heading "Average Annual Return for the Decades 1926–1989." This is a summary of the profits you would have made, per year, by investing your money in the S&P 500 stocks, small-company stocks, long-term government bonds, long-term corporate bonds, and short-term Treasury bills. The results are shown in Table I-1.

The investment geniuses among us could have put all their money into the S&P 500 stocks in the 1920s, switched in 1929 to long-term corporate bonds and held these throughout the 1930s, moved into small-company stocks in the 1940s, back into the S&P 500 in the 1950s, back to small companies in the 1960s and the 1970s, and returned to the S&P 500 in the 1980s. The people who followed that inspired strategy are now all billionaires and living on the coast of France. I would have recommended it myself, had I been clever enough to know beforehand what was going to happen. In hindsight, it's quite obvious.

Since I've never met a single billionaire who made his or her fortune exactly in this fashion, I must assume that they are in short supply relative to the rest of us who exhibit normal intelligence. The rest of us have no way of predicting the next rare period in which bonds will outperform stocks. But the fact that it's only happened in one decade out of seven, the 1930s (the 1970s was a standoff), gives the dedicated stockpicker an advantage. By sticking with stocks all the time, the odds are six to one in our favor that we'll do better than the people who stick with bonds.

Moreover, the gains enjoyed by the bondholders in the rare decade when bonds beat stocks cannot possibly hope to make up for the huge advances made by stocks in periods such as the 1940s and the 1960s. Over the entire 64 years covered in the table, a $100,000 investment in long-term government bonds would now be worth $1.6 million, whereas the same amount invested in the S&P 500 would be worth $25.5 million. This leads me to Peter's Principle #2:

> **Gentlemen who prefer bonds don't know what they're missing.**

Table 1-1. AVERAGE ANNUAL RETURN

	1920s*	1930s	1940s	1950s	1960s	1970s	1980s
S&P 500	19.2%	0.0%	9.2%	19.4%	7.8%	5.9%	17.5%
Small-Company Stocks	– 4.5%	1.4%	20.7%	16.9%	15.5%	11.5%	15.8%
Long-Term Government Bonds	5.0%	4.9%	3.2%	– 0.1%	1.4%	5.5%	12.6%
Long-Term Corporate Bonds	5.2%	6.9%	2.7%	1.0%	1.7%	6.2%	13.0%
Treasury Bills	3.7%	0.6%	0.4%	1.9%	3.9%	6.3%	8.9%
Inflation	– 1.1%	–2.0%	5.4%	2.2%	2.5%	7.4%	5.1%

*Based on the period 1926–29.

SOURCE: *Ibbotson SBBI Yearbook, 1993*

The Growth in Common Stocks
S&P 500, 1926–present

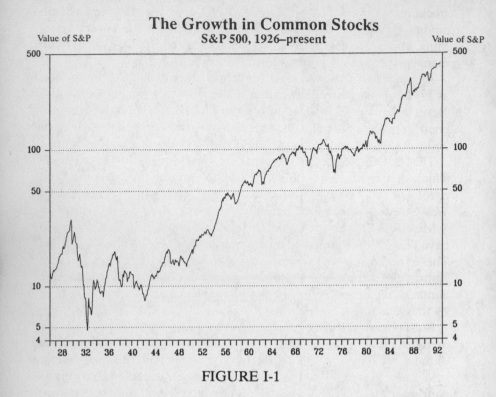

Value of S&P

Value of S&P

FIGURE I-1

Yet we continue to be a nation of bondholders. Millions of people are devoted to collecting interest, which may or may not keep them slightly ahead of inflation, when they could be enjoying a 5–6 percent boost in their real net worth, above and beyond inflation, for years to come. Buy stocks! If this is the only lesson you learn from this book, then writing it will have been worth the trouble.

The debate over whether to invest in small stocks or big stocks, or how to choose the best stock mutual fund (all subjects of later chapters), is subordinate to the main point—whichever way you do it, big stocks, small stocks, or medium-sized stocks, buy stocks! I'm assuming, of course, that you go about your stockpicking or fund-picking in an intelligent manner, and that you don't get scared out of your stocks during corrections.

A second reason I've taken on this project is to further encourage the amateur investor not to give up on the rewarding pastime of stockpicking. I've said before that an amateur who devotes a small amount of study to companies in an industry he or she knows something about can outperform 95 percent of the paid experts who manage the mutual funds, plus have fun in doing it.

A sizable crowd of mutual fund managers dismisses this notion as hooey, and some have called it "Lynch's ten-bagger of wind." Nevertheless, my 2½ years away from Magellan have only strengthened my conviction that the amateur has the advantage. For nonbelievers on this point, I've stumbled onto some additional proof.

This can be found in Chapter 1, "The Miracle of St. Agnes," which describes how a bunch of seventh graders at a Boston area parochial school have produced a two-year investment record that Wall Street professionals can only envy.

Meanwhile, a larger bunch of adult amateur investors claims to have bested their professional counterparts for many years in a row. These successful stockpickers belong to the hundreds of investment clubs sponsored by the National Association of Investors, and their annual rates of return have been just as enviable as those turned in by the students at St. Agnes.

Both bunches of amateurs have this in common: their stockpicking methods are much simpler and generally more rewarding than many of the more baroque techniques used by highly paid fund managers.

Whatever method you use to pick stocks or stock mutual funds, your ultimate success or failure will depend on your ability to ignore the worries of the world long enough to allow your investments to succeed. It isn't the head but the stomach that determines the fate of the stockpicker. The skittish investor, no matter how intelligent, is always susceptible to getting flushed out of the market by the brush beaters of doom.

A group of us investment seers meets every January to participate in a panel discussion sponsored by *Barron's* magazine, which later publishes the transcript. If you had bought many of the stocks that we recommended, you would have made money, but if you paid attention to our expert opinions on the direction of the market and the economy you would have been too scared to own stocks for the last seven years. Chapter 2 deals with the pitfalls of this "weekend worrying" and how to ignore it.

Chapter 3, "A Tour of the Fund House," is my attempt to devise a strategy for mutual fund investing. Although I remain a stockpicker at heart, my retirement gives me the opportunity to discuss a subject

I was reluctant to tackle as a fund manager. When you're still in the business, almost anything you say about it could be construed as either self-serving or a sneaky way to attract new customers— charges that I trust will not be leveled against me now.

Recently, I helped a not-for-profit organization in New England devise a new portfolio strategy. (This organization shall remain nameless because its identity isn't relevant to the exercise.) We first had to decide how much of the money to put into stocks and how much into bonds, and then how to invest each portion. These are the same decisions that every household CEO must make, which is why I've provided a detailed description of how we approached the problem.

Chapters 4, 5, and 6 are a three-part retrospective: how I managed Magellan during 13 years and 9 major corrections. This exercise gave me an excuse to go back and figure out exactly what factors contributed to whatever successes I had. Some of the conclusions have surprised even me, and I was there.

In this part of the book I've tried to concentrate on methodology and to downplay the idle reminiscence. Perhaps there's something to be learned from my occasional triumphs and my numerous mistakes.

In Chapters 7 through 20, which account for more than half of these pages, I describe how I went about picking the 21 stocks I recommended to the readers of *Barron's* magazine in January 1992. I've talked before about theories of investing, but in making these selections I took notes as I went along. With these notes in hand, I've tried to analyze my stockpicking habits in as much detail as possible. This includes both how to identify promising situations and how to go about researching them.

The 21 stocks that I've used to illustrate this Lynch Method cover many of the important categories and industry groups (banks and S&Ls, cyclicals, retailers, utilities) in which people routinely invest. I've arranged the chapters so that each one deals with a specific kind of company. Chapter 21, "The Six-Month Checkup," describes the regular process of reviewing the story of each company in a portfolio.

I have no pat formulas to offer. There are no bells that ring when you've bought the right stock, and no matter how much you know about a company you can never be certain that it will reward you for investing in it. But if you know the factors that make a retailer or a bank or an automaker profitable or unprofitable, you can improve your odds. Many of these factors are laid out here.

The text is fortified with liberal doses of Peter's Principles, such as the two you've already had to tolerate. Many of these lessons I've learned from experience, which is always an expensive teacher, so you're getting them here at a discount.

(The stock prices of the 21 companies that I describe in the second half of this book were constantly changing in the course of my research. For example, Pier 1 was selling for $7.50 when I began looking into it and $8 when I finally recommended it in *Barron's*. On one page, I may refer to Pier 1 as a $7.50 stock, and on another as an $8 stock. Several such anomalies may appear in the text.)

ONE

THE MIRACLE
OF ST. AGNES

Amateur stockpicking is a dying art, like pie-baking, which is losing out to the packaged goods. A vast army of mutual-fund managers is paid handsomely to do for portfolios what Sara Lee did for cakes. I'm sorry this is happening. It bothered me when I was a fund manager, and it bothers me even more now that I have joined the ranks of the nonprofessionals, investing in my spare time.

This decline of the amateur accelerated during the great bull market of the 1980s, after which fewer individuals owned stocks than at the beginning. I have tried to determine why this happened. One reason is that the financial press made us Wall Street types into celebrities, a notoriety that was largely undeserved. Stock stars were treated like rock stars, giving the amateur investor the false impression that he or she couldn't possibly hope to compete against so many geniuses with M.B.A. degrees, all wearing Burberry raincoats and armed with Quotrons.

Rather than fight these Burberried geniuses, large numbers of average investors decided to join them by putting their serious money into mutual funds. The fact that up to 75 percent of these mutual funds failed to perform even as well as the stock market averages proves that genius isn't foolproof.

But the main reason for the decline of the amateur stockpicker has to be losses. It's human nature to keep doing something as long as it's pleasurable and you can succeed at it, which is why the world population continues to increase at a rapid rate. Likewise, people continue to collect baseball cards, antique furniture, old fishing lures, coins, and stamps, and they haven't stopped fixing up houses and reselling them, because all these activities can be profitable as well as enjoyable. So if they've gotten out of stocks, it's because they're tired of losing money.

It's usually the wealthier and more successful members of society who have money to put into stocks in the first place, and this group is used to getting A's in school and pats on the back at work. The stock market is the one place where the high achiever is routinely shown up. It's easy to get an F here. If you buy futures and options and attempt to time the market, it's easy to get all F's, which must be what's happened to a lot of people who have fled to the mutual funds.

This doesn't mean they stop buying stocks altogether. Somewhere down the road they get a tip from Uncle Harry, or they overhear a conversation on a bus, or they read something in a magazine and decide to take a flier on a dubious prospect, with their "play" money. This split between serious money invested in the funds and play money for individual stocks is a recent phenomenon, which encourages the stockpicker's caprice. He or she can make these frivolous side bets in a separate account with a discount broker, which the spouse doesn't have to know about.

As stockpicking disappears as a serious hobby, the techniques of how to evaluate a company, the earnings, the growth rate, etc., are being forgotten right along with the old family recipes. With fewer retail clients interested in such information, brokerage houses are less inclined to volunteer it. Analysts are too busy talking to the institutions to worry about educating the masses.

Meanwhile, the brokerage-house computers are busily collecting a wealth of useful information about companies that can be regurgitated in almost any form for any customer who asks. A year or so ago, Fidelity's director of research, Rick Spillane, interviewed several top-producing brokers about the data bases and so-called screens that are now available. A screen is a computer-generated list of companies that share basic characteristics—for example, those that have raised dividends for 20 years in a row. This is very useful to investors who want to specialize in that kind of company.

At Smith Barney, Albert Bernazati notes that his firm can provide 8–10 pages of financial information on most of the 2,800 companies in the Smith Barney universe. Merrill Lynch can do screens on ten different variables, the *Value Line Investment Survey* has a "value screen," and Charles Schwab has an impressive data service called "the Equalizer." Yet none of these services is in great demand. Tom Reilly at Merrill Lynch reports that less than 5 percent of his customers take advantage of the stock screens. Jonathan Smith at Lehman Brothers says that the average retail investor does not take advantage of 90 percent of what Lehman can offer.

In prior decades, when more people bought their own stocks, the stockbroker per se was a useful data base. Many old-fashioned brokers were students of a particular industry, or a particular handful of companies, and could help teach clients the ins and outs. Of course, one can go overboard in glorifying the old-fashioned broker as the Wall Street equivalent of the doctor who made house calls. This happy notion is contradicted by public opinion surveys that usually ranked the stockbroker slightly below the politican and the used-car salesman on the scale of popularity. Still, the bygone broker did more independent research than today's version, who is more likely to rely on information generated in house by his or her own firm.

Newfangled brokers have many things besides stocks to sell, including annuities, limited partnerships, tax shelters, insurance policies, CDs, bond funds, and stock funds. They must understand all of these "products" at least well enough to make the pitch. They have neither the time nor the inclination to track the utilities or the retailers or the auto sector, and since few clients are invested in individual stocks, there's little demand for their stockpicking advice. Anyway, the broker's biggest commissions are made elsewhere, on mutual funds, underwritings, and in the options game.

With fewer brokers offering personal guidance to fewer stock-pickers, and with a climate that encourages capricious speculation with "fun" money and an exaggerated reverence for professional skills, it's no wonder that so many people conclude that picking their own stocks is hopeless. But don't tell that to the students at St. Agnes.

THE ST. AGNES PORTFOLIO

The fourteen stocks shown in Table 1-1 were the top picks of an energetic band of seventh-grade portfolio managers who attended the St. Agnes School in Arlington, Massachusetts, a suburb of Boston, in 1990. Their teacher and CEO, Joan Morrissey, was inspired to test the theory that you don't need a Quotron or a Wharton M.B.A., or for that matter even a driver's license, to excel in equities.

You won't find these results listed in a Lipper report or in *Forbes*, but an investment in the model St. Agnes portfolio produced a 70 percent gain over a two-year period, outperforming the S&P 500 composite, which gained 26 percent in the same time frame, by a whopping margin. In the process, St. Agnes also outperformed 99 percent of all equity mutual funds, whose managers are paid considerable sums for their expert selections, whereas the youngsters are happy to settle for a free breakfast with the teacher and a movie.

Table 1-1. ST. AGNES PORTFOLIO

Company	1990–91 Performance (%)
Wal-Mart	164.7
Nike	178.5
Walt Disney	3.4
Limited	68.8
L.A. Gear	− 64.3
Pentech	53.1
Gap	320.3
PepsiCo	63.8
Food Lion	146.9
Topps	55.7
Savannah Foods	− 38.5
IBM	3.6
NYNEX	− .22
Mobil	19.1
Total Return for Portfolio	69.6
S&P 500	26.08

Total return performance January 1, 1990–December 31, 1991

I was made aware of this fine performance via the large scrapbook sent to my office, in which the seventh graders not only listed their top-rated selections, but drew pictures of each one. This leads me to Peter's Principle #3:

Never invest in any idea you can't illustrate with a crayon.

This rule ought to be adopted by many adult money managers, amateur and professional, who have a habit of ignoring the understandably profitable enterprise in favor of the inexplicable venture that loses money. Surely it would have kept investors away from Dense-Pac Microsystems, a manufacturer of "memory modules," the stock of which, alas, has fallen from $16 to 25 cents. Who could draw a picture of a Dense-Pac Microsystem?

In order to congratulate the entire St. Agnes fund department (which doubles as Ms. Morrissey's social studies class) and also to learn the secrets of its success, I invited the group to lunch at Fidelity's executive dining room, where, for the first time, pizza was served. There, Ms. Morrissey, who has taught at St. Agnes for 25 years, explained how her class is divided every year into teams of four students each, and how each team is funded with a theoretical $250,000 and then competes to see who can make the most of it.

Each of the various teams, which have adopted nicknames such as Rags to Riches, the Wizards of Wall Street, Wall Street Women, The Money Machine, Stocks R Us, and even the Lynch Mob, also picks a favorite stock to be included in the scrapbook, which is how the model portfolio is created.

The students learn to read the financial newspaper *Investor's Business Daily.* They come up with a list of potentially attractive companies and then research each one, checking the earnings and the relative strength. Then they sit down and review the data and decide which stocks to choose. This is a similar procedure to the one that is followed by many Wall Street fund managers, although they aren't necessarily as adept at it as the kids.

"I try to stress the idea that a portfolio should have at least ten companies, with one or two providing a fairly good dividend," says Ms. Morrissey. "But before my students can put any stock in the portfolio, they have to explain exactly what the company does. If they can't tell the class the service it provides or the products it makes, then they aren't allowed to buy. Buying what you know about is one of our themes." Buying what you know about is a very sophisticated strategy that many professionals have neglected to put into practice.

One of the companies the students at St. Agnes knew about was Pentech International, a maker of colored pens and markers. Their favorite Pentech product, with a marker on one end and a highlighter on the other, was introduced into the class by Ms. Morrissey. This pen was very popular, and some of the kids even used it to highlight their stock selections. It wasn't long before they were investigating Pentech itself.

The stock was selling for $5 at the time, and the students discovered that the company had no long-term debt. They were also impressed by the fact that Pentech made a superior product, which, judging by its popularity in house, was likely to be just as popular in classrooms nationwide. Another positive, from their point of view, was that Pentech was a relatively unknown company, as compared, say, to Gillette, the maker of Paper Mate pens and the Good News razors they saw in their fathers' bathrooms.

Trying to come to the aid of a colleague, the St. Agnes fund managers sent me a Pentech pen and suggested I look into this wonderful company. This advice I wish I had taken. After I received the research tip and neglected to act on it, the stock nearly doubled, from 5⅛ to a high of 9½.

This same kid's-eye approach to stockpicking led the 1990 St. Agnes fund managers to the Walt Disney Company, two sneaker manufacturers (Nike and L.A. Gear), the Gap (where most of them buy their clothes), PepsiCo (which they know four different ways via Pepsi-Cola, Pizza Hut, Kentucky Fried Chicken, and Frito-Lay), and Topps (a maker of baseball cards). "We were very much into trading cards within the seventh grade," Ms. Morrissey says, "so there was no question about whether to own Topps. Again, Topps produced something the kids could actually buy. In doing so, they felt they were contributing to the revenues of one of their companies."

They got to the others as follows: Wal-Mart because they were shown a videotaped segment of "Lifestyles of the Rich and Famous" that featured Wal-Mart's founder, Sam Walton, talking about how investing benefits the economy; NYNEX and Mobil because of their excellent dividends; Food Lion, Inc., because it was a well-run company with a high return on equity and also because it was featured in the same video segment that introduced them to Sam Walton. Ms. Morrissey explains:

"The focus was on eighty-eight citizens of Salisbury, North Carolina, who each bought ten shares of Food Lion stock for one hundred dollars when the company went public back in 1957. A thousand dollars invested then had become fourteen million dollars. Do you believe it? All of these eighty-eight people became millionaires. These facts impressed all the kids, to say the least. By the end of the year they had forgotten a lot of things, but not the story of Food Lion."

The only clunker in the model portfolio is IBM, which I don't have to tell you has been the favorite of professional adult money managers for 20 years (yours truly included—grown-ups keep buying it and keep wishing they hadn't). The reason for this destructive obsession is not hard to find: IBM is an approved stock that everybody knows about and a fund manager can't get into trouble for losing money on it. The St. Agnes kids can be forgiven this one foolish attempt to imitate their elders on Wall Street.

Let me anticipate some of the criticisms of the St. Agnes results that are sure to come from the professional ranks. (1) "This isn't real money." True, but so what? Anyway, the pros ought to be relieved that St. Agnes isn't working with real money—otherwise, based on St. Agnes's performance, billions of dollars might be pulled from the regular mutual funds and turned over to the kids. (2) "Anybody could have picked those stocks." If so, why didn't anybody? (3) "The kids got lucky with a bunch of their favorite picks." Perhaps, but some of the smaller portfolios chosen by the four-person teams in Ms. Morrissey's class did as well as or better than the model portfolio selected by the class at large. The winning foursome in 1990 (Andrew Castiglioni, Greg Bialach, Paul Knisell, and Matt Keating) picked the following stocks for the reasons noted:

100 shares of Disney ("Every kid can explain this one.")
100 shares of Kellogg ("They liked the product.")
300 shares of Topps ("Who doesn't trade baseball cards?")
200 shares of McDonald's ("People have to eat.")
100 shares of Wal-Mart ("A remarkable growth spurt.")
100 shares of Savannah Foods ("They got it from *Investor's Daily.*")

5,000 shares of Jiffy Lube ("Cheap at the time.")
600 shares of Hasbro ("It's a toy company, isn't it?")
1,000 shares of Tyco Toys (Ditto.)
100 shares of IBM ("Premature adulthood.")
600 shares of National Pizza ("Nobody can turn down a pizza.")
1,000 shares of Bank of New England ("How low could it go?")

This last stock I owned myself and lost money on, so I can appreciate the mistake. It was more than counteracted by the boys' two best picks, National Pizza and Tyco Toys. These four-baggers would have done wonders for any portfolio. Andrew Castiglioni discovered National Pizza by scanning the NASDAQ list, and then he followed up on his discovery by doing some research on the company—the crucial second step that many adult investors continue to omit.

The winning foursome in 1991 (Kevin Spinale, Brian Hough, David Cardillo, and Terence Kiernan) divided their pretend money among Philip Morris, Coca-Cola, Texaco, Raytheon, Nike, Merck, Blockbuster Entertainment, and Playboy Enterprises. Merck and Texaco got their attention because of the good dividends. Playboy got their attention for reasons that had nothing to do with the fundamentals of the company, although they did notice that the magazine had a large circulation and that Playboy owned a cable channel.

The entire class was introduced to Raytheon during the Gulf War, when Ms. Morrissey's students sent letters to the troops in Saudi Arabia. They developed a regular correspondence with Major Robert Swisher, who described how a Scud missile hit within a couple of miles of his camp. When the portfolio managers learned that Raytheon made the Patriot missile, they couldn't wait to research the stock. "It was a good feeling," Ms. Morrissey says, "knowing we had a theoretical financial interest in the weapon that was keeping Major Swisher alive."

THE ST. AGNES CHORUS

After visiting Fidelity, eating pizza in the executive dining room, and giving me the Pentech advice I wish I had taken, the St. Agnes stock experts returned the favor by inviting me to address the school and to visit their portfolio department, a.k.a. the classroom. In response to my visit to this 100-year-old institution, which offers classes from kindergarten through eighth grade, I received a cassette tape the students had recorded.

This remarkable tape included some of their own stockpicking ideas and stratagems, as well as a few that I'd suggested and they decided to repeat back to me, if only to make certain that I wouldn't forget them myself. Here are some of their comments:

Hi, this is Lori. One thing I remember you telling us is over the last seventy years the market has declined forty times, so an investor has to be willing to be in the market for the long term. . . . If I ever invest money in the market I will be sure to keep the money in.

Hi, this is Felicity. I remember you telling us the story about Sears and how when the first shopping malls were built, Sears was in ninety-five percent of them. . . . Now when I invest in a stock, I'll know to invest in a company that has room to grow.

Hi, this is Kim. I remember talking to you and you said that while K mart went into all the big towns, Wal-Mart was doing even better because it went into all the small towns where there was no competition, and I remember you said you were the guest speaker at Sam Walton's award ceremony, and just yesterday Wal-Mart was sixty dollars and they announced a two-for-one split.

This is Willy. I just want to say that all the kids were relieved when we had pizza for lunch.

Hi, this is Steve. I just want to tell you that I convinced my group to buy a lot of shares of Nike. We bought at fifty-six dollars a share; it is currently at seventy-six dollars a share. I own a lot of pairs of sneakers and they are comfortable shoes.

Hi, this is Kim, Maureen, and Jackie. We remember you were telling us that Coke was an OK company until five years ago when they came out with diet Coke and the adults went from drinking coffee and tea to diet Coke. Recently, Coke just split its stock at eighty-four dollars and is doing quite well.

At the end of the tape, the entire seventh-grade portfolio department repeated the following maxims in unison. This is a chorus that we should all memorize and repeat in the shower, to save ourselves from making future mistakes:

A good company usually increases its dividend every year.

You can lose money in a very short time but it takes a long time to make money.

The stock market really isn't a gamble, as long as you pick good companies that you think will do well, and not just because of the stock price.

You can make a lot of money from the stock market, but then again you can also lose money, as we proved.

You have to research the company before you put your money into it.

When you invest in the stock market you should always diversify.

You should invest in several stocks because out of every five you pick one will be very great, one will be really bad, and three will be OK.

Never fall in love with a stock; always have an open mind.

You shouldn't just pick a stock—you should do your homework.

Buying stocks in utility companies is good because it gives you a higher dividend, but you'll make money in growth stocks.

Just because a stock goes down doesn't mean it can't go lower.

Over the long term, it's better to buy stocks in small companies.

You should not buy a stock because it's cheap but because you know a lot about it.

Ms. Morrissey continues to do her best to promote amateur stock-picking, not only with students but with her fellow teachers, whom she inspired to start their own investment club, the Wall Street Wonders. There are twenty-two members, including me (honorary) and also Major Swisher.

The Wall Street Wonders have had a decent record, but not as good as the students'. "Wait until I tell the other teachers," Ms. Morrissey said after we had gone over the numbers, "that the kids' stocks have done better than ours."

10,000 INVESTMENT CLUBS CAN'T BE WRONG

Evidence that adults as well as children can beat the market averages with a disciplined approach to picking stocks comes from the

National Association of Investors Corporation, based in Royal Oak, Michigan. This organization represents 10,000 stockpicking clubs, and publishes a guidebook and a monthly magazine to help them.

Over the decade of the 1980s, the majority of NAIC chapters outperformed the S&P 500 index, and three-quarters of all equity mutual funds to boot. The NAIC also reports that in 1991, 61.9 percent of its chapters did as well as or better than the S&P 500. Sixty-nine percent beat that average again in 1992. The key to the success of these investment clubs is that they invest on a regular timetable, which takes the guesswork out of whether the market is headed up or down, and does not allow for the impulse buying and impulse selling that spoil so many nest eggs. People who invest in stocks automatically, the same amount every month, through their retirement accounts or other pension plans, will profit from their self-discipline just as the clubs have.

The following calculations, made at my request by Fidelity's technical department, have strengthened the argument for investing on a schedule. If you had put $1,000 in the S&P 500 index on January 31, 1940, and left it there for 52 years, you'd now have $333,793.30 in your account. This is only a theoretical exercise, since there were no index funds in 1940, but it gives you an idea of the value of sticking with a broad range of stocks.

If you'd added $1,000 to your initial outlay every January 31 throughout those same 52 years, your $52,000 investment would now be worth $3,554,227. Finally, if you had the courage to add another $1,000 every time the market dropped 10 percent or more (this has happened 31 times in 52 years), your $83,000 investment would now be worth $6,295,000. Thus, there are substantial rewards for adopting a regular routine of investing and following it no matter what, and additional rewards for buying more shares when most investors are scared into selling.

All 10,000 clubs in the NAIC held to their timetables during and after the Great Correction of October 1987, when the end of the world and the end of the banking system were widely predicted. They ignored the scary rhetoric and kept on buying stocks.

An individual might be scared out of stocks and later regret it, but in the clubs nothing can be accomplished without a majority vote. Rule by committee is not always a good thing, but in this case it helps ensure that no foolish proposal to sell everything will be carried out by the group. Collective decision making is one of the principal reasons that club members tend to do better with the money they invest with the group than with the money they invest in their private accounts on the side.

The clubs meet once a month, either in members' houses or in rented conference rooms at local hotels, where they trade ideas and decide what to buy next. Each person is responsible for researching one or two companies and keeping tabs on the latest developments. This takes the whimsy out of stockpicking. Nobody is going to get up and announce: "We've got to buy Home Shopping Network. I overheard a taxicab driver say it's a sure thing." When you know your recommendations will affect the pocketbooks of your friends, you tend to do your homework.

For the most part, the NAIC groups buy stocks in well-managed growth companies with a history of prosperity, and in which earnings are on the rise. This is the land of the many-bagger, where it's not unusual to make 10, 20, or even 30 times your original investment in a decade.

In 40 years of experience, the NAIC has learned many of the same lessons I learned at Magellan, beginning with the fact that if you pick stocks in five different growth companies, you'll find that three will perform as expected, one will run into unforeseen trouble and will disappoint you, and the fifth will do better than you could have imagined and will surprise you with a phenomenal return. Since it's impossible to predict which companies will do better than expected and which will do worse, the organization advises that your portfolio should include no fewer than five stocks. The NAIC calls this the Rule of Five.

The NAIC Investors Manual, which the directors kindly sent to my office, contains several important maxims that can be added to the repertoire of the St. Agnes chorus. These can be chanted as you mow the lawn, or, better yet, recited just before you pick up the phone to call the stockbroker:

Hold no more stocks than you can remain informed on.

Invest regularly.

You want to see, first, that sales and earnings per share are moving forward at an acceptable rate and, second, that you can buy the stock at a reasonable price.

It is well to consider the financial strength and debt structure to see if a few bad years would hinder the company's long term progress.

Buy or do not buy the stock on the basis of whether or not the growth meets your objectives and whether the price is reasonable.

Understanding the reasons for past sales growth will help you form a good judgment as to the likelihood of past growth rates continuing.

To assist investors in delving more deeply into these matters, the NAIC offers its investors manual and a home study course that teach how to calculate earnings growth and sales growth; how to determine, on the basis of earnings, if a stock is cheap, expensive, or fairly priced; and how to read a balance sheet to tell whether or not a company has the wherewithal to survive hard times. For people who enjoy working with numbers and who want to do more sophisticated investment homework than they've done up to now, this is a good place to start.

The NAIC also publishes a monthly magazine, *Better Investing,* which recommends stocks in promising growth companies and provides regular updates on their status. For further information, write to the organization at P.O. Box 220, Royal Oak, MI 48068, or call (313) 543-0612. This completes my unpaid and unsolicited advertisement.

TWO

THE WEEKEND WORRIER

The key to making money in stocks is not to get scared out of them. This point cannot be overemphasized. Every year finds a spate of books on how to pick stocks or find the winning mutual fund. But all this good information is useless without the willpower. In dieting and in stocks, it is the gut and not the head that determines the results.

In the case of mutual funds, for which the investor isn't required to analyze companies or follow the market, it's often what you know that can hurt you. The person who never bothers to think about the economy, blithely ignores the condition of the market, and invests on a regular schedule is better off than the person who studies and tries to time his investments, getting into stocks when he feels confident and out when he feels queasy.

I'm reminded of this lesson once a year, at the annual gathering of the *Barron's* Roundtable, when a group of supposed experts, yours truly included, gets involved in weekend worrying. Every year since 1986, I've participated in this event. In January we meet for eight hours to trade quips and tips, most of which end up in the publication in the following three weekly issues.

Since *Barron's* is owned by Dow Jones, its offices are located in the new Dow Jones complex overlooking the right bank of the Hudson River on the southern end of Manhattan. For marble and high ceilings, the lobby is the equal of St. Peter's in Rome. You enter it via moving walkways similar to the ones installed at international airports. There is a thorough security system that begins with the check-in station, where you must reveal your identity and state the nature of your visit. Once you are approved at the check-in station, you are handed a piece of paper, which you must then show to the guard outside the elevator.

After you've passed this test, you're permitted to ride to the appropriate floor, where you have to pass through another locked door that is opened with a credit card. If all goes well, you eventually find yourself in the Roundtable conference room, where the table isn't round. It used to be U-shaped, but lately the organizers have collapsed one of the sides to form a giant triangle. We financial wizards sit along the hypotenuse while our hosts from *Barron's* question us from the base. This friendly inquisition is directed by *Barron's* editor Alan Abelson, the resident wit, who has done for finance what Dorothy Parker did for romance.

Above us are hanging microphones and a powerful bank of 13 1,000-watt spotlights, which are flipped on and off for the convenience of the photographers. While one of them takes candid shots with a zoom lens from about 13 feet away, another (a woman wearing kneepads) crouches just below our nostrils and aims upward for the close-ups. Aside from the photographers, the room is filled with *Barron's* editors, sound experts, and technicians, some of whom lurk behind a glass wall. Eggs could hatch in the heat from the overhead bulbs.

This is a lot of fuss to be made over a bunch of money managers of advancing age and graying sideburns, but we thrive on it. Occasionally a new panelist is added and an old one subtracted, but the regulars include Mario Gabelli and Michael Price, both of whom run highly regarded "value" funds that have recently come back into vogue; John Neff of the Vanguard Windsor Fund, who already was a legend when I started running Magellan in 1977; Paul Tudor Jones, a whiz at commodities; Felix Zulauf, an international banker and frequent worrywart who for all I know may be regarded as a raging optimist in his native Switzerland, where people tend to worry about everything; Marc Perkins, a money manager whom I got to know when he was a bank analyst; Oscar Schafer, who concentrates on "special situations"; Ron Baron, who looks for stocks that Wall Street doesn't bother to follow; and Archie MacAllaster, a savvy investor in the over-the-counter market.

On the 1992 panel, Paul Tudor Jones's spot was taken by Barton Biggs, chairman of Morgan Stanley Asset Management and a bargain hunter with a global perspective. Marc Perkins's spot was opened up in 1991, when Jimmy Rogers, a *Barron's* fixture for five straight years, gave up Wall Street in favor of following the old silk trade route across China on a motorcycle. The last I'd heard, Jimmy had shipped his motorcycle to Peru and was riding around the Andes, 1,000 miles from the nearest broker. (He's since resurfaced on a nightly business show.)

Whereas most people's friendships are based on their experiences in college, or the army, or summer camp, ours go back to stocks. I can't see Ron Baron without thinking of Strawbridge & Clothier, an issue we both owned at the same time and sold prematurely.

Over the years, we've tried to develop a comeback capability, to keep up with Abelson's one-liners. In the actual transcript as published in *Barron's,* Abelson is identified only as *Barron's* or as "Q," but he deserves personal credit for all of the following except the Schafer retort, which I've included because it lives up to an Abelson line.

> JIM ROGERS: I do own one European company called Steyr-Daimler-Puch, which is a company that has been losing money for several years now.
> ABELSON: . . . What else does it have going for it?

> ABELSON (to Oscar Schafer): Are you short anything?
> SCHAFER: Let me talk about one more long and then I'll talk about a short, if I'm boring you.
> ABELSON: No more than usual.

> ED GOODNOW (former panelist who touted Philippine Long Distance Telephone): I understand the service is not so good out in the provinces. One of the problems is that it's hard to get the guys to go up the poles to fix the lines because they sometimes get picked off by snipers. But other than that, they've got a very solid operation.
> ABELSON: Do you call that a long shot?

> PETER LYNCH: I still like my ultimate savings and loan, which is Fannie Mae. It has a lot to go.
> ABELSON: In which direction?

> JOHN NEFF (recommending Delta Air Lines): What people are missing on the airline side . . .

ABELSON: Or near-missing . . .

MICHAEL PRICE: We have, in real stocks, maybe forty-five percent of our fund.
OSCAR SCHAFER: Unreal stocks make up the other fifty-five percent?

MARIO GABELLI: And as you know, I've been recommending Lin Broadcasting for twenty years.
ABELSON: Too bad it never worked out!

MARIO GABELLI: I am talking about a multifaceted approach to a multifaceted problem.
ABELSON: Please, Mario, this is a family magazine.

JOHN NEFF: And in the past eight recessions, when you went down that much in the first two months of a quarter . . . I am inventing all this.
ABELSON: Like everything else you say!

The Roundtable starts promptly at noon and is divided into two parts. The first part is an overview of the financial markets, in which we are encouraged to discuss where the economy is headed and whether or not the world is coming to an end. This is the part that gets us into trouble.

These overview discussions are worth analyzing because they are no different from the thousands of similar exchanges that take place among amateur investors at the breakfast table, or at the health club or the golf course on weekends. It is on weekends that people have extra time to ponder the distressing news that comes our way via TV stations or the daily newspaper wrapped in a plastic bag by the delivery boys. Maybe there's a hidden message here: they are trying to protect us from the contents.

When we make the mistake of letting the news out of the bag, we are confronted with the latest reasons that mankind is doomed: global warming, global cooling, the evil Soviet empire, the collapse of the evil Soviet empire, recession, inflation, illiteracy, the high cost of health care, fundamentalist Muslims, the budget deficit, the brain drain, tribal warfare, organized crime, disorganized crime, sex scandals, money scandals, sex and money scandals. Even the sports pages can make you sick.

While catching up on the news is merely depressing to the citizen who has no stocks, it is a dangerous habit for the investor. Who wants to own shares in the Gap if the AIDS virus is going to kill half the consumers, and the hole in the ozone the other half, either before or after the rain forest disappears and turns the Western Hemisphere into the new Gobi Desert, an event that will likely be preceded, if not followed, by the collapse of the remaining savings and loans, the cities, and the suburbs?

You may never admit to yourself, "I decided to sell my Gap shares because I read an article in the Sunday magazine about the effects of global warming," but that's the kind of weekend logic that's in force, sub rosa, when the sell orders come pouring in on Mondays. It's no accident that Mondays historically are the biggest down days in stocks and that Decembers are often losing months, when the annual tax-loss selling is combined with an extended holiday during which millions of people have extra time to consider the fate of the world.

Weekend worrying is what our panel of experts, in the first half of the *Barron's* session, practices year after year. In 1986, we worried about M-1 versus M-3, the Gramm-Rudman deficit reduction package, what the Group of Seven would do, and whether the "J Curve effect" would begin to reduce the trade deficit. In 1987, we worried that the dollar was collapsing, foreign companies were dumping their products in our markets, the Iran-Iraq War would cause a global oil shortage, foreigners would stop buying our stocks and bonds, the consumer was deeply in hock and unable to buy merchandise, and President Reagan was not allowed to run for a third term.

You couldn't worry all the panelists all the time. Some worried more than others, and some who worried one year were unworried the next, and a couple of us were often optimistic about the future, which added a bit of emotional buoyancy to the generally dire proceedings. In fact, the year we were the most optimistic about the future for the economy and the stock market was 1987, which ended with the famous 1000-point drop. The lone panelist to sound an alarm that year was Jimmy Rogers, who in 1988 rang the alarm bell once again, warning of an impending collapse of stock prices around the world. Rogers is famous for "shorting" stocks when he expects them to falter, yet in spite of his gloomy premonition, he had few shorts to recommend in *Barron's* that year or the next. A successful investor does not let weekend worrying dictate his or her strategy.

Here is a group of influential professionals who manage billions of dollars that belong to other people, and from one Roundtable to the next we can't agree on whether we are facing an imminent global depression or an economic upswing.

It is worth noting that our worrying peaked in the 1988 Roundtable session, held two months after the Great Correction. We'd just suffered this major collapse in the stock market, so of course we were looking for another one for the following year. This leads to Peter's Principle #4:

You can't see the future through a rearview mirror.

Mr. Zulauf set the tone in 1988 with his opening statement that "the honeymoon, from 1982 to 1987, is over." This was the most optimistic thing said all day. The rest of the time, we debated whether we were going to have a standard bear market, which would take the Dow average down to 1500 or lower, or a killer bear market that would "wipe out most people in the financial community and most investors around the world" (Jimmy Rogers's fret) and bring about a "worldwide depression like we saw in the early thirties" (Paul Tudor Jones's).

In between worrying about the killer bear market and the worldwide depression, we worried about the trade deficit, unemployment, and the budget deficit. I rarely sleep well the night before I'm scheduled to meet with the *Barron's* panel, but after this one I had bad dreams for three months.

The 1989 panel was somewhat cheerier than 1988, although Mr. Zulauf brought up the fact that this was the Year of the Snake, a bad sign in Chinese cosmology. When we convened in 1990, the oft-predicted Depression was nowhere in evidence and the Dow had climbed back to 2500 points. Still, we found new reasons to stay out of stocks. There was the collapse in real estate, another calamity to add to the list. We were unsettled by the fact that after seven straight years of up markets (1987 ended with a slight gain over 1986, in spite of the Great Correction), a down market was inevitable. Here was a worry that things had been going too well! Friends of mine, sophisticated people and not easily frightened, were talking about taking the money out of banks and hiding it at home, because they thought the money-center banks might fail and collapse the banking system.

The pessimism of 1990 beat the pessimism of 1980–82, when investors were so depressed about stocks that whenever the subject came up they changed it to earthquakes, funerals, or even the futile pennant hopes of the Boston Red Sox. In 1990, they weren't simply avoiding the subject, they were eager to tell you how they were betting *against* the market. I actually heard cabdrivers recommending bonds, and barbers bragging about how they'd bought "puts," which increase in value as stocks decline.

Barbers are a segment of the population that I assumed had never heard of put options, but here they were making these complicated wagers with their own paychecks. If Bernard Baruch was right about selling all stocks when the shoeshine boys are buying, then surely the right time to be buying is when the barbers discover puts.

I collected a sample of some of the happier headlines to re-create the public mood in the fall of 1990:

"Layoffs This Time Hit Professional Ranks with Unusual Force,"
    Wall Street Journal, October 4.
"How Safe Is Your Job?," *Newsweek,* November 5.
"Scraping By," *New York Times,* November 25.
"The Real Estate Bust," *Newsweek,* October 1.
"High Rents Could Be Keeping Young from Setting Up House,"
    Business Week, October 22.
"Housing Slump Hammering Home Remodelers," *Business
    Week,* October 22.
"How the Real Estate Crash Threatens Financial Institutions,"
    U.S. News, November 12.
"Housing Recession That Began in Northeast Three Years Ago
    Now Engulfs Entire Nation," *New York Times,* December 16.
"Deficit Plan Will Face Dicey Fate in Congress and Isn't a Cure-
    All," *Wall Street Journal,* October 1.
"Uncertainty Rains for U.S. Economy," *Wall Street Journal,* December 3.
"The Consumer Has Seen the Future, and Gotten Depressed,"
    Business Week, December 10.
"A Survival Guide for the Age of Anxiety," *Newsweek,* December 31.
"Can America Still Compete?," *Time,* October 29.
"Can Your Bank Stay Afloat?," *U.S. News,* November 12.
"Can You Compete? The Americas Are Falling Behind and What
    Can Be Done to Pick Up the Pace," *Business Week,* December 17.

To top it all off, there was a war in the desert to fight. Cameras were rolling in the Pentagon briefing rooms, where millions of viewers learned for the first time where Iraq and Kuwait were located. Military strategists debated how many body bags would be needed to ship home the casualties from the chemical and biological weapons soon to be loosed on our soldiers by the well-trained Iraqi army, fourth-largest in the world, hunkered down in reinforced bunkers hidden in the sand dunes.

This Mother of All Worries had a predictable effect on the fearful forecasters. By January 15, 1991, when we convened at the *Barron's* offices, the specter of body bags hung over our spirits. In our "wither the economy" discussion, Zulauf, though gloomy as usual, once again was outgloomed. He foresaw a fall in the Dow to somewhere between 2000 and the lows of the 1987 Big Correction, while Michael Price saw a 500-point downside, Marc Perkins an eventual fall to 1600–1700. Yours truly volunteered that in the worst case we could have a major recession, and if the war was as terrible as some had expected we'd see a 33 percent drop in the price of stocks.

Since you can't get onto the *Barron's* panel without being a successful investor, it's safe to assume that all of us have somehow managed to develop a disciplined approach to investing that enables us to block out our own distress signals. Along with the rest of the country, I knew there was a chance that Operation Desert Storm would turn into a long and bloody conflict, but meanwhile, the stockpicker in me couldn't help notice the amazing bargains that had resulted from the widespread selling by investors. I was no longer dealing in millions of shares as I had at Magellan, but I was adding to my holdings in my own account, and buying for the charitable trusts and public foundations whose portfolios I help manage. In October 1990, *The Wall Street Journal* noticed that I'd increased my personal stake in W. R. Grace and Morrison-Knudsen, two companies on whose boards I serve. I told the reporter, Georgette Jasen, that these were just "two of about ten stocks I added to . . . if they go lower, I'll buy more." I also went on record as having purchased another 2,000 shares in Magellan to add to my holdings, just as I had after I retired.

This was the perfect scenario for the disciplined stockpicker to search his or her buy lists for likely prospects. The headlines were negative, the Dow Jones average had lost 600 points over the summer and the early fall, cabdrivers were recommending bonds, mutual-fund managers had 12 percent of their fund assets in cash, and at least five of my fellow panelists were predicting a severe recession.

Of course, we now know that the war wasn't as terrible as some had expected (unless you were an Iraqi) and what we got from the stock market instead of a 33 percent drop was a 30 percent gain in the S&P 500 average, a 25 percent gain in the Dow, and a 60 percent gain in smaller stocks, which added up to making 1991 the best year in two decades. You would have missed it had you paid the slightest attention to our celebrated prognostications.

Moreover, if you had paid close attention to the negative tone of most of our "whither the economy" sessions over the past six years, you would have been scared out of your stocks during the strongest leg of the greatest market advance in modern history, when investors who maintained their blissful ignorance of the world coming to an end were merrily tripling or quadrupling their money. Remember this the next time you find you're being talked out of a good investment by somebody who convinces you that Japan is going bankrupt or that a rogue meteor is hurtling toward the New York Stock Exchange.

"Suspense and dread cast a heavy pall over the markets," said *Barron's* the week of our gathering for the 1991 Roundtable and just prior to the great upward spurt in the market that would carry the Dow to a record high.

THE EVEN BIGGER PICTURE

It's simple enough to tell yourself, "Gee, I guess I'll ignore the bad news the next time the stock market is going down and pick up some bargains." But since each crisis seems worse than the last, ignoring bad news is getting harder and harder to do. The best way not to be scared out of stocks is to buy them on a regular schedule, month in and month out, which is what many people are doing in the 401(k) retirement plans and in their investment clubs, as mentioned before. It's no surprise that they've done better with this money than the money they move in and out of the market as they feel more and less confident.

The trouble with the Dr. Feelgood method of stockpicking is that people invariably feel better after the market gains 600 points and stocks are overvalued and worse after it drops 600 points and the bargains abound. If you don't buy stocks with the discipline of adding so much money a month to your holdings, you've got to find some way to keep the faith.

Keeping the faith and stockpicking are normally not discussed in the same paragraph, but success in the latter depends on the former. You can be the world's greatest expert on balance sheets or p/e ratios, but without faith, you'll tend to believe the negative headlines. You can put your assets in a good mutual fund, but without faith you'll sell when you fear the worst, which undoubtedly will be when the prices are their lowest.

What sort of faith am I talking about? Faith that America will survive, that people will continue to get up in the morning and put their pants on one leg at a time, and that the corporations that make the pants will turn a profit for the shareholders. Faith that as old enterprises lose momentum and disappear, exciting new ones such as Wal-Mart, Federal Express, and Apple Computer will emerge to take their place. Faith that America is a nation of hardworking and inventive people, and that even yuppies have gotten a bad rap for being lazy.

Whenever I am confronted with doubts and despair about the current Big Picture, I try to concentrate on the Even Bigger Picture. The Even Bigger Picture is the one that's worth knowing about, if you expect to be able to keep the faith in stocks.

The Even Bigger Picture tells us that over the last 70 years, stocks have provided their owners with gains of 11 percent a year, on average, whereas Treasury bills, bonds, and CDs have returned less than half that amount. In spite of all the great and minor calamities that have occurred in this century—all the thousands of reasons that the world might be coming to an end—owning stocks has continued to be twice as rewarding as owning bonds. Acting on this bit of information will be far more lucrative in the long run than acting on the opinion of 200 commentators and advisory services that are predicting the coming depression.

Moreover, in this same 70 years in which stocks have outperformed the other popular alternatives, there have been 40 scary declines of 10 percent or more in the market. Of these 40 scary declines, 13 have been for 33 percent, which puts them into the category of terrifying declines, including the Mother of All Terrifying Declines, the 1929–33 sell-off.

I'm convinced that it's the cultural memory of the 1929 Crash more than any other single factor that continues to keep millions of investors away from stocks and attracts them to bonds and to money-market accounts. Sixty years later, the Crash is still scaring people out of stocks, including people in my generation who weren't even born in 1929.

If this is a post-Crash trauma syndrome we suffer from, it's been very costly. All the people who've kept their money in bonds, money-market accounts, savings accounts or CDs to avoid being involved in another Crash have missed out on 60 years of stock-market gains and have suffered the ravages of inflation, which over time has done more damage to their wealth than another crash would have done, had they experienced one.

Because the famous Crash was followed by the Depression, we've learned to associate stock-market collapses with economic collapses, and we continue to believe that the former will lead to the latter. This misguided conviction persists in the public mind, even though we had an underpublicized crash in 1972 that was almost as severe as the one in 1929 (stocks in wonderful companies such as Taco Bell declined from $15 to $1) and it didn't lead to an economic collapse, nor did the Great Correction of 1987.

Perhaps there will be another Big One, but since I'm not equipped to predict such matters—nor, obviously, are my learned colleagues on the *Barron's* panel—what's the sense of trying to protect myself in advance? In 39 out of the 40 stock-market corrections in modern history, I would have sold all my stocks and been sorry. Even from the Big One, stocks eventually came back.

A decline in stocks is not a surprising event, it's a recurring event—as normal as frigid air in Minnesota. If you live in a cold climate, you expect freezing temperatures, so when your outdoor thermometer drops below zero, you don't think of this as the beginning of the next Ice Age. You put on your parka, throw salt on the walk, and remind yourself that by summertime it will be warm outside.

A successful stockpicker has the same relationship with a drop in the market as a Minnesotan has with freezing weather. You know it's coming, and you're ready to ride it out, and when your favorite stocks go down with the rest, you jump at the chance to buy more.

After the Great Correction, when 508 points were shaved from the Dow Jones average in a single day, a symphony of experts predicted the worst, but as it turned out, the 1000-point decline in the

Dow (33 percent from the August high) did not bring on the apocalypse that so many were expecting. It was a normal, albeit severe, correction, the latest in a string of 13 such 33 percent drops in this century.

The next 10 percent decline, which may already have occurred since I've written this, will be the 41st in recent history, or, if it happens to be a 33 percent decline, the 14th. In Magellan's annual reports, I often reminded the shareholders that such setbacks were inevitable.

The story of the 40 declines continues to comfort me during gloomy periods when you and I have another chance in a long string of chances to buy great companies at bargain prices.

THREE

A TOUR OF THE FUND HOUSE

Mutual funds were supposed to take the confusion out of investing—no more worrying about which stock to pick. Not anymore. Now you have to worry about which mutual fund to pick. There are 3,565 of them at recent count: 1,266 equity funds, 1,457 bond and income funds, 566 taxable money-market funds, and 276 short-term municipal bond funds. This compares with 452 funds (278 of them equity) in existence in 1976.

This jolly fundmaking shows no signs of any letup. We've got country funds and region funds, hedge funds and sector funds, value funds and growth funds, simple funds and hybrid funds, contrary funds, index funds, and even funds of funds. Soon we'll probably see the all-dictators fund, the fund of countries with no vowels, the fund of funds of funds. The latest emergency instructions for every firm on Wall Street? In Case of a Sudden Drop in Profits, Start Another Fund.

We've lately reached an important milestone in fundmaking history: the number of funds now exceeds the number of individual stocks traded on the New York and American stock exchanges combined. This is even more remarkable when you consider that 328 of these individual stocks are actually funds in disguise. (See the discussion of closed-end funds on page 73.) So how can we begin to sort this muddle out?

DESIGNING A PORTFOLIO

Two years ago, a group of wizened (as opposed to wise) investors in New England asked ourselves precisely that question. We'd been invited to help the nonprofit organization I mentioned earlier (which shall continue to remain nameless) restructure its portfolio. Like most nonprofit organizations, this one was in constant need of capital. For years its investments were handled by a single manager, who divided the money between bonds and stocks, the way most investors do.

The issues we confronted in advising this organization how to redeploy its money were the same as those faced by the average person who must figure out the same thing.

First, we had to determine whether the mix of stocks and bonds should be changed. This was an interesting exercise. No investment decision has greater consequence for a family's future net worth than the initial growth-versus-income decision.

In my own family portfolio I've had to become slightly more bond oriented, since I now rely on investment income to make up for the absence of a salary. But I'm still heavily invested in stocks. Most people err on the side of income, and shortchange growth. This is truer today than it was in 1980, when 69 percent of the money invested in mutual funds went into stock funds. By 1990, only 43 percent of mutual-fund assets were invested in stocks. Today, approximately 75 percent of all mutual fund dollars is parked in bond and money-market funds.

The growing popularity of bonds has been fortunate for the government, which has to sell an endless supply of them to finance the national debt. It is less fortunate for the future wealth of the bondholders, who ought to be in stocks. As I hope I convinced you in the introduction, stocks are more generous companions than bonds, having returned to their owners 10.3 percent annually over 70 years, compared to 4.8 percent for long-term government debt.

The reason that stocks do better than bonds is not hard to fathom. As companies grow larger and more profitable, their stockholders share in the increased profits. The dividends are raised. The dividend is such an important factor in the success of many stocks that you could hardly go wrong by making an entire portfolio of companies that have raised their dividends for 10 or 20 years in a row.

Moody's *Handbook of Dividend Achievers,* 1991 edition—one of my favorite bedside thrillers—lists such companies, which is how I know that 134 of them have an unbroken 20-year record of dividend increases, and 362 have a 10-year record. Here's a simple way to succeed on Wall Street: buy stocks from the Moody's list, and stick with them as long as they stay on the list. A mutual fund run by Putnam, Putnam Dividend Growth, adheres to this follow-the-dividend strategy.

Whereas companies routinely reward their shareholders with higher dividends, no company in the history of finance, going back as far as the Medicis, has rewarded its bondholders by raising the interest rate on a bond. Bondholders aren't invited to annual meetings to see the slide shows, eat hors d'oeuvres, and get their questions answered, and they don't get bonuses when the issuers of the bonds have a good year. The most a bondholder can expect is to get his or her principal back, after its value has been shrunk by inflation.

One reason bonds are so popular is that elderly people have most of the money in this country, and elderly people tend to live off interest. Young people, who have earning power, are supposed to buy all the stocks, to build up their assets until they, too, are old and need to live off interest. But this popular prescription—stocks for the young, bonds for the old—is becoming obsolete. People aren't dying as readily as they used to.

Today, a healthy 62-year-old is looking at a life expectancy of 82: 20 more years of spending, 20 more years of inflation to erode the buying power of his or her money. Senior citizens who assumed they could retire happily on bonds and CDs are finding out otherwise. With 20 years of bill paying ahead of them, they need to put some growth back into the portfolio to maintain their standard of living. With interest rates low, even people with huge portfolios are having trouble living off interest.

This has created a situation in which senior citizens around the nation are all asking, "How can I survive on a three and a half percent return from my CDs?"

Consider what happens to the retired couple whose entire net worth, $500,000, is invested in short-term bonds or CDs. If interest rates go down, they have to roll over their CDs at much lower interest rates, and their income is drastically reduced. If interest rates go up, their income goes up, but so does the inflation rate. If they put the entire $500,000 into long-term bonds paying 7 percent, their income is a steady $35,000. But with an inflation rate of 5 percent, the buying power of this $35,000 will be cut in half in 10 years, and cut two-thirds in 15.

So at some point in their retirement, our generic couple may be forced to cancel some of the trips they wanted to take, or they may have to spend some of their capital, which reduces their future income as well as any inheritance they planned to leave to their children. Except among the very rich, the good life cannot long be preserved without stocks.

Obviously, how much you should invest in stocks depends on how much you can afford to invest in stocks and how quickly you're going to need to spend this money. That said, my advice is to increase the stock part of the mix to the limit of your tolerance.

I proposed as much to the trustees of the nameless organization. Before they decided to remodel the portfolio, the mix was 50 percent stocks and 50 percent bonds. The bond portion (invested in five- to six-year maturities) was yielding about 9 percent at the time, and the stock portion was giving them a 3 percent dividend, so the combined portfolio had a 6 percent return.

Normally, bonds are held to maturity and redeemed for the original purchase price, so there was no potential for growth in that half of the portfolio. The stock portion, on the other hand, could be expected to increase in value at 8 percent a year, above and beyond the dividend.

(Historically, stocks return nearly 11 percent, 3 percent of which is dividends, and 8 percent of which is due to stock prices going up. Of course, the big reason that stock prices go up is that companies continue to raise their dividends, which in turn makes stocks more valuable.)

With 50 percent of the money invested in stocks that grow at 8 percent, and 50 percent in bonds that don't appreciate at all, the combined portfolio had a growth rate of 4 percent—barely enough to keep up with inflation.

What would happen if we adjusted the mix? By owning more stocks and fewer bonds, the organization would sacrifice some current income in the first few years. But this short-term sacrifice would be more than made up for by the long-term increase in the value of the stocks, as well as by the increases in dividends from those stocks.

What you can expect to gain in growth and lose in income by adjusting the percentages of bonds and stocks in any portfolio is shown in Table 3-1. These numbers were crunched on my behalf by Bob Beckwitt, who has turned in a winning performance at the Fidelity Asset Manager Fund, which he runs.

Beckwitt is one of our resident quants. A quant is a complex thinker who deals in concepts beyond the grasp of most linear imaginations, and speaks a language that is understood only by other quants. Beckwitt is a rarity: a quant who can switch out of quant mode and communicate in normal English.

In all three scenarios analyzed by Beckwitt, $10,000 is invested. We're assuming here that the bonds are paying 7 percent interest and that the stocks are paying the current 3 percent dividend, and appreciate at the standard 8 percent a year.

In Case A, the entire $10,000 is put into bonds. In 20 years, the owner of this money will receive $14,000 in interest income, and then get back his or her original $10,000.

In Case B, the $10,000 is divided 50/50 between bonds and stocks. The result after 20 years is that the owner receives $10,422 in interest income from the bonds, plus $6,864 in dividend income from the stocks, and ends up with a portfolio worth $21,911.

In Case C, the entire $10,000 is put into stocks. Here the owner gets $13,729 in dividend income from the stocks, and ends up with a portfolio worth $46,610.

Since dividends continue to grow, eventually a portfolio of stocks will produce more income than a fixed yield from a portfolio of bonds. That's why after 20 years in Case B you actually receive $3,286 more in income than in Case A, and in Case C you're only losing $271 in income to get the full benefit of all the appreciation from putting your entire bankroll into stocks.

If you take this analysis a step further, you realize that theoretically it makes no sense to put any money into bonds, even if you do need income. This radical conclusion comes from another set of numbers I asked Beckwitt to crunch. The result is shown here in Table 3-2.

Let's say you have $100,000 to invest, and have determined that you need to make $7,000 in income to maintain your standard of living. The commonsense advice given to people who need income is to buy bonds. But instead, you veer off in a wild and crazy direction and turn the $100,000 into a portfolio of stocks that pay a combined 3 percent dividend.

TABLE 3-1. RELATIVE MERITS OF STOCKS VERSUS BONDS

	End-of-Year Value of Bonds	Bond Income	End-of-Year Value of Stocks	Stock Income	Total Income	End-of-Year Principal
Case A:						
100%						
Bonds						
Year 1	$10,000	$ 700	—	—	$ 700	$10,000
Year 2	10,000	700	—	—	700	10,000
Year 10	10,000	700	—	—	700	10,000
Year 20	10,000	700	—	—	700	10,000
Total 20 years	10,000	14,000	—	—	14,000	10,000
*Case B:						
50%						
Bonds,						
50%						
Stocks						
Year 1	5,000	350	5,400	150	500	10,400
Year 2	5,200	364	5,616	162	526	10,816
Year 10	7,117	498	7,686	300	798	14,803
Year 20	10,534	737	11,377	647	1,384	21,911
Total 20 years	10,534	10,422	11,377	6,864	17,286	21,911
Case C:						
100%						
Stocks						
Year 1	—	—	10,800	300	300	10,800
Year 2	—	—	11,664	324	324	11,664
Year 10	—	—	21,589	600	600	21,589
Year 20	—	—	46,610	1,295	1,295	46,610
Total 20 years	—	—	46,610	13,729	13,729	46,610

*To maintain a 50-50 ratio, a portfolio must be periodically "rebalanced"—that is, money must be added to the bond portion to make up for the gain in the stocks.

TABLE 3-2. 100% STOCKS INVESTMENT STRATEGY
Begin with 3% dividend on stocks; assume 8% growth in dividends and in stock
prices; spend a minimum of $7,000*

Year	100% Stocks Beginning-of-Year Stocks	Dividend Income	End-of-Year Stocks	Spending	End of Year
1	$100,000	$ 3,000	$108,000	$ 7,000	$104,000
2	104,000	3,120	112,320	7,000	108,440
3	108,440	3,250	117,200	7,000	113,370
4	113,370	3,400	122,440	7,000	118,840
5	118,840	3,570	128,350	7,000	124,910
6	124,910	3,750	134,900	7,000	131,650
7	131,650	3,950	142,180	7,000	139,130
8	139,130	4,170	150,260	7,000	147,440
9	147,440	4,420	159,230	7,000	156,660
10	156,660	4,700	169,190	7,000	166,890
Total (1–10)		37,330		70,000	166,890
11	166,890	5,010	180,240	7,000	178,250
12	178,250	5,350	192,510	7,000	190,850
13	190,850	5,730	206,120	7,000	204,850
14	204,850	6,150	221,230	7,000	220,380
15	220,380	6,610	238,010	7,000	237,620
16	237,620	7,130	256,630	7,130	256,630
17	256,630	7,700	277,160	7,700	277,160
18	277,160	8,310	299,330	8,310	299,330
19	299,330	8,980	323,280	8,980	323,280
20	323,280	9,700	349,140	9,700	349,140
Total (11–20)		70,660		76,820	349,140
Total (1–20)		107,990		146,820	349,140

*All dollar amounts have been rounded to the nearest $10.

During the first year, your 3 percent dividend puts $3,000 into
your account. That's not enough income. How do you cover this
shortfall? You sell $4,000 worth of stock. If your stock prices have
gone up at the normal rate of 8 percent, the portfolio will be worth
$108,000 at the end of the year, so your $4,000 dip into capital leaves
you with $104,000.

The second year, the dividend income from the portfolio has
increased to $3,120, so you only have to sell $3,880 worth of stock.
Every year thereafter, the dip into capital gets smaller and the div-

idends get larger, until the 16th year, when the portfolio produces more than $7,000 in income from your dividend checks alone. At this point, you can maintain your standard of living without having to sell a single share.

At the end of 20 years, your original $100,000 has grown into $349,140, and you're nearly four times richer than you were when you started, in addition to your having spent $146,820 worth of income along the way.

Once and for all, we have put to rest the last remaining justification for preferring bonds to stocks—that you can't afford the loss in income. But here again, the fear factor comes into play. Stock prices do not go up in orderly fashion, 8 percent a year. Many years, they even go down. The person who uses stocks as a substitute for bonds not only must ride out the periodic corrections, but also must be prepared to sell shares, sometimes at depressed prices, when he or she dips into capital to supplement the dividend.

This is especially difficult in the early stages, when a setback for stocks could cause the value of the portfolio to drop below the price you paid for it. People continue to worry that the minute they commit to stocks, another Big One will wipe out their capital, which they can't afford to lose. This is the worry that will keep you in bonds, even after you've studied Tables 3-1 and 3-2 and are convinced of the long-range wisdom of committing 100 percent of your money to stocks.

Let's assume, then, that the day after you've bought all your stocks, the market has a major correction and your portfolio loses 25 percent of its value overnight. You berate yourself for gambling away the family nest egg, but as long as you don't sell, you're still far better off than if you'd bought a bond. Beckwitt's computer run shows that 20 years later, your portfolio will be worth $185,350, or nearly double the value of your erstwhile $100,000 bond.

Or let's imagine an even worse case: a severe recession that lasts 20 years, when instead of dividends and stock prices increasing at the normal 8 percent rate, they do only half that well. This would be the most prolonged disaster in modern finance, but if you stuck with the all-stock portfolio, taking out your $7,000 a year, in the end you'd have $100,000. This still equals owning a $100,000 bond.

I wish I'd had Beckwitt's numbers when I made my presentation to the nonprofit organization we've been talking about, because then

I might have tried to talk them out of owning any bonds. At least we decided to increase the percentage of assets invested in stocks, which is a step in the right direction.

BONDS VERSUS BOND FUNDS

The mix of assets having been decided, the next step is to figure out how to invest the bond portion. I'm no bond fan, which explains why this discussion is going to be short. That I'd rather be touting stocks should be apparent by now, but I'll put aside my favorite subject to say something about bonds as a safe place to keep your money. They aren't.

People who sleep better at night because they own bonds and not stocks are susceptible to rude awakenings. A 30-year Treasury bond that pays 8 percent interest is safe only if we have 30 years of low inflation. If inflation returns to double digits, the resale value of an 8 percent bond will fall by 20–30 percent, if not more. In such a case, if you sell the bond, you lose money. If you hold on to it for the entire 30 years you're guaranteed to get your money back, but that money (the principal) will be worth only a fraction of what it's worth today. Unlike wine and baseball cards, money is cheapened with age. For example, the 1992 dollar is worth one third of its 1962 ancestor.

(It's interesting to note that at present the much-disparaged money-market fund is not necessarily the disaster it's made out to be. With inflation at 2.5 percent and the money markets paying 3.5 percent, at least you're 1 percent ahead of the game. If interest rates rise, so will the money-market yields. I'm not saying you can live on a 3.5 percent return, but in the money market at least you run no risk of losing your capital. The low-fee money-market funds now offered by several investment houses have made this product more attractive. And since low interest rates are not likely to last forever, this is a far safer place to be invested than long-term bonds.)

Another fallacy about bonds is that it's safer to buy them in a fund. No doubt it is, if you're talking about corporate bonds or low-rated junk bonds, because a fund can limit the risk of default by investing in a variety of issues. But a bond fund offers no protection against higher interest rates, which is by far the greatest danger in owning a long-term IOU. When rates go higher, a bond fund loses value as quickly as an individual bond with a similar maturity.

You can make a halfway decent case for investing in a junk-bond fund, or in a blended fund that offers a mix of corporate and government paper that produces a better overall yield than you could get from investing in a lone bond. What I can't figure out is why anybody would want to invest all his money in an intermediate- or long-term government bond fund. A lot of people do. More than $100 billion is invested in government bond funds today.

I may lose some friends in the bond-fund department for saying this, but their purpose in life eludes me. Anyone who buys an intermediate-term government bond fund and pays the .75 percent in annual expenses for salaries, accounting fees, the cost of producing reports, etc., could just as easily buy a 7-year Treasury bond, pay no fee, and get a higher return.

Treasury bonds and bills can be purchased through a broker, or directly from a Federal Reserve bank, which charges no commission. You can buy a 3-year note, or T-bill, for as little as $5,000 and a 10-year or 30-year Treasury bond for as little as $1,000. The interest on the T-bill is paid up front, and the interest on the bond is automatically deposited in your brokerage account or your bank account. There's no fuss.

The promoters of government-bond funds like to argue that expert managers can get you a better return via their well-timed buying, selling, and hedging of positions. Apparently, this doesn't happen very often. A study done by the New York bond dealer Gabriele, Hueglin & Cashman concludes that in a six-year period from 1980 to 1986, bond funds were consistently outperformed by individual bonds, sometimes by as much as 2 percent a year. Moreover, the bond funds did worse relative to bonds the longer the funds were held. The benefits of expert management were exceeded by the expenses that were extracted from the funds to support the experts.

The authors go on to suggest that bond funds try to maximize current yield at the expense of total return later. I have no evidence of my own to support or refute their conclusion, but I do know that the owner of a 7-year bond can at least be confident of getting his or her money back at the end of 7 years, whereas the owner of an intermediate-term bond fund had no such assurance. The price this investor gets on the day he or she sells the fund will depend on the bond market.

Another mystifying aspect of bond-fund mania is why so many people are willing to pay an upfront sales charge, a.k.a. load, to get into government funds and the so-called Ginnie Mae funds. It makes sense to pay the load on a stock fund that consistently beats the market—you'll get it back and then some in the fund's performance. But since one U.S. Treasury bond or Ginnie Mae certificate is the same as the next, there is little a manager of one of these kinds of funds can do to distinguish himself from competitors. In fact, the performance of nonload bond funds and funds with loads is almost identical. This leads us to Peter's Principle #5:

There's no point paying Yo-Yo Ma to play a radio.

To handle the bond portion of the portfolio for our nonprofit organization, we hired seven people—two traditional bond managers to invest the bulk of the money, three convertible bond managers (see page 72), and two junk bond managers. Junk can be very lucrative, if you buy the right junk, but we didn't want to bet the ranch on it.

STOCKS VERSUS STOCK FUNDS

In one respect, a stock fund is no different from a stock. The only way to benefit from it is to keep owning it. This requires a strong will. For people who can be scared out of stocks, investing in a stock fund doesn't solve the problem. It's a common occurrence for the best-performing funds to decline more than the average stock during a correction. During my turn at the helm at Magellan, on the nine occasions when the average stock lost 10 percent of its value the fund sank deeper than the market, only to rise higher than the market on the rebound—as I'll explain in more detail later. To benefit from these comebacks, you had to stay invested.

In letters to the shareholders, I warned of Magellan's tendency to get swamped in choppy waters, on the theory that when people are prepared for something it may disturb them, but it won't unnerve them. Most, I think, remained calm and held on to their shares. Some did not. Warren Buffett's admonition that people who can't tolerate seeing their stocks lose 50 percent of their value shouldn't own stocks also applies to stock funds.

People who can't tolerate seeing their mutual funds lose 20–30 percent of their value in short order certainly shouldn't be invested in growth funds or general equity funds. Perhaps they should choose a balanced fund that contains both stocks and bonds, or an asset allocation fund—either of which offers a smoother ride than the ride they'd get on a pure growth stock fund. Of course, there's less reward at the end of the trip.

Turning our attention to the baffling assortment of 1,127 equity funds on the market today, we arrive at Peter's Principle #6:

As long as you're picking a fund, you might as well pick a good one.

This is easier said than done. Over the last decade, up to 75 percent of the equity funds have been worse than mediocre, failing to outgain the random baskets of stocks that make up the market indexes, year in and year out. In fact, if a fund manager has even matched the market's performance, he or she has ranked in the top quartile of all funds.

The fact that so many funds with investments in the stocks that make up the averages can manage to do worse than the averages is a modern paradox. It seems illogical that a majority of fund managers cannot achieve an average result, but that's the way it's been—1990 was the eighth year in a row in which this widespread failure to match the gains recorded by the popular S&P 500 index occurred.

The causes of this strange phenomenon are not entirely known. One theory is that fund managers are generally lousy stockpickers and would do better to scrap their computers and throw darts at the business page. Another is that the herd instinct on Wall Street has produced so many camp followers that fund managers only pretend to pursue excellence, when actually they are closet indexers whose goal in life is to match the market averages. Tragically, their residual creativity gets in their way, so they cannot do even a decent bad job, as also occurs with brilliant writers who try and fail to produce simpleminded best-sellers.

A third and more charitable theory is that the stocks that make up the averages—especially the S&P 500 index—tend to represent large companies that in recent years have enjoyed a great run. It was harder to beat the market in the 1980s than it was in the 1970s. In the 1980s, you had massive buyouts of companies that were included in the S&P indexes, which caused the prices of the stocks in the indexes to go up. You had a lot of foreigners investing in our market, and these foreigners preferred to buy large-company stocks with famous names. This added to the upward momentum.

In the 1970s, on the other hand, many of these popular brand-name stocks (Polaroid, Avon Products, Xerox, the steels, the automakers) faltered because the companies themselves were doing badly. Quality growth companies such as Merck continued to thrive, but their stocks went nowhere because they were overpriced. A fund manager who avoided these big stocks had a huge advantage back then.

A fourth theory is that the popularity of index funds has created a self-fulfilling prophecy. As more big institutions invest in indexes, more money is poured into index stocks, causing them to rise in price, which results in index funds outperforming the competition.

So should you forget about picking a managed fund from among the hundreds on the market, invest in an index fund or a couple of index funds, and be done with it? I discussed this option with Michael Lipper, the number-one authority on mutual funds. He provided Table 3-3. It compares the record of a large group of managed funds, here called the General Equity Funds, with the S&P 500 Reinvested, which is essentially the same thing as an index fund, minus the very small fees charged by index-fund operators.

Lipper's chart illustrates what we've already said, that throughout the recent decade the index funds beat the managed funds, and often by a wide margin. If you had put $100,000 in the Vanguard 500 index fund on January 1, 1983, and had forgotten about it, you would have celebrated January 1, 1991, with $308,450 in your pocket, but you'd have had only $236,367 in your pocket if you had put the money in the average managed equity fund. The eight-year winning streak for the indexes was finally broken in 1991.

Over 30 years, the managed funds and the indexes are running neck and neck, with the managed funds having the slightest edge. All the time and effort that people devote to picking the right fund, the hot hand, the great manager, have in most cases led to no advantage. Unless you were fortunate enough to pick one of the few funds that consistently beat the averages (more on this later), your research came to naught. There's something to be said for the dart-board method of investing: buy the whole dart board.

Table 3-3. MUTUAL FUND MANAGERS VERSUS S&P 500®
The S&P 500 Index has outperformed the average mutual fund manager in 8 of
the past 10 years . . .

Calendar Year	General Equity Funds (%)	S&P 500 Reinvested (%)
1992	9.1	7.6
1991	35.9	30.4
1990	− 6.0	− 3.1
1989	24.9	31.6
1988	15.4	16.6
1987	.9	5.2
1986	14.4	18.7
1985	28.1	31.7
1984	− 1.2	6.3
1983	21.6	22.6

. . . but, over the long term, managed funds have a slight edge

1982	26.0	21.6
1981	− .6	− 4.9
1980	34.8	32.5
1979	29.5	18.6
1978	11.9	6.6
1977	2.5	− 7.1
1976	26.7	23.9
1975	35.0	37.2
1974	− 24.2	− 26.5
1973	− 22.3	− 14.7
1972	13.2	19.0
1971	21.3	14.3
1970	− 7.2	3.9
1969	− 13.0	− 8.4
1968	18.1	11.0
1967	37.2	23.9
1966	− 4.9	− 10.0
1965	23.3	12.5
1964	14.3	16.5
1963	19.2	22.8
1962	− 13.6	− 8.7
1961	25.9	26.9
1960	3.6	.5

Cumulative Total Return Performance (%)

| 1960–92 | 2548.8 | 2470.5 |

Source: Lipper Analytical Services, Inc.

Lipper himself sees the futility in the annual search to find tomorrow's winning fund manager. The evidence tells us that it's probably a useless exercise. Still, hope springs eternal. The human spirit is alive and well on Wall Street, and investors are not about to stop sifting through the fund lists, looking for a fund that can consistently beat the averages.

Several colleagues and I took on this challenge for the nonprofit organization already mentioned. We spent hours reviewing the résumés and performance records of 75 different money managers, and from this number we chose to interview 25.

We had decided to hire a group of managers and give each a portion of the stock portfolio. You could do the same by buying several funds of varying styles and philosophies. Our thinking was as follows: markets change and conditions change and one style of manager or one kind of fund will not succeed in all seasons. What applies to stocks also applies to mutual funds. You just never know where the next great opportunities will be, so it pays to be eclectic.

If you own only one fund, you may find yourself stuck in a situation in which the managers have lost their touch, or in which the stocks in the fund have gone out of favor. A value fund, for instance, can be a wonderful performer for three years and awful for the next six. Prior to the Great Correction in 1987, value funds led the market for eight years while growth funds fell behind. Recently the growth funds led the market, but then they lost their advantage in 1992.

Here we get into the increasingly complex universe of types of funds. For the purposes of this discussion, the most important basic types are as follows:

1. Capital appreciation funds, in which the managers have leeway to buy any and all kinds of stocks and are not forced to adhere to any particular philosophy. Magellan is one of these.
2. Value funds, in which the managers invest in companies whose assets, not their current earnings, are the main attraction. These include natural resource companies, companies that own real estate, cable TV companies, pipeline companies, and bottling companies. Many of these so-called value companies have gone deep into debt to buy assets. They plan to reap the benefits later as the debts are paid off.
3. Quality growth funds, in which the managers invest in medium-

sized and large companies that are well established, expanding at a respectable and steady rate, and increasing their earnings 15 percent a year or better. This cuts out the cyclicals, the slower-growing blue chips, and the utilities.

4. Emerging growth funds, in which managers invest mostly in small companies. These small-cap stocks lagged the market for several years and suddenly came into their own in 1991.

5. Special situations funds, in which managers invest in stocks of companies that have nothing in particular in common except that something unique has occurred to change their prospects.

Knowing what kind of fund you have helps you make an informed judgment as to whether or not you should keep it. That Mario Gabelli's value fund has lagged the market for four years is not in itself a good reason for abandoning Gabelli. (In fact, Gabelli's fund rebounded in 1992). When value stocks are out of favor, there is no way Gabelli or Kurt Lindner or Michael Price can be expected to perform as well as the manager of a growth fund that is in favor.

The only fair point of comparison is one value fund versus another. Over many years, if Gabelli has achieved a better result than Lindner, that's an argument for sticking with Gabelli. But if Gabelli has been outperformed by John Templeton, the well-known growth-fund manager, it's no reflection on Gabelli. It's a reflection on the value style of investing.

Likewise, it would be silly to blame the manager of a gold fund that was down 10 percent last year, when gold stocks in general were down by the same 10 percent. When any fund does poorly, the natural temptation is to want to switch to a better fund. People who succumb to this temptation without considering the kind of fund that failed them are making a mistake. They tend to lose patience at precisely the wrong moment, jumping from the value fund to a growth fund just as value is starting to wax and growth is starting to wane.

In fact, when a value fund does better than its rivals in a lousy year for value funds, it's not necessarily any cause for celebration. (This also applies to growth funds or any other kind of fund.) It may be that the manager has gotten disenchanted with value stocks and has invested some of the money in blue chips or utilities. He or she has gotten frustrated with the value style, especially when it hasn't been working.

The manager's lack of discipline may produce good results in the short run, but the benefits may be fleeting. When value stocks come back, this manager won't be fully invested in them, and his or her shareholders won't be getting what they paid for.

The sophisticated investor can check up on a fund by reading the semiannual and annual reports to determine whether the manager is buying the kinds of stocks he or she is supposed to be buying. For instance, you wouldn't want to find Microsoft in the portfolio of your value fund. Second-guessing the fund manager, I realize, is beyond the scope of the average investor, but it's the kind of thing we stockaholics have fun doing.

THE ALL-STAR TEAM

To increase the odds that at least some of the assets would be invested in the right place at the right time, we ended up picking 13 different funds and managers for our nonprofit organization. These included one value manager, two quality growth managers, two special situations funds, three capital appreciation funds, one emerging growth fund, a fund that invests only in companies that have consistently raised their dividends, and three convertible securities funds (as described on page 72).

Out of this team of funds and managers, we expect to produce a different all-star to outperform the market every year, and with enough all-stars to counteract the mediocre performers, we hope to beat the dreaded market averages.

If you are an average investor, you can duplicate this strategy in a simpler way by dividing your portfolio into, say, six parts and investing in one fund from each of the five fund types mentioned above, plus a utility fund or an equity-and-income fund for ballast in a stormy market.

Since 1926, emerging growth stocks have outperformed the S&P 500 by a substantial margin, so it's always a good idea to keep something invested here. You could throw in a couple of index funds to go along with the managed funds. You might, for instance, buy an S&P 500 index fund to cover the quality growth segment; the Russell 2000 index fund to cover the emerging growth stocks; Gabelli Asset, the Lindner Fund, or Michael Price's Mutual Beacon for the value stocks; and Magellan (is one plug allowed here?) for capital appreciation.

The easiest approach is to divide up your money into six equal parts, buy six funds, and be done with the exercise. With new money to invest, repeat the process. The more sophisticated approach is to adjust the weighting of the various funds, putting new money into sectors that have lagged the market. This you should do *only* with new money. Since individuals have to worry about tax consequences (which charities don't), it's probably not a good idea to do a lot of buying and selling and switching around among funds.

So how do you know which sectors have lagged the market? We looked at this issue in our planning for our nonprofit organization in the fall of 1990. At the time, I was convinced that some of the major growth stocks, such as Bristol-Myers, Philip Morris, and Abbott Labs, which Wall Street had taken on a giddy scramble to new highs, were overpriced and due for a comeuppance, or at least a decent rest. How I divined this is explained in more detail on page 142.

These are typical corporate giants in the drug and food businesses that make up the S&P 500 index. The Dow Jones average, on the other hand, is heavily weighted in cyclicals, while the NASDAQ and the Russell 2000 represent smaller emerging growth enterprises—restaurant chains, technology companies, etc.

By comparing the S&P 500 index with the performance of the Russell 2000 Index going back 10 years, you can begin to see a pattern. First of all, emerging growth stocks are much more volatile than their larger counterparts, dropping and soaring like sparrow hawks around the stable flight path of buzzards. Also, after small stocks have taken one of these extended dives, they eventually catch up to the buzzards.

In the five years prior to 1990, the emerging growth stocks turned in a dismal performance relative to the S&P 500, with the S&P up 114.58 percent, while the Russell 2000 was up only 47.65 percent. But emerging growth caught up with a vengeance in 1991, when the Russell index gained 62.4 percent in 12 months. Some emerging growth funds did better, even, than the Russell 2,000, posting 70 or even 80 percent gains.

Obviously, 1990 would have been a good year to add money to the emerging growth sector of your portfolio. You would have been inclined to do just that had you paid attention to the progress of the various indexes, as reported in *Barron's, The Wall Street Journal,* and elsewhere.

Another useful way to decide whether to put more money into the emerging growth sector or to invest in a larger, S&P-type fund is to follow the progress of T. Rowe Price New Horizons. New Horizons is a popular fund created in 1961 to invest in small companies. In fact, whenever a company gets too big, the managers at New Horizons remove it from the portfolio. This is as close as you'll get to a barometer of what is happening to emerging growth stocks.

Figure 3-1, published with periodic updates by T. Rowe Price, is a comparison of the p/e ratio of the stocks in the New Horizons fund and the p/e ratio of the S&P 500 overall. Since small companies are expected to grow at a faster rate than the big companies, small stocks generally sell at a higher p/e ratio than big stocks. Theoretically, you would expect the p/e ratio of the New Horizons fund to be higher than the p/e ratio of the S&P at all times.

In practice, this is not always the case, which is what makes this table so useful. During certain periods when emerging growth sector

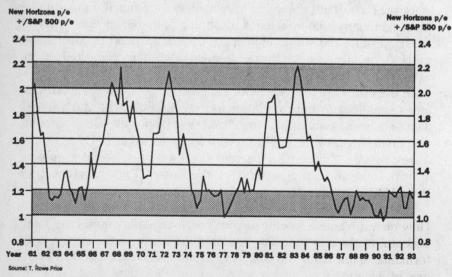

FIGURE 3-1

is unpopular with investors, these small stocks get so cheap that the
p/e ratio of New Horizons falls to the same level as that of the S&P.
(This rare condition is indicated here by the number 1.0.)

In other periods, when small stocks are wildly popular and bid
up to unreasonably high levels, the p/e ratio of New Horizons will
rise to double that of the S&P 500 (shown here by the number 2.0).

As you can see, only twice in the past 20 years (1972 and 1983)
has this lofty 2.0 level been reached. In both cases, small stocks got
clobbered for several years afterward. In fact, small stocks missed
most of the bull market from 1983 to 1987. When the New Horizons
indicator approaches the dreaded 2.0, this is a huge hint that it's
time to avoid the emerging growth sector and concentrate on the
S&P.

Clearly, the best time to buy emerging growth stocks is when the
indicator falls to below 1.2. Once again, to reap the reward from
this strategy you have to be patient. The rallies in small stocks can
take a couple of years to gather steam, and then several more years
to fully develop. For example, in 1977, after the emerging growth
sector had had a year or two of good performance, the prevailing
opinion on Wall Street was that this sector had played itself out, and
it was time to abandon small stocks in favor of big stocks. As a
young fund manager, I ignored that opinion and stuck with small
stocks, a decision that helped Magellan outperform the market for
five years after that.

The same sort of comparison can be applied to growth funds versus
value funds. Lipper Analytical Services publishes an index of 30
value funds and an index of 30 growth funds that appears in every
issue of *Barron's*. Between 1989 and 1991, the Lipper growth-fund
index soared by 98 percent while the value-fund index managed to
gain only 36 percent. When value underperforms growth for several
years, you might want to add money to the value pot.

PICKING A WINNER

How do you choose a value fund, growth fund, or capital appreciation fund that will outdo its rivals? Most people look at past performance. They study the Lipper guide published in *Barron's* or any
one of a number of similar sources that track fund performance.
They look at the record for 1 year, 3 years, 5 years, and beyond.

This is another national pastime, reviewing the past performance of funds. Thousands of hours are devoted to it. Books and articles are written about it. Yet with few exceptions, this turns out to be a waste of time.

Some people take last year's biggest winner, the one at the top of the Lipper list of 1-year achievers, and buy that fund. This is particularly foolish. The 1-year winner tends to be a fund managed by someone who bet on one industry or one kind of company in a hot sector and got lucky. Why else would he or she have been able to run so far ahead of the pack? Next year, when this fund manager is not so lucky, his or her fund will be on the bottom of the Lipper list.

Alas, this picking future winners from past performance doesn't seem to work even when you use a 3-year or 5-year record. A study done by *Investment Vision* magazine (now *Worth*) shows the following: if every year between 1981 and 1990 you invested in the fund that had performed the best over the prior 3 years, in the end you would have lagged the S&P 500 by 2.05 percent. If you invested in similar fashion in the funds with the best 5- and 10-year records, you would have beaten the S&P by .88 and 1.02 percent respectively. This would not have made up for the cost of getting in and out of these funds.

What if you had bought the funds with the best 5- and 10-year performances and held on to them for 5 years? In the case of the best 5-year performers, you would have done no better than the S&P index, and in the case of the 10-year performers you would actually have ended up lagging the S&P by .61 percent.

The lesson here is: don't spend a lot of time poring over the past performance charts. That's not to say you shouldn't pick a fund with a good long-term record. But it's better to stick with a steady and consistent performer than to move in and out of funds, trying to catch the waves.

Another major issue is what happens to a fund in a bear market. This, too, is a complicated subject. Some funds lose more than others, but gain more on the rebound; some lose less and gain less; and some lose more and gain less. This last group is the one to avoid.

One excellent source of information on this subject is the *Forbes* Honor Roll, published in that magazine every September. To make the *Forbes* list, a fund has to have some history behind it—two bull markets and at least two bear markets. *Forbes* grades each fund (from A to F) on how it has fared in both situations. It gives the name of the fund manager and how long he or she has held the post, the fund expenses, the p/e ratio, and the average annual return over ten years.

Getting on the *Forbes* Honor Roll is tough, which is what makes this a good place to shop for funds. You can hardly go wrong by choosing one with an A or B rating in both kinds of markets.

Out of the 1,200 or so equity funds in existence, only 264 go back as far as 1978, and of those 264, only 9 have shown a gain in every calendar year since. This list includes: Phoenix Growth, Merrill Lynch Capital A, Investment Company of America, John Hancock Sovereign, CGM Mutual, Nationwide, Eaton Vance Investors, Pax World, and Mutual of Omaha Income. The best performer of these, Phoenix Growth, has compiled a remarkable record—a compound annual gain of 20.2 percent since 1977. Eight of the nine have produced an annual gain of 13 percent or better.

LOAD VERSUS NO-LOAD

Another matter that needs to be addressed is load versus no-load. If you buy a fund that carries a load (translation: sales commission), does that mean you're getting a better product? Not necessarily. Some successful funds charge a load, while other equally successful funds don't. If you plan to stick with a fund for several years, the 2–5 percent you paid to get into it will prove insignificant. You should not buy a fund because it has a load, nor refuse to buy one for the same reason.

The ongoing fees and expenses of a fund can certainly hamper its performance, which is where the index funds have the advantage, as we've seen. In comparing the past performance of one managed fund against another, you can ignore the fees. A fund's annual return is calculated after fees and expenses are deducted, so they're automatically factored into the equation.

Some people worry about the size of a fund, especially Magellan. Beginning in 1983, when Magellan's assets passed the $1 billion mark, I first began to hear the words "too big to succeed." It was too big to succeed at $2 billion, and at $4 billion, and at $10 billion, and by the time I left it was too big to succeed at $14 billion. Presumably, it was too big to succeed at $20 billion, the size it reached under Morris Smith.

For a year after Morris took over, *The Boston Globe* ran its "Morris Smith Watch" column, which might as well have been called "Watch Morris Smith Fail with a Fund That's Too Big." After Morris's excellent results in 1991, the *Globe* dropped the column, but many people are still singing the "Your Fund's Too Big" blues. Now that Morris has left, it's Jeff Vinik's turn to succeed with a fund that's too big.

There are certain drawbacks to running a big fund. It's like a linebacker trying to survive on a diet of petits fours. He has to eat a considerable pile to get any nourishment out of them. A fund manager has the same predicament with shares. He can't buy enough shares of a wonderful small company for it to make any difference to the performance of the fund. He has to buy shares in big companies, and even with big companies it takes months to amass a meaningful quantity and more months to unload it.

These disadvantages can be overcome by skillful management. Michael Price has proved it with his Mutual Shares (this fund is now closed to new investors; Price also runs Mutual Beacon), and so did Morris Smith, my successor at Magellan.

Before we leave this subject, there are four other types of funds I'd like to discuss: sector funds, convertible funds, closed-end funds, and country funds.

SECTOR FUNDS

Sector funds have been around since the 1950s. In 1981, Fidelity offered the first group of sector funds, allowing investors to switch back and forth between sectors at relatively low cost. An investor who was bullish on an industry (oil, for example) but had no time to study specific companies in the oil business could simply buy the oil and gas sector fund.

These sector funds were not designed to give the whimsical stock-picker a new opportunity to follow hunches. Alas, that's sometimes how they're used. Buying the oil and gas fund, as opposed to buying Exxon, will hardly protect you from losses if oil prices head south just as you've acted on a gut feeling that oil prices are headed north.

The best candidate for investing in sector funds is a person with special knowledge about a commodity or the near-term prospects for a certain kind of business. It could be a jewelry store owner, a builder, an insurance adjuster, a gas station manager, a doctor, or a scientist, each of whom is in a position to follow the latest developments in, respectively, gold and silver prices, lumber prices, insurance rates, oil prices, government approvals for new drugs, or whether the biotech firms are beginning to turn out a marketable product.

If you're in the right sector at the right time, you can make a lot of money very fast, as investors in Fidelity Biotechnology discovered in 1991. The value of that sector fund increased by 99.05 percent in one year. But such profits can also disappear as quickly as they are made. Fidelity Biotech was down 21.5 percent through the first nine months of 1992. Technology sector funds were big winners in mid-'82–mid-'83, and big losers for several years after. Over the past decade, health care, financial services, and utilities have been the most profitable sectors, and precious metals the least.

On the theory that every sector in the stock market eventually has its day, I've begun to get interested in the gold sector again.

In my earliest years at Magellan, gold prices were soaring and people were avoiding the dentist because they feared having to pay for a gold cap even more than they feared the drill. In this era, the best-performing funds were gold funds, which had names like Strategic Investments or International Investors or United Services. To the casual observer, the gold funds sounded like general equity funds, a confusion that I found infuriating.

In the Lipper rankings for best-performing mutual funds over a five-year period, usually I'd be beaten out by a gold fund, which many people didn't realize was a gold fund. To the average investor, it looked as if other equity managers were doing a better job than I was, when in fact these number-one performers were specialists in a hot sector. Soon enough, the gold funds disappeared from the top of the Lipper list, and in recent years they've hit the bottom.

For the decade that ended June 1992, 5 of the 10 worst-performing funds in the U.S. market were gold funds. U.S. Goldshares, for instance, was up only 15 percent for this entire stretch when the average mutual fund tripled and quadrupled. You'd have done better in a money market, or U.S. savings bonds, even, than in a gold fund.

But with gold having been highly prized by the world's population since before the time of the Egyptians and the Incas, I doubt that we've seen its last hurrah. One of the charities in which I'm involved owns some gold shares, and I recently heard a presentation from some well-informed gold bugs. They point out that in the 1980s the decline in South African output was more than offset by new production from U.S., Canadian, Brazilian, and Australian mines. This created a gold glut, exacerbated by the dumping of gold by the former Soviet republics. They doubt the glut will continue.

The gold supply in new mines will run out soon, and meanwhile, the decade of low prices has discouraged companies from further exploration and development. This is likely to set up a nice situation in mid-decade. The demand for gold for jewelry and industrial uses will go up, while the supply goes down. And if inflation returns to double digits, people will once again buy gold as a hedge.

In addition, there is a "China factor" pushing up the gold prices. Chinese workers are becoming more prosperous, but they lack things to buy with their money. There's a limited supply of big-ticket items (cars, appliances, houses, etc.) that can be purchased, so the government is trying to relieve the frustration by allowing people to own gold. This policy is creating a whole new demand for the metal. The situation may repeat itself for other developing countries.

There are 34 gold sector funds on the market today—some that buy shares in South African mining companies, others that buy shares only in non–South African mining companies. A couple of hybrid funds are 50 percent invested in gold and 50 percent in government bonds. For the extremely skittish investor who worries about both the coming Depression and the coming Hyperinflation, this is an appealing mix.

CONVERTIBLE FUNDS

This is an underrated way to enjoy the best of two worlds: the high performance of secondary and small-cap stocks and the stability of bonds. Generally, it is the smaller companies that issue convertible bonds, which pay a lower rate of interest than regular bonds. Investors are willing to accept this lower rate of interest in return for the conversion feature, which allows them to exchange their convertible bonds for common stock at some specific conversion price.

Customarily, the conversion price is 20–25 percent higher than the current price of the common stock. When the price of the common stock reaches this higher level and beyond, the conversion feature becomes valuable. While waiting for this to happen, the bondholder is collecting interest on the bond. And whereas the price of a common stock can fall very far very fast, the price of a convertible bond is less volatile. The yield holds it up. In 1990, for instance, the common stocks connected to the various convertible bonds were down 27.3 percent, while the convertible bonds themselves lost only 13 percent of their value.

Still, there are certain pitfalls to investing in convertible bonds. This is one field that's best left to the experts. The amateur investor can do well in one of the numerous convertible funds, which deserve more recognition than they get. Today, a good convertible fund yields 7 percent, which is far better than the 3 percent dividend that you get from the average stock. The Putnam Convertible Income Growth Trust, to name one such fund, has a 20-year total return of 884.8 percent, which beats the S&P 500. Few managed funds can make such a claim, as we've already seen.

At the nameless New England charity, we invested in no fewer than three convertible funds, because at the time convertibles seemed undervalued. How could we tell? Normally, a regular corporate bond yields 1½ to 2 percent more than a convertible bond. When this spread widens, it means convertibles are becoming overpriced, and when it narrows, the reverse is true. In 1987, just before the Great Correction, regular corporate bonds yielded 4 percent more than convertibles, which meant that the convertibles were extremely overpriced. But during the Saddam Sell-off in October 1990, convertible bonds were actually yielding 1 percent more than regular bonds issued by the same companies. This was a rare opportunity to pick up convertibles at a favorable rate.

Here's a good strategy for convertible investing: buy into convertible funds when the spread between convertible and corporate bonds is narrow (say, 2 percent or less), and cut back when that spread widens.

CLOSED-END FUNDS

Closed-end funds trade as stocks on all the major exchanges. There are 318 of these at current count. They come in all sizes and varieties:

closed-end bond funds, municipal bond funds, general equity funds, growth funds, value funds, etc.

The main difference between a closed-end fund and an open-ended fund such as Magellan is that a closed-end fund is static. The number of shares stays the same. A shareholder in a closed-end fund exits the fund by selling his or her shares to somebody else, the same as if he or she were selling a stock. An open-ended fund is dynamic. When an investor buys in, new shares are created. When the investor sells out, his or her shares are retired, or "redeemed," and the fund shrinks by that amount.

Both closed-end funds and open-ended funds are basically managed the same way, except that the manager of a closed-end fund has some extra job security. Since the fund cannot shrink in size due to a mass exodus of customers, the only way he or she can fail is to generate losses in the portfolio itself. Running a closed-end fund is like having tenure at a university—you can be dismissed, but you have to do something really awful to make it happen.

I've never seen a definitive study of whether closed-end funds, as a group, do better or worse than open-ended funds. On casual inspection, neither kind has any particular advantage. Superior performers in both categories appear on the *Forbes* Honor Roll of mutual funds, which proves that it's possible to excel with either format.

One intriguing feature of the closed-end funds is that since they trade like stocks they also fluctuate like stocks—a closed-end fund sells at either a premium or a discount to the market value (or net asset value) of its portfolio. Bargain hunters have excellent opportunities in market sell-offs to buy a closed-end fund at a substantial discount to its net asset value.

IF IT'S TUESDAY, IT MUST BE THE BELGIUM FUND

Many closed-end funds are more popularly known as country funds. These enable us to invest in our favorite countries, a more romantic prospect than investing in companies. After a nice bottle of wine in the piazza near the Trevi Fountain, who but the most coldhearted lout wouldn't want to invest in the Italy Fund? Here's a tip for the marketing department: attach 800 numbers for country funds to the telephones in the major foreign hotels.

There are at least 75 country funds and/or region funds in existence today. With the breakup of the communist bloc, this number is sure to grow. Two Cuba funds are being launched in Miami, in anticipation of the restoration of capitalism to Havana, and Castro hasn't even packed his bags

The best argument for country funds as long-term investments is that foreign economies are growing faster than the U.S. version, which causes their stock markets to advance at a faster pace than ours. In the last decade, this certainly has been the case. Even in Magellan, my ratio of winners to losers was higher in foreign stocks than in the made-in-the-U.S.A. stocks.

But to succeed in a country fund you have to have patience and a contrarian's bent. Country funds arouse a desire for instant gratification. They can be traps for weekend thinkers. A good example is the Germany Fund, and its offshoot the New Germany Fund, both of which were conceived as the Berlin Wall was coming down, and Germans from both sides were hugging each other in the streets, with the rest of the world cheering them on. The great German renaissance was about to begin.

Behind the Wall, as an emotional backdrop, you had the magical reunification of Europe. By the appointed witching hour in 1992, centuries of animosity were supposed to disappear overnight: the French would kiss and make up with the Germans and the English would kiss and make up with the Germans and the French, the Italians would give up their lire and the Dutch their guilders for a common currency, and unity, peace, and prosperity would prevail. Personally, I found it much easier to believe in the turnaround in Pier 1 Imports.

As triumphant Berliners danced on the rubble of the Wall, the price of the two Germany funds was bid up to 25 percent above the value of the underlying stocks. These funds were going up 2 points a day on nothing but a wing and a prayer for an economic boom. The same overblown expectations now exist for the merger of North and South Korea, which I predict will come to a similar short-term end.

Six months later, when investors finally noticed the problems in this great German renaissance, euphoria turned to despair and the Germany funds quickly sold off at a 20–25 percent discount to the value of the underlying stocks. They've been selling at a discount ever since.

Meanwhile, in 1991, when people were still euphoric about German prospects, the stock market there did poorly, whereas in the first half of 1992, when the news from Germany was all gloomy, the stock market did well. It's hard enough to fathom these developments at home, much less from abroad.

Clearly, the best time to buy a country fund is when it is unpopular and you can get it for a 20–25 percent discount. Sooner or later, Germany will have its renaissance, and patient investors who bought the Germany funds on the dips will be glad they did.

There are many drawbacks to the country funds. Fees and expenses are generally quite high. It's not enough that the companies in which the fund has invested have done well. The currency of the country in question has to remain strong relative to the dollar, otherwise your gains will all be lost in translation. The government can't ruin the party with extra taxes or regulations that hurt business. The manager of the country fund has to do his or her homework.

Just who is that manager? Is it someone who once visited this country and has a travel poster to prove it, or someone who has lived and worked there, has contacts in the major companies, and can follow their stories?

I'd like to add my two cents to the U.S.-versus-the-world debate. These days, it's fashionable to believe that foreign-made anything is superior to the domestic version: the Germans are more efficient and make the best cars, the Japanese work harder and make the best TVs, the French are more fun-loving and make the best bread, the Singaporeans are better educated and make the best disk drives, etc. From all my trips abroad, I've concluded that the U.S. still has the best companies and the best system for investing in them.

Europe is filled with big conglomerates that are the equivalent to our blue chips, but Europe lacks the number of growth companies that we have. Those that do exist tend to be overpriced. There was L'Oréal, a French cosmetics company that Carolyn discovered in her fundamental analysis at the perfume counter. I liked the stock, but not at 50 times earnings.

I'm certain that hundreds of U.S. companies have increased their earnings 20 years in a row. In Europe, I'd be hard-pressed to find even 10. Even the European blue chips have no record of the sustained earnings that are commonplace here.

Information about foreign companies is sketchy and often misleading. Only in Britain is there a semblance of the careful coverage that companies get on Wall Street. On the Continent, securities analyst is an obscure profession. In Sweden there is scarcely an analyst in sight. The only one that I could find had never visited Volvo, a company with the clout of a General Motors or an IBM.

Earnings estimates can be quite imaginative. We chide U.S. analysts for being wrong much of the time, but compared to European analysts, they are nearly infallible. In France, I read an upbeat analyst's report on a conglomerate called Matra. Filled with joyous expectations, I visited the company. A spokesman there reviewed the prospects for each division. The news was mostly bad: ruinous competition in one division, an unexpected write-off in another, a labor strike in a third, etc. "This doesn't sound like the same company I've been reading about, that's going to double its earnings this year," I remarked. He sort of stared at me.

If you do your own research in Europe, you can turn the poor coverage to your advantage, for instance by discovering that Volvo was selling for the same price as the cash in its vault. That's why I was able to do so well with foreign stocks in Magellan. In the U.S., what makes stockpicking difficult is that 1,000 people smarter than you are studying the same stocks you are. It's not that way in France, or Switzerland, or Sweden. There all the smart people are studying Virgil and Nietzsche, instead of Volvo and Nestlé.

What about the Japanese, those champions of capitalism and overtime at the office, owners of Rockefeller Center and Columbia Pictures, and soon to be owners of the Seattle Mariners and maybe the Washington Monument after that? If you had come along on one of my research trips to Japan, you would have realized that this whole business of Japanese superiority was malarkey from the start.

Japan is the richest country in the universe where the people have trouble making ends meet. The Japanese admire us Americans for our closet space, our low prices, and our weekend homes. An apple costs them $5, and dinner costs them $100, and it's not even much of a dinner. They cram themselves into subway cars, and after an hour and a half they still haven't left greater Tokyo, which is bigger than Rhode Island. Along the way, they dream about moving to Hawaii, where they might get something for their money, but they have to stay in Japan and dedicate themselves to paying the mortgage on their $1 million, 1,000-square-foot hutch; if they sold the hutch, they'd have to move into another $1 million hutch, or else rent a $15,000-a-month apartment.

The Japanese predicament reminds me of the story about the man who brags about having once owned a $1 million dog, and you ask him how he knew it was $1 million dog and he says because he traded it for two $500,000 cats. Maybe the Japanese do have some $500,000 cats to go along with their $500,000 golf club memberships, and until recently they could have traded these for a few $100,000 stocks.

The advertising slogan "When E. F. Hutton Talks, People Listen" would have been an understatement in Japan. There, the slogan would have been "When Nomura Securities Commands, People Obey." Brokers were entirely trusted, and their advice was taken as gospel. The Japanese bought $500,000 cats on cue.

The result was a wondrous market of stocks with p/e ratios of 50, 100, 200, which were so out of line with rational levels that bystanders began to theorize that the high Japanese p/e was a cultural trait. Actually, U.S. investors exhibited that same trait in the late 1960s, when our market was so overvalued that it took 22 years, until 1991, for the Dow Jones average, adjusted for inflation, to reach the all-time high it set in 1967.

The Japanese market has been subject to behind-the-scenes finagling to a degree unknown on Wall Street since the 1920s. Large investors in Japan had a money-back guarantee from the brokerage firms—when they lost money, the brokers paid them back. If only Merrill Lynch and Smith Barney would be so accommodating, it would put some confidence back into *our* stocks.

I got a hint that Japan was a finagled market on my first visit, in 1986. The trip was arranged through the Fidelity office in Tokyo, which employed 80 people. In his book *The Money Game,* Adam Smith wrote a chapter on Fidelity's founder, the industrious Mr. Johnson. Ever since it was published in Japanese, Fidelity has been famous in Japan.

Nevertheless, it took many letters and phone calls before a series of meetings could be arranged between me and some Japanese companies. I got the annual reports in advance and had them translated into English, and wrote out my questions. I used the same technique I follow at home, warming up with polite banter, peppering my questions with facts to show that I cared enough to do the homework.

Japanese firms are very formal and the meetings were ceremonial in nature, with a lot of bowing and coffee tippling. At one company, I asked a question about capital spending, which took about 15 seconds in English, but the translator took five minutes to relay it to the Japanese expert, who then took another seven minutes to answer in Japanese, and what finally came back to me in English was "One hundred and five million yen." This is a very flowery language.

At a later interview with one of the best-known brokers in the country, I got a hint of the extent to which Japanese stock prices are controlled. He was describing his favorite stock—I don't remember what the name was—and he kept referring to a number—something like 100,000 yen. I wasn't sure if he was talking about sales, earnings, or what, so I asked for clarification. It turned out he was picking the stock price 12 months hence. A year later, I checked, and he was exactly right.

Japan was a nightmare for a fundamental analyst. I saw example after example of companies with bad balance sheets and spotty earnings, and overpriced stocks with wacky p/e ratios, including the company that launched the biggest public offering in financial history: Nippon Telephone.

When a telephone company is privatized, I normally can't wait to buy it (see Chapter 17), but Sushi Bell was the exception. This was not a fast grower in an underdeveloped country with a hunger for a handset. This was a regulated Japanese utility in its mature phase, something like the old Ma Bell before it was split up, which could be expected to grow at 6 or 7 percent a year, but not double digits.

The initial offering was sold out in 1987 at a price of 1.1 million yen per share. I thought this was a crazy price then, and in the aftermarket the price nearly tripled. At this point, Nippon Telephone was selling for something like 3,000 times earnings. It had a market value of $350 billion, more than the entire German stock market and more than the top 100 companies in our *Fortune* 500.

On this deal, not only did the emperor have no clothes, but the people lost their shirts. After the Great Correction, the Japanese government was able to foist more overpriced Nippon on the Japanese public via two additional offerings: one for 2.55 million yen a share and the next for 1.9 million yen a share. It's been all downhill since. As of this writing, a share of Nippon sells for 575,000 yen, an 85 percent discount from the 1987 discounted price. For investors on Wall Street to lose a similar amount, the entire *Fortune* 100 list of companies would have to be wiped out.

Even at 575,000 yen per share, Nippon's market value exceeds that of Philip Morris, the largest company in the U.S. with 30 straight years of increased earnings. After all its losses, Nippon is still over-priced at 50 times earnings.

Japanese investors, we hear, paid little heed to earnings and focused their attention on cash flow—perhaps due to a shortage of the former. Companies that spend money like drunken sailors, especially on acquisitions and real estate, are left with a huge depreciation allowance and a lot of debts to pay off, which gives them a high cash flow/low earnings profile.

Students of the Japanese market will tell you that the Japanese fondness for cash flow is another cultural trait, but there's nothing cultural about red ink. Red ink is the problem facing Japanese banks that lent money to all the purchasers of the $1 million dogs and the $500,000 cats.

Speculation plays a much larger role in the Japanese economy than in the U.S. economy. Merrill Lynch in its best years never appeared among the top 100 U.S. companies in the *Fortune* 500, but at one point, 5 of the top 25 companies in Japan were brokerage houses, and another 5 to 10 were banks.

U.S. banks are criticized for making stupid loans to the Reichmanns and the Trumps, but even the dumbest of these real-estate loans were backed by some sort of collateral. Japanese banks were making 100 percent loans on zero collateral for office buildings where in the most optimistic scenario the rents would barely cover the expenses.

Until the recent sell-off, the only bargains in Japanese stocks were small companies that in my opinion are the key to Japan's future growth and prosperity, just as they are in the U.S. Small Japanese companies were ignored in the early stages of the great stock mania, and I concentrated my purchases there. When these small stocks reached the same crazy prices as the rest, I got out. All things considered, I'd rather be invested in a solid emerging-growth stock mutual fund in the good old U.S.A.

To summarize our discussion of mutual fund strategies:

- Put as much of your money into stock funds as you can. Even if you need income, you will be better off in the long run to own dividend-paying stocks and to occasionally dip into capital as an income substitute.
- If you must own government bonds, buy them outright from the

Treasury and avoid the bond funds, in which you're paying management fees for nothing.

- Know what kinds of stock funds you own. When evaluating performance, compare apples to apples, i.e., value funds to value funds. Don't blame a gold-fund manager for failing to outperform a growth stock fund.
- It's best to divide your money among three or four types of stock funds (growth, value, emerging growth, etc.) so you'll always have some money invested in the most profitable sector of the market.
- When you add money to your portfolio, put it into the fund that's invested in the sector that has lagged the market for several years.
- Trying to pick tomorrow's winning fund based on yesterday's performance is a difficult if not futile task. Concentrate on solid performers and stick with those. Constantly switching your money from one fund to another is an expensive habit that is harmful to your net worth.

FOUR

MANAGING MAGELLAN

The Early Years

Recently, I cleared the latest red herrings (the name for prospectuses on Wall Street) off my desk, pulled the thick loose-leaf books of Magellan's reports to shareholders from their perch on a dusty shelf, and attempted to make sense of 13 years of managing the fund. I was aided in this effort by Fidelity computer whizzes Guy Cerundolo, Phil Thayer, and especially Jacques Perold, who produced printouts of my biggest gains and losses. This list is more instructive than I thought it would be—even I am surprised by some of the results. The popular theory that small growth stocks were the major factor in Magellan's success falls wide of the mark.

I offer this review in the hope that it will serve some practical benefit to other fund managers and also amateur investors who might want to learn from my mistakes, or, if not that, anyone who might be curious about what worked for me and what didn't. I have divided the material into three chapters dealing with the early years, the middle years, and the later years, in the style of diplomats who write their memoirs, only because it's a convenient way to organize things and not because there's any highfalutin importance about the life of a stockpicker, which I was and still am.

Fidelity is not a public company. If it had been I'd like to think I would have been sensible enough to recommend that people buy shares in it, having seen firsthand every day the new money pouring in and the new funds launched, and the other effects of brilliant management, first by Mr. Johnson and then by his son, Ned.

The Magellan Fund did not start with me. Ned Johnson started it in 1963 as the Fidelity International Fund, but a tax on foreign investments, promoted by then-President Kennedy, forced the managers of international funds to sell their foreign stocks and buy domestic stocks. For two years the International Fund was really a domestic fund in disguise, until it became Magellan on March 31, 1965. Magellan's biggest position then was Chrysler, which came back from the edge of bankruptcy 20 years later to become my biggest position, proving that you can never give up on certain companies.

When Magellan was launched, I was a student at Boston College, caddying golf games on weekends. This was during the great fund boom, when everybody wanted to buy funds. The fund mania even reached my own mother, a widow of limited resources. A schoolteacher who was moonlighting as a part-time fund salesman convinced her to buy Fidelity Capital. She liked the fact that "a Chinese guy" was running it, because she believed in the brilliant Oriental mind. The Chinese guy was Gerry Tsai; he, along with Ned Johnson at Fidelity Trend, were fund managers *sui generis* in that era.

My mother never would have known that a Chinese guy was running the Fidelity Capital Fund if the salesman hadn't told her. A flotilla of fund floggers traveled the countryside, many of them part-timers, making house calls along with the vacuum cleaner, insurance, burial plot, and encyclopedia salesmen. My mother agreed to a plan in which she would invest $200 a month, forever, to secure us a prosperous future. This was money she did not have, but Fidelity Capital outperformed the S&P, as it tripled in the 1950s and doubled again during the first six years of the 1960s.

The stock market is a fickle business, although it's difficult to believe that today, after so many years of exciting gains. Severe corrections lead to long stretches when nothing happens, Wall Street is shunned by the magazine editors, nobody is bragging about stocks at cocktail parties, and the investor's patience is sorely tested. Dedicated stockpickers begin to feel as lonely as vacationers at off-season resorts.

When I hired on as an analyst at Fidelity, the market was just entering one of those doldrums. Stock prices had peaked and were headed toward the 1972–74 collapse, the worst since the 1929–32 collapse that preceded the Depression. Suddenly, nobody wanted to buy mutual funds. There was no interest at all. Business was so terrible that the flotilla of floggers was forced to disband. The sales-men returned to selling vacuum cleaners or car wax or whatever else they'd sold before the funds got hot.

As people fled the stock funds, they put the cash into money-market and bond funds. Fidelity made enough profit from these sorts of funds to keep at least some of the unpopular equity funds alive. These survivors had to compete for the few customers who were interested in stocks, an endangered species that was vanishing at a fast clip.

There was little to distinguish one equity fund from another. Most of them were called "captial appreciation funds," a vague term that gave managers the leeway to buy cyclicals, utilities, growth com-panies, special situations, whatever. While the mix of stocks would differ from one capital appreciation fund to another, to the fund shopper they all looked like the same product.

In 1966, Fidelity Magellan was a $20 million fund, but the steady outflow of money from the customer's redemptions reduced it to a $6 million fund by 1976. It's hard to pay the electric bill, much less any salaries, from a $6 million fund when the management fee of .6 percent generates $36,000 for annual operating expenses.

So in 1976, in an effort to economize by doubling up, Fidelity merged the $6 million Magellan Fund with another casualty of inves-tor lack of interest, the $12 million Essex Fund. At one point, Essex had been a $100 million fund, but it had done so poorly in the bad market that it had produced a $50 million tax-loss carryforward. This was its major attraction. The management and trustees at Fi-delity thought that the Magellan Fund, which had been capably managed by Dick Haberman since 1972, and from 1969 to 1972 by Haberman and Ned Johnson, could take advantage of the tax losses of the Essex Fund. The combined entity didn't have to pay any taxes on the first $50 million in capital gains.

This was the situation I inherited in 1977 when I was named fund manager: two funds rolled into one, $18 million in assets, the $50 million tax-loss carryforward, a terrible stock market, a small and rapidly declining number of skittish customers, and no way of attracting new ones because Fidelity had closed Magellan to buyers.

It wasn't until four years later, in 1981, that Magellan was reopened and people could buy shares again. This long shutdown has been widely misinterpreted in the press. The popular view is that Fidelity had devised a clever strategy of waiting for its funds to compile a decent performance record before bringing them out, in order to stimulate sales. Magellan is often identified as one of several so-called incubator funds that were given an extended tryout.

The truth is much less flattering. Fidelity would have been delighted to attract more shareholders all along. What stopped us was the lack of interested parties. The fund business was so dismal that brokerage houses had disbanded their sales departments, so there was nobody left to sell the shares to the few oddballs who might have been interested in buying.

I'm convinced that the obscurity in which I operated for the first four years was more of a blessing than a curse. It enabled me to learn the trade and make mistakes without being in a spotlight. Fund managers and athletes have this in common: they may do better in the long run if they're brought along slowly.

There's no way an analyst who is familiar with perhaps 25 percent of the companies in the stock market (in my case, mostly textiles, metals, and chemicals) can feel adequately prepared to run a capital appreciation fund, in which he or she can buy anything. Having been director of research at Fidelity from 1974 to 1977 and having served on the investment committee gave me some familiarity with other industries. In 1975, I had begun to help a Boston charity manage its portfolio. This was my first direct experience with a fund.

My diaries of visits with companies, which I have kept as religiously as a Casanova kept his datebooks, remind me that on October 12, 1977, I visited General Cinema, which must not have impressed me, because the stock doesn't show up on my buy list. It was selling for less than $1 then and is selling for more than $30 today—imagine missing this 30 bagger right off the bat. (This $30 figure has been adjusted for stock splits. We've done the same with stock prices throughout the book. Therefore, the prices you see here may not correspond with the ones that you see in the business section, but the gains and losses described in this text are absolute and correct.)

My diaries are full of such missed opportunities, but the stock market is merciful—it always gives the nincompoop a second chance.

During my first months, I was preoccupied with getting rid of my predecessor's favorite selections and replacing them with my own picks, and with constantly selling shares to raise cash to cover the endless redemptions. By the end of December 1977, my biggest positions were Congoleum (51,000 shares worth a whopping $833,000—this would be an insignificant holding 10 years later), Transamerica, Union Oil, and Aetna Life and Casualty. I'd also discovered Hanes (thanks to my wife, Carolyn, who was crazy about their L'eggs), Taco Bell ("What's that, the Mexican telephone company?" asked Charlie Maxfield, my first trader, when I placed the buy order), and Fannie Mae, of which I'd bought 30,000 shares.

Congoleum I liked because it had invented a new vinyl flooring without seams that could be rolled out across an entire kitchen as if it were a carpet. Besides doing floors, this company was also building battle frigates for the Defense Department with the same modular techniques that were used on prefab houses. The Congoleum prefab frigate was said to have a promising future. Taco Bell I liked because of its tasty tacos, because 90 percent of the country had not yet been exposed to the tasty tacos, and because the company had a good record, a strong balance sheet, and a home office that resembled a neighborhood garage. This leads me to Peter's Principle #7:

> **The extravagance of any corporate office is directly proportional to management's reluctance to reward the shareholders.**

Aside from being public companies, my original picks (Congoleum, Kaiser Steel, Mission Insurance, La Quinta Motor Inns, Twentieth Century–Fox, Taco Bell, Hanes, etc.) seem to have nothing in common. From the beginning, I was attracted to a mystifying assortment, the most notable absence being the chemical sector that I had researched so thoroughly as an analyst.

The March 31, 1978, annual report for Magellan came out ten months into my tenure. The cover is illustrated with an elaborate and ancient map of the coast of South America, showing the names of various inlets and rivers. Three charming little galleons, presumably Magellan's, were drawn on the margins, sailing happily toward Cape Horn. In later years, as the fund got larger and more complicated, the illustrations got simpler. Soon, the Spanish names were erased from the inlets and the rivers, and the flotilla was reduced from three ships to two.

I'm reminded from that March 1978 report that the fund was up 20 percent in the prior 12 months, while the Dow Jones average lost 17.6 percent and the S&P 500 lost 9.4 percent in the same period.

Some of this success must have resulted from my rookie's contribution. In my letter to shareholders, in which I was always obliged to try to explain the inexplicable, I described my strategy as follows: "Reduced holdings in autos, aerospace, railroads, pollution, utilities, chemicals, electronics, and energy; added to positions in financial institutions, broadcasting, entertainment, insurance, banking and finance, consumer products, lodging, and leasing." All this for a ten-month stint on a $20 million portfolio with fewer than 50 stocks!

The fact is that I never had an overall strategy. My stockpicking was entirely empirical, and I went sniffing from one case to another like a bloodhound that's trained to follow a scent. I cared much more about the details of a particular story—for instance, why a company that owned TV stations was going to earn more money this year than last—than about whether my fund was underweighted or overweighted in broadcasting. What could happen is that I would meet with one broadcaster who would tell me that business was improving, and then he'd give me the name of his strongest competitor, and I'd check out the details, and often end up buying the second broadcaster's stock. I followed scents in every direction, proving that a little knowledge about a lot of industries is not necessarily a dangerous thing.

Since Magellan was a capital appreciation fund, I was allowed to buy anything—domestic stocks of all varieties, foreign stocks, even bonds. This gave me the latitude to fully exploit my bloodhound style. I was not constrained the way a manager of a growth fund was. When the entire growth sector was overvalued, which happened every few years, the growth-fund manager was forced into buying the overpriced inventory, otherwise he didn't have a growth fund. He had to choose from the best of a terrible lot. I was free to wander off and learn that Alcoa's earnings were on the rebound because the price of aluminum was going up.

In January 1978, we told the shareholders that "the portfolio is dominated by three categories of companies: special situations, undervalued cyclicals, and small and medium-sized growth companies." If this didn't cover the waterfront, the definition was expanded a year later as follows:

The goal of Magellan Fund is capital appreciation through investing in relatively attractive common stocks found primarily in five categories: small and medium-sized growth companies, companies whose prospects are improving, depressed cyclicals, high yielding and growing dividend payers, and finally, companies where the market has overlooked or underestimated the real value of the firm's assets . . . at some point in the future, foreign stocks could represent a substantial portion of the fund.

In other words, if it's sold on a stock exchange, we'll buy it.

Flexibility was the key. There were always undervalued companies to be found somewhere. Two of my biggest gainers in this early stage were major oil companies: Unocal and Royal Dutch. You'd expect a $20 million fund to ignore major oil companies and concentrate on smaller stocks with better growth rates, but I learned that Royal Dutch was turning around and Wall Street apparently hadn't realized it, so I bought Royal Dutch. At one point when Magellan was still a pip-squeak fund, I put 15 percent of the assets into utilities. I owned Boeing and Todd Shipyards right along with Pic 'N' Save and Service Corporation International, the McDonald's of funeral homes. I doubt that I was ever more than 50 percent invested in the growth stocks to which Magellan's success is so often attributed.

Rather than being constantly on the defensive, buying stocks and then thinking of new excuses for holding on to them if they weren't doing well (a great deal of energy on Wall Street is still devoted to the art of concocting excuses), I tried to stay on the offensive, searching for better opportunities in companies that were more undervalued than the ones I'd chosen. In 1979, a good year for stocks in general, Magellan was up 51 percent while the S&P rose 18.44. In the annual report to shareholders, once again I faced the challenge of explaining my strategy, as if I'd had one to begin with. "Increased holdings in lodging, restaurants, and retail" was the best I could do.

I was attracted to fast-food restaurants because they were so easy to understand. A restaurant chain that succeeded in one region had an excellent chance of duplicating its success in another. I'd seen how Taco Bell had opened many outlets in California and, after proving itself there, had moved eastward, growing its earnings at 20 to 30 percent a year in the process. I bought Cracker Barrel and later visited the Cracker Barrel country store located in Macon, Georgia. I'd flown to Atlanta to attend an investment conference sponsored by Robinson-Humphrey, and decided to make a side trip to the restaurant. On the rental car map, Macon appeared to be a few miles away from my downtown Atlanta hotel.

A few miles turned out to be more like 100, and in the rush-hour traffic my little foray took three hours, but in the end I had a delicious catfish dinner and came away impressed with the entire Cracker Barrel operation. This 50-bagger did well for Magellan, which is why I've included it in my 50 most important stocks list on page 136.

I did a similar bit of on-site research at a do-it-yourself handyman's supermarket also located in the Atlanta area. It was called Home Depot. Again I was impressed with the courteous service, not to mention the vast inventory of screws, bolts, bricks, and mortar, the cheap prices, and the knowledgeable employees. Here the sunshine painter and the weekend plumber were liberated from the high-priced and poorly stocked local paint and hardware store.

This was the infancy of Home Depot, with the stock (adjusted backward for later splits) selling for 25 cents a share, and I'd seen it with my own eyes and bought it, but then lost interest and sold it a year later. Figure 4-1 has caused me eternal remorse. Imagine a stock that goes from 25 cents to $65, a 260-bagger in 15 years, and I was on the scene at the creation and didn't see the potential.

Perhaps if Home Depot had begun in New England, or if I'd known the difference between a Phillips screwdriver and a sloe gin fizz, I wouldn't have misjudged this wonderful company. That and Toys "R" Us, which I also unloaded too soon, were the two worst sell orders of my entire career.

Even without Home Depot, Magellan's successes in 1979 were duplicated and then some in 1980, when my tiny club of shareholders enjoyed a 69.9 percent gain, while the S&P rose 32 percent. My latest big positions were in gaming (Golden Nugget and Resorts International, to be exact), insurance, and retail. I liked the convenience stores so much that I bought Hop-In Foods, Pic 'N' Save, Shop & Go, Stop & Shop, and Sunshine Jr. all at once.

In reviewing this early phase of my stewardship, I'm amazed at the turnover rate in the fund: 343 percent in the first year, when the portfolio contained 41 stocks, and 300 percent in each of the three years thereafter. Beginning on August 2, 1977, when I sold 30 percent of the holdings, I maintained a dizzy pace of buying and selling as oil companies, insurance companies, and consumer stocks came and went from month to month.

In September 1977 I purchased a few cyclicals, and by November I was getting rid of them. Fannie Mae and Hanes, both of which

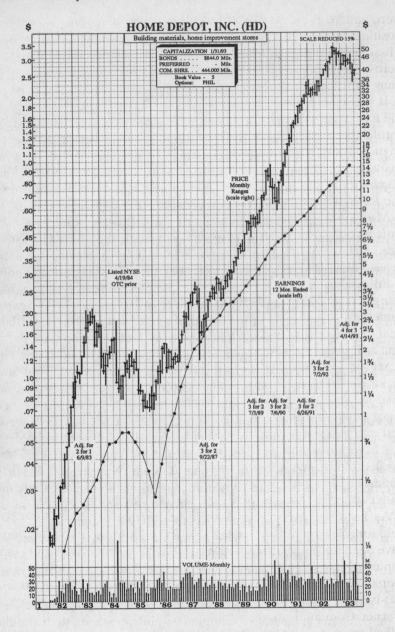

HOME DEPOT, INC. (HD)

Building materials, home improvement stores

SCALE REDUCED 15%

CAPITALIZATION 1/31/93
BONDS . . . . . $844.0 Mils.
PREFERRED . .   - Mils.
COM. SHRS. . .   444.000 Mils.
Book Value -   5
Options: PHIL

PRICE
Monthly
Ranges
(scale right)

Listed NYSE
4/19/84
OTC prior

EARNINGS
12 Mos. Ended
(scale left)

Adj. for
4 for 3
4/14/93

Adj. for
3 for 2
7/2/92

Adj. for   Adj. for   Adj. for
3 for 2   3 for 2   3 for 2
7/3/89   7/6/90   6/26/91

Adj. for
2 for 1
6/9/83

Adj. for
3 for 2
9/22/87

VOLUME-Monthly

FIGURE 4-1

were added to the fund that fall, were gone by spring. My largest position went from Congoleum to Signal Companies, and then to Mission Insurance, followed by Todd Shipyards, and then the Ponderosa steak house. Pier 1 appears and disappears, so does a company with the intriguing name of Four-Phase.

It seems that I was in and out of Four-Phase with every cycle of the moon. Eventually it was bought out by Motorola (much to Motorola's later regret) so I had to stop trading it back and forth. I vaguely recall it had something to do with computer terminals, but I couldn't really explain it then or now. Fortunately, I never invested much money in things I didn't understand, which included most of the technology companies along Route 128 in the Boston area.

Most of my abrupt changes in direction were caused not by any shift in policy but by my having visited some new company that I liked better than the last. I might have preferred to own both, but in a small fund in which shareholders continued to seek redemptions, I did not have that luxury. In order to raise the cash to buy something, I had to sell something else, and since I always wanted to buy something, I had to do a lot of selling. Every day, it seemed I would hear about some new prospect—Circle K, House of Fabrics, etc.— that was more exciting than yesterday's prospects.

My frequent trading continued to lead to the annual challenge: making whatever I'd done sound sensible to the shareholders who read the progress report. "Magellan shifts from cyclicals that had appreciated in value to noncyclicals which seem likely to have sales and earnings gains" was my strategic recap for one year, followed by "Magellan reduced positions in companies whose earnings could be affected by an economic slowdown. Nevertheless, the Fund continues to be heavily invested in cyclicals that appear to be undervalued."

As I study these reports now, I realize that many stocks that I held for a few months I should have held a lot longer. This wouldn't have been unconditional loyalty, it would have been sticking to companies that were getting more and more attractive. The seller's remorse list includes Albertson's, a great growth stock that became a 300-bagger; Toys "R" Us, ditto; Pic 'N' Save, already mentioned; Warner Communications, which a technical analyst, of all things, talked me out of; and Federal Express, a stock I bought at $5 and promptly sold at $10, only to watch it soar to $70 in two years.

By abandoning these great companies for lesser issues, I became a victim of the all-too-common practice of "pulling out the flowers and watering the weeds," one of my favorite expressions. Warren Buffett, renowned for his investing acumen as well as his skill as a writer, called me up one night seeking permission to use it in his annual report. I was thrilled to be quoted there. Some investors, the rumor goes, own a share of Buffett's Berkshire Hathaway company (these cost $11,000 apiece) simply to get on the mailing list for Buffett's reports. This makes Berkshire Hathaway the most expensive magazine subscription in history.

TAKING UNION CARBIDE TO LUNCH

During the four-year stretch when Magellan was closed to new customers and the heavy redemptions (one third of all the shares) forced me to sell in order to buy, I acquainted myself with a wide range of companies and industries and learned the factors that caused the ups and down in each. At the time, I wouldn't have guessed that I was getting an education in how to run a multibillion-dollar fund.

One of the most important lessons was the value of doing my own research. I visited dozens of companies at their headquarters, and was introduced to dozens more at regional investment conferences, and a growing number (200 a year or so in the early 1980s) came to Fidelity.

Fidelity began a policy of taking a corporation to lunch. This superseded the old system, under which we had lunch with cronies in the office or with stockbrokers and talked about our golf games or the Boston Red Sox. Stockbrokers and cronies were amiable enough, but not as valuable as CEOs or investor relations people who knew what business was like in the insurance or aluminum sector.

Lunches soon escalated into breakfasts and dinners, until you could have eaten your way through the S&P 500 in the Fidelity dining rooms. Every week, Natalie Trakas put out a printed menu, similar to the one that school systems send home with children (spaghetti on Monday, hamburgers on Tuesday), except that ours was a menu of guests (Monday, AT&T or Home Depot; Tuesday, Aetna, Wells Fargo, or Schlumberger; and so forth). There were always several choices.

Since I couldn't possibly attend all the informational meals, I made a point to see the companies in which I wasn't invested, just to see what I'd been missing. If I was underweighted in oil, for instance, I'd be sure to show up at the lunch with the oil company, and these conversations often led to my getting a jump on the latest developments in this cyclical industry.

This is the sort of information that is always available to the people directly or indirectly involved in a business, either as producers or suppliers, or, in the case of the oil business, as tanker salesmen or gas station owners or equipment suppliers, who can see the changes and take advantage of them.

Boston's being the capital of the mutual-fund industry made it easy for us to see hundreds of corporations a year without having to leave town. Their executives and their finance people could make the rounds of Putnam, Wellington, Massachusetts Financial, State Street Research, Fidelity, or numerous potential stops, seeking buyers for their latest public offerings or for their shares in general.

In addition to taking companies to breakfast, lunch, and/or dinner, analysts and fund managers were encouraged to attend the afternoon chitchats with additional corporate sources in one of the Fidelity conference rooms. Often our visitors had invited themselves to come in and talk to us, but we initiated many of these exchanges as well.

When a company wanted to tell us a story, it was usually the same story that everybody else on Wall Street was hearing, which is why the talks tended to be more useful if we sent out the invitations.

I'd spend an hour or so with the guy from Sears and find out about carpet sales. A vice-president of Shell Oil would give me a rundown on the oil, gas, and petrochemical markets. (A timely tip from Shell led me to sell shares in an ethylene company that soon enough fell apart.) An emissary from Kemper would tell me if insurance rates were on the rise. In 2 out of 10 of these random encounters, I'd discover something important.

My personal rule was that once a month I ought to have at least one conversation with a representative of each major industry group, just in case business was starting to turn around or there were other new developments that Wall Street had overlooked. This was a very effective early-warning system.

I always ended these discussions by asking: which of your competitors do you respect the most? When a CEO of one company admits that a rival company is doing as good a job or better, it's a powerful endorsement. The upshot was that I often went out and bought the other guy's stock.

The information we sought wasn't esoteric, or top secret, either, and our guests were happy to share what they knew. I found that the vast majority of corporate representatives were both objective and candid about the strengths and weaknesses in their own operations. When business was lousy, they admitted it, and they told me when they thought it was turning around. We humans tend to get cynical and suspicious of one another's motives, especially where money is involved, but in my thousands of encounters with people who wanted me to invest in their companies I was lied to only a handful of times.

In fact, there may be fewer liars on Wall Street than on Main Street. Remember, you heard it here first! It isn't that financial types are closer to the angels than the merchants down the street, it's that they are so widely distrusted that their every claim is reviewed by the SEC, so they aren't allowed to lie. The lies that do get through cannot survive the next quarterly earnings report.

I was always careful to write down the name of everyone I met at the lunches and meetings. Many of these people became valuable sources I called upon repeatedly over the years. In industries with which I was only vaguely familiar, they taught me the basics of what to look for on the balance sheet and what questions to ask.

I didn't know a thing about insurance until I met with executives at Aetna, Travelers, and Connecticut General in Hartford. In a couple of days they gave me a crash course in the business. I never had the same sort of edge that an insurance professional has, but I learned to identify the factors that make the earnings rise and fall. Then I could ask the right questions.

(I've explained elsewhere that the insurance professional ought to take advantage of this edge, and not blow it by shunning the insurance stocks and buying railroads or waste management companies, the workings of which he or she is entirely ignorant. If ignorance is bliss, then bliss can be very expensive.)

Speaking of insurance, by March 1980 I'd put 25.4 percent of the fund in either property or casualty underwriters, and I owned so many of these out-of-favor issues that the industry asked me to give a speech at its annual conference as insurance's best friend. The underwriters might not have invited me had they suspected that a year later I would be out of insurance stocks entirely and into bank stocks.

Interest rates had risen to record levels in 1980, at the tail end of the Carter administration, when the Federal Reserve was putting the brakes on the economy. In this atmosphere, the bank stocks were selling below book value despite the industry's superb growth prospects. I didn't discover this by sitting at my desk and imagining what would happen when interest rates declined. I discovered it at a regional investment conference in Atlanta organized by Robinson-Humphrey.

Actually, it was outside the conference that I started thinking about banks. During a lull in the proceedings, tired of presentations from companies with no track records and no earnings, I took a side trip to visit First Atlanta. This was a company with 12 years of continuously higher earnings. Its earnings were greater than the sales of many companies that were making flashy presentations downtown. Obviously, investors had overlooked First Atlanta, which was a 30-bagger by the time it merged with Wachovia of North Carolina five years later.

Wall Street was excited about all sorts of companies that might or might not survive, yet solid banks like this one were selling for half the p/e ratio of the market.

From the day I heard the First Atlanta story, I've been impressed with the quality of regional banks and perplexed by investors' lack of appreciation of them. They get little notice from the investment houses. Ask a fund manager to guess which companies produced the wonderful results shown in Figures 4-2, 4-3, and 4-4 and he or she will probably mention Wal-Mart, Philip Morris, or Merck. These look like the tracks of fast-growth companies—who would suspect they're all banks? The company shown in Figure 4-2, the stock price of which increased 10-fold in ten years, is Wachovia; Figure 4-3 is Norwest of Minneapolis; and Figure 4-4 is NBD Bancorp of Detroit.

I'm still amazed by the fact that a bank like NBD, which for years has been growing at the same 15 percent rate as a Pep Boys or a Dunkin' Donuts or any other fast grower, is given a low p/e multiple in the stock market. The way banks are treated by investors, you'd think they were mature utilities, just plodding along.

This mispricing of regional banks creates a lot of buying opportunities, which is why Magellan consistently had four or five times the market weighting in bank stocks. One of my favorites, a $2-to-$80 shot, was Fifth Third—how could you resist a bank with a name like that? Then there was Meridian, whose headquarters no other investor had visited in years; and KeyCorp, which had the "frost belt" theory, acquiring small banks and thrifts in mountainous areas

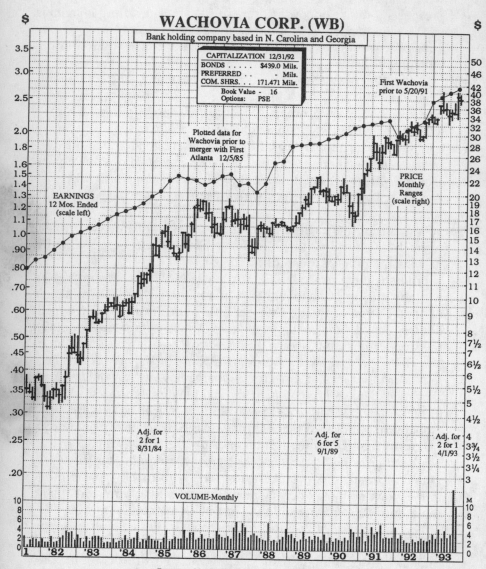

WACHOVIA CORP. (WB)

Bank holding company based in N. Carolina and Georgia

CAPITALIZATION 12/31/92	
BONDS	$439.0 Mils.
PREFERRED . .	- Mils.
COM. SHRS. . .	171.471 Mils.
Book Value -	16
Options:	PSE

First Wachovia
prior to 5/20/91

Plotted data for
Wachovia prior to
merger with First
Atlanta 12/5/85

EARNINGS
12 Mos. Ended
(scale left)

PRICE
Monthly
Ranges
(scale right)

Adj. for
2 for 1
8/31/84

Adj. for
6 for 5
9/1/89

Adj. for
2 for 1
4/1/93

VOLUME-Monthly

'1 '82 '83 '84 '85 '86 '87 '88 '89 '90 '91 '92 '93

Chart courtesy of: Securities Research Co.
A division of Babson-United Investment Advisors, Inc.
101 Prescott Street, Wellesley Hills, Ma. 02181-3319

FIGURE 4-2

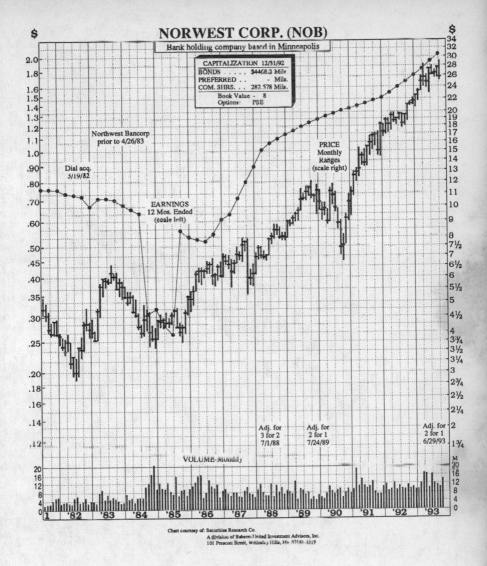

NORWEST CORP. (NOB)

Bank holding company based in Minneapolis

CAPITALIZATION 12/31/92
BONDS . . . . . $4468.2 Mils.
PREFERRED . . . . - Mils.
COM. SHRS. . . 282.578 Mils.
Book Value - 8
Options: PSE

Northwest Bancorp prior to 4/26/83

Dial acq. 3/19/82

EARNINGS
12 Mos. Ended
(scale left)

PRICE
Monthly
Ranges
(scale right)

Adj. for
3 for 2
7/1/88

Adj. for
2 for 1
7/24/89

Adj. for
2 for 1
6/29/93

VOLUME-Monthly

'82 '83 '84 '85 '86 '87 '88 '89 '90 '91 '92 '93

Chart courtesy of: Securities Research Co.
A division of Babson-United Investment Advisors, Inc.
101 Prescott Street, Wellesley Hills, Ma 02181-3319

FIGURE 4-3

where the people tend to be frugal and conservative and less likely to default.

But my biggest winners in the bank group have been the regionals, such as the three shown on pages 96–98. I always look for banks that have a strong local deposit base, and are efficient and careful commercial lenders. Magellan's 50 most important bank stocks are listed on page 137.

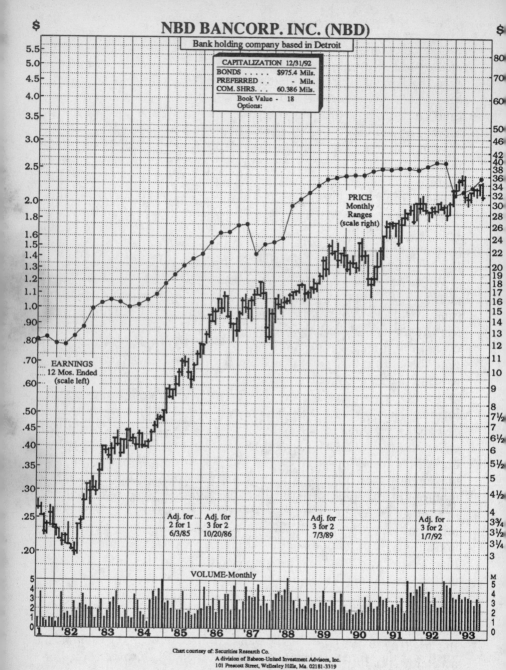

NBD BANCORP. INC. (NBD)

Bank holding company based in Detroit

CAPITALIZATION 12/31/92
BONDS . . . . . $975.4 Mils.
PREFERRED . .   - Mils.
COM. SHRS. . .   60.386 Mils.
Book Value -   18
Options:

PRICE
Monthly
Ranges
(scale right)

EARNINGS
12 Mos. Ended
(scale left)

Adj. for
2 for 1
6/3/85

Adj. for
3 for 2
10/20/86

Adj. for
3 for 2
7/3/89

Adj. for
3 for 2
1/7/92

VOLUME-Monthly

'82 '83 '84 '85 '86 '87 '88 '89 '90 '91 '92 '93

FIGURE 4-4

One bank led to another, and by the end of 1980 I had 9 percent of the fund invested in 12 different banks.

In the annual report of March 1981, I was pleased to note that Magellan's shareholders had nearly doubled their money—the fund's net asset value had risen 94.7 percent from the previous March, as compared to 33.2 percent for the S&P 500.

While Magellan had beaten the market four years in a row, the number of shareholders continued to decline, and one third of the shares were redeemed in this period. I can't be sure why this happened, but my guess is that people who got into Magellan by default when we merged with Essex waited until they'd recovered most of their losses and then cashed out. It's possible to lose money even in a successful mutual fund, especially if your emotions are giving the buy and sell signals.

With the many redemptions counteracting the capital gains, Magellan's growth was retarded. What should have been an $80 million fund, thanks to a fourfold increase in the value of the portfolio over four years, was only a $50 million fund. In mid-1980, Magellan owned 130 stocks, an increase from the 50 to 60 I'd held at any one time during the first two years. A surge in redemptions forced me to scale back to 90 stocks.

In 1981, Magellan was merged with the Salem Fund, bringing the Puritans on board with the Portuguese explorers. Salem was another of Fidelity's small operations that had gone nowhere. It used to be called the Dow Theory Fund, and its losses had produced another big tax-loss carryforward. Warren Casey had done a superb job of managing Salem in the two years after the merger was first announced in 1979, but still the fund was too small to be economical.

Only at this point, after the merger with Salem, was Magellan finally offered for sale to the public. That it took this long is an indication of how unpopular investing in stocks had become. Rather than return to the outside brokers who had sold the fund door-to-door a decade earlier, Ned Johnson, Fidelity's chief executive, decided to give the job to Fidelity's in-house sales force.

Our first offer was that you could buy Magellan with a 2 percent sales charge, or load. This worked so well that we decided to raise the load to 3 percent to slow down the rush. Then we tried to accelerate the rush by offering a 1 percent discount on the 3 percent load to anyone who bought the fund within 60 days.

This clever marketing ploy almost came to ruin when we published the wrong phone number in the notice to shareholders. Interested parties who thought they were calling Fidelity's sales department were connected to the switchboard at the Massachusetts Eye and Ear Infirmary. For several weeks, the hospital had to deny it was a mutual fund, which is probably the worst thing ever said about it.

Between the existing assets, the merger with Salem, and the new offer, Magellan crossed the $100 million mark for the first time in 1981. Here we'd gotten the first flurry of interest from the public, and what happened? The stock market fell apart. As is so often the case, just when people began to feel it was safe to return to stocks, stocks suffered a correction. But Magellan managed to post a 16.5 percent gain for the year in spite of it.

No wonder Magellan had a good beginning. My top 10 stocks in 1978 had p/e ratios of between 4 and 6, and in 1979, of between 3 and 5. When stocks in good companies are selling at 3–6 times earnings, the stockpicker can hardly lose.

Many of my favorite picks in those years were the so-called secondary stocks, small or mid-sized companies including the retailers, banks, etc., that I've already described. At the end of the 1970s, fund managers and other experts were advising me that secondary stocks had had their day, and that it was time to invest in the big blue chips. I'm glad I didn't take their advice. The big blue chips did not have exciting stories to tell, and they were twice as expensive as the secondaries. Small is not only beautiful, it also can be lucrative.

FIVE

MAGELLAN

The Middle Years

FAR FROM A ONE-MAN SHOW

My working day began at 6:05 A.M., when I would meet the Saab driven by Jeff Moore, a friend from Marblehead who gave me a ride into town. Next to him in the front seat was his wife, Bobbie. Both were radiologists.

It was still dark. While Jeff drove, Bobbie held X rays up to a small light on the passenger side. I was in the back with another small light, perusing annual reports and my chart books, which fortunately for Bobbie's patients never got mixed up with the medical records in the front seat. There wasn't much conversation.

By 6:45, I was in my office, but not alone. Fidelity was a no-nonsense New England institution, where even on weekends you could have gotten up a basketball game with analysts and fund managers who arrived before dawn. I doubt our competitors could have gotten up a double solitaire game.

But we didn't play basketball, we worked. Ned Johnson loved the idea of people working extra hard. His customary business hours were 9:30 A.M. to 9:30 P.M.

From the mess on my desk, I retrieved the sophisticated tools of my trade, the S&P stock guide available free from any brokerage house, the antique Rolodex, the empty yellow legal pads, the 2½ pencils, and the clunky Sharp Compet calculator with the oversize buttons that I've used for 15 years. Copies of outdated S&P guides would pile up on my desk. Behind the desk on a separate stand was the Quotron.

The earliest version of the Quotron required that you type in a stock symbol and push the enter button before the current price would appear. Otherwise, the screen was blank. Later versions, which you've probably seen, display an entire portfolio and the prices for all the stocks, which are updated automatically as the day's trading progresses. The blank screen was a better system because you couldn't stare at it all day and watch your stocks go up and down, as many contemporary fund managers do. When I got a newfangled Quotron, I had to turn it off because it was too exciting.

In the precious hours before the market opened and before the phones began to ring, I reviewed the summary of the buys and sells from the day before, prepared by Fidelity clerks. These so-called night sheets indicated what Fidelity fund managers were doing. I read the in-house summary of what our analysts had learned from their talks with various companies. I read *The Wall Street Journal*.

By 8:00 A.M. or so, I had written out a new buy and sell list, largely made up of companies that I'd bought the day before and the day before that, in an attempt to slowly build up a sizable stake at reasonable prices. I called my head trader, Barry Lyden, who worked in the trading room on a lower floor, to give him the orders.

Between me and the trading floor was a walkway or bridge that crossed a nine-floor drop and gave you the sensation of walking a tightrope over a deep canyon. Fidelity must have designed it that way to keep the fund managers from bothering the traders in person. In my case, it worked.

At first, my head trader was my only trader, but by the end of 1983, when Magellan had grown and the buys and sells got more complicated, I was assigned a second person, Carlene DeLuca. Lyden did buys and DeLuca did sells. Both were very patient with me, and I tried to give them the leeway to do their jobs.

Trading was the least of my worries. In retrospect, I probably spent more time on it than I should have—an hour a day instead of 10 minutes. It was fun to buy and sell, but I would have been better off using the extra 50 minutes to call two more companies. This is one of the keys to successful investing: focus on the companies, not on the stocks.

Once my trading list was sent down, I returned to my main task—

keeping up with the companies. My methods were not much different from those of an investigative reporter—reading the public documents for clues, talking with intermediaries such as analysts and investor relations people for more clues, and then going directly to the primary sources: the companies themselves.

After every contact I made, on the phone or in person, I'd scribble a notation in a loose-leaf binder—the name of the company and the current stock price, followed by a one- or two-line summary of the story I'd just heard. Every stockpicker, I think, could benefit from keeping such a notebook of stories. Without one, it's easy to forget why you bought something in the first place.

As Magellan grew, so did my library of notebooks, and the amount of time it took to review all the stories. I cut back on the corporate lunches, as useful as those had been, in favor of the more efficient practice of munching on a sandwich in between phone calls. I'd developed enough sources from the earlier lunches that I could get most of the information I needed on the phone.

Outside my cubicle door, four secretaries, led by the unflappable Paula Sullivan, were busy routing the calls. They'd yell, "So-and-so on line one," and I'd pick up. Rarely did anyone venture into my office for long. Since the seats of the chairs had become extra file cabinets, there was no convenient place to sit, except on the floor.

If I left my post, it was either to get another diet Coke from the office refrigerator or to use the bathroom. Between me and the nearest bathroom was a small lobby where corporate guests and visiting analysts waited for their meetings with the various fund managers on our floor. Usually there were people I knew out there. I avoided them by sneaking down a back stairway to a more secluded bathroom. Otherwise, I would have had to waste time making small talk, or snub these friends and acquaintances, which I didn't want to do.

MY NOT-SO-SILENT PARTNERS

Magellan was far from a one-man show. From 1981 forward, I always had one or more talented assistants who did the same thing I did, calling companies or calling analysts to keep me up to date on developments. My first assistant, Rich Fentin, set the standard for quality. He went on to run the Fidelity Growth and Fidelity Puritan funds. Fentin was followed by several others who learned so much from my mistakes that they, too, ran successful funds: Danny Frank at Special Situations; George Noble, who started the Overseas Fund; Bob Stansky who took over Growth; Will Danoff at Contrafund; and Jeff Vinik, who now runs Magellan. Then there were Jeff Barmeyer, now deceased; Deb Wheeler; George Domolky; Kari Firestone; and Bettina Doulton, now Vinik's assistant.

These energetic surrogates enabled me to be in several places at once. They proved that the best way to get the most out of a staff is to give people full responsibility. Usually, they will live up to it.

Fidelity put this theory into practice by making all the fund managers responsible for doing our own research. This requirement was revolutionary, and not always popular with my colleagues. In the traditional setup, a fund manager chooses stocks that the analysts have recommended, based on the analysts' research. This is very convenient for the fund managers, and excellent for their job security, since if the stocks go kaput they can blame the analysts for providing faulty information. It's the same dodge that the average investor uses when he loses money on a stock tip from Uncle Harry. "How could Uncle Harry have been so stupid?" he says to his wife after she hears the bad news. This is exactly what the fund manager says to his bosses about the analysts.

Knowing that the blame will be passed along to them, the analysts soon learn to protect themselves by not sticking their necks out. Instead of making imaginative recommendations to the fund managers, they prefer to tout acceptable, worn-out companies like IBM. Because they recommend acceptable stocks, they don't get criticized as much when the fund managers have a lousy quarter.

At Fidelity, this didn't happen. For better or worse, fund managers did independent research and were held accountable for the results. Analysts did their own parallel research and passed it along to the fund managers, who were free to take or leave the analysts' advice. Thus, there was twice as much investigating going on as there would have been with the customary division of labor.

Each new Fidelity fund required a new fund manager, who also would function as a fact gatherer for the others, so as the number of funds increased, so did the quality of our in-house intelligence. My colleagues' tips and leads were particularly valuable to me because Magellan was a capital appreciation fund, and therefore I had the widest latitude to buy stocks that the special situations person, the small-stock person, the growth person, the value person, or the over-the-counter stock person had recommended.

I was a passionate advocate of launching new funds, such as the OTC Portfolio, the Overseas Fund, and the Retirement Growth Fund. Most have turned out to be quite popular, but even if they hadn't, they gave us more researchers to snoop in new areas of the market. I took full advantage of their discoveries. Danny Frank of Special Situations was the first to see the potential in Fannie Mae, and also several turnarounds; George Vanderheiden of the Destiny Fund led me to Owens-Corning; Tom Sweeney of Capital Appreciation gave me one of my best stocks, Envirodyne.

The new funds also gave us new slots into which we could promote our talented young analysts, who otherwise might have been lured away to rival firms. The result was one of the greatest teams of stock sleuths ever assembled.

Early in my tenure, we formalized the swapping of information. Our random powwows in the hallway near the refrigerator were superseded by a scheduled event in a conference room, where all the analysts and fund managers presented our picks of the week.

Later, I presided over these meetings with a small kitchen timer, which I pretended to set at three minutes—the official time limit for any defense or explanation of a pick. In fact, I was setting the timer at progressively shorter intervals, until I got it down to a minute and a half. I'm confessing this now that it's too late for anyone to demand a chance to make up the lost time.

People were too excited about their favorite subject to notice that I was fooling with the timer. Anyway, 90 seconds is plenty of time to tell the story of a stock. If you're prepared to invest in a company, then you ought to be able to explain why in simple language that a fifth grader could understand, and quickly enough so the fifth grader won't get bored.

These sessions of ours were not put-down contests. Wall Street tends to be a combative environment where only the glibbest survive, but combat is not the best way to arrive at the truth about stocks. When you are openly criticized for your ideas, you may tend to hold back the next time. And when there's a chorus of criticism, you're likely to lose faith in your own research.

A hostile reception might not affect your confidence immediately, but the brain never forgets a painful experience. It will remember that every person in the room ridiculed the notion that Chrysler was an exceptional bargain at $5 a share. Then one night a year or more later, when the stock's at $10 and the brain has nothing better to do, it will remind you that "maybe all those smart people were right," and the next day you'll wake up and sell your Chrysler about $30 a share too soon.

To avoid undermining one another's confidence, we allowed no feedback at our presentations—the listeners were free to follow up on the leads or ignore them as they chose. I tried to focus on the quality of each idea, as opposed to the quality of the speaker. Often, the most valuable leads came from people whose stockpicking skills far exceeded their forensic skills, and I made it a point to pick the brains of the nonverbal contingent outside the meetings, with the egg timer turner off.

Eventually, the weekly sessions were replaced by daily research notes, because we had too many analysts and fund managers to fit into one room.

Two other sources of leads that often proved valuable were analysts and fund managers from outside Fidelity. At least once a week, I'd talk to the manager of a competing fund, and occasionally we'd bump into each other on the street or at a meeting. "What do you like?" we'd say as soon as we'd gotten beyond "Hello." This is the way stockpickers communicate. It's never "How's your wife?" or "Gee, did you see the shot that Larry Bird made?" It's always "What do you like?" followed by "Gee, things are getting better at Delta," or "I'm expecting a turnaround in Union Carbide."

We were competitors in the sense that our funds' performance was compared by Lipper, *Barron's, Forbes,* etc., and how well we did relative to the others would determine how much new money we attracted the following year. But the competition did not stop us from revealing our favorite stocks to one another at every opportunity—at least after we'd acquired all the shares we were planning to buy.

You wouldn't expect the coach of the Washington Redskins to share his favorite plays with the coach of the Chicago Bears, but we were eager to share our buy lists. If one of us gave a competitor a good idea, he or she would return the favor.

The advice of the analysts from other firms and salespeople from the brokerage community I took more selectively. There is great variation in quality here, and it's dangerous to follow a recommendation put out by a brokerage house without knowing something about the person who made it. Some highly regarded analysts are resting on their laurels in air-conditioned comfort. They may be listed as all-stars in *Institutional Investor* magazine, but that doesn't mean they've talked to Colgate-Palmolive in the last two years.

The out-of-touch expert is part of a growing crowd on Wall Street. Analysts spend more and more time selling and defending ideas to their superiors and/or clients, and less and less researching the ideas. It's unusual to find an analyst who calls several companies each day, and even rarer to find one who gets out and visits them.

Whenever I ran across such a person, I made it a point to keep in touch. Maggie Gilliam at First Boston, who saw the virtue in Home Depot and provided astute coverage of the Limited, is a good example. Others include John Kellenyi of NatWest on utilities; Elliot Schneider at Gruntal on financial services; and George Shapiro at Salomon Brothers on aerospace. Analysts of this caliber are always worth listening to, especially when you've called them, rather than vice versa.

Analysts love to brag about how they "initiated coverage" on a company when the stock was selling for 25 cents, and ten years later it is selling for $25. What's more important is whether they reinforced their opinion with a second or third and fourth favorable report when the stock hit $5, then $10, then $15. An initial buy signal is quickly forgotten, and if that's all the analyst has provided, the audience has missed the chance to profit from the stock farther up the line.

IT PAYS TO BE PATIENT

By the time Magellan was opened to the public in 1981, I had become a more patient investor. So had the shareholders. Redemptions were down, which meant I wasn't forced to sell stocks to raise cash. The fund's annual turnover rate dropped by nearly two thirds, from 300 percent to 110 percent. My biggest positions (Nicor, a natural gas producer; Fedders, the air conditioner people; Service Corporation International, the funeral home chain) now stayed that way for several months in a row.

Magellan was still small, $100 million, which put it in the bottom fifth of all general equity funds. I divided the money among 200 different stocks in every kind of company imaginable: John Blair, a broadcaster; Tandy, owner of Radio Shack; Quixote, which made plastic safety barriers used by construction crews on highways; Telecredit; Zapata Corporation, which added to George Bush's fortune; ChemLawn; Seven Oaks, a processor of grocery store coupons; Irving Bank; and Chart House and Skipper's, both fast-food restaurant chains.

I was progressively more impressed with the long-range potential of restaurant chains and retailers. By expanding across the country, these companies could keep up a 20 percent growth rate for 10 to 15 years. The math was, and continues to be, very favorable. If earnings increase 20 percent per annum, they double in 3½ years and quadruple in 7. The stock price follows suit, and often outpaces the earnings, as investors are willing to pay a considerable premium for the company's future prospects. (A list of my 50 most important retailers appears on page 138.)

The Rule of 72 is useful in determining how fast money will grow. Take the annual return from any investment, expressed as a percentage, and divide it into 72. The result is the number of years it will take to double your money. With a 25 percent return, your money doubles in less than 3 years: with a 15 percent return, it doubles in less than 5.

From watching the ups and downs of the various industries, I learned that whereas it was possible to make two to five times your money in cyclicals and undervalued situations (assuming that all went well), there were bigger payoffs in the retailers and the restaurants. Not only did they grow as fast as the high-tech growth companies (computer manufacturers, software manufacturers, medical enterprises), but they were generally less risky. A computer company can lose half its value overnight when a rival unveils a better product, but a chain of donut franchises in New England is not going to lose business when somebody opens a superior donut franchise in Ohio. It may take a decade for the competitor to arrive, and investors can see it coming.

At the end of 1981, I'd taken my profit in Circle K Convenience Stores and Penn Central, a turnaround from bankruptcy. I sold Bally, the slot-machine company and casino operator, and bought two other gaming stocks, Elsinore and Resorts International. In early 1982, I bought back Circle K. My biggest holding was Mattel, the toy maker, which was 3 percent of the fund. Other companies in my top 10 at the time were Chemical Bank; Pic 'N' Save, a chain of discount stores in California; Verbatim, a manufacturer of floppy disks (once again, I'd fallen for a high-tech stock); Horn & Hardart, the owners of Bojangles restaurants and a mail-order gift business; and Pep Boys—Manny, Moe & Jack, not to be confused with the

Three Stooges. These were the Three Sages when it came to making money in auto parts.

Pep Boys, Seven Oaks, Chart House, Telecredit, Cooper Tire— now I was beginning to see that some of my favorite stocks did have something in common. These were companies with strong balance sheets and favorable prospects but most portfolio managers wouldn't dare buy them. As I've mentioned before, a portfolio manager who cares about job security tends to gravitate toward acceptable holdings such as IBM, and to avoid offbeat enterprises like Seven Oaks, the aforementioned servicer with a plant in Mexico. If Seven Oaks fails, the person who recommended putting it in the portfolio gets the blame, but if IBM fails, the blame is put on IBM itself, for "disappointing the Street."

What made it possible for me to deviate from this stultifying norm? In a wide-open fund like Magellan, nobody was looking over my shoulder. In many firms there is a hierarchy of shoulders, with each person judging the work of the person directly in front of him, while worrying about how he's being judged from behind.

When you have to concern yourself with what the person behind you thinks about your work, it seems to me that you cease to be a professional. You are no longer responsible for what you do. This creates a doubt in your mind as to whether you are capable of succeeding at what you do—otherwise, why would they be monitoring your every move?

I was spared the indignity of being second guessed by my superiors. I had the luxury of buying shares in companies that nobody had heard of, or of selling shares at $40 and changing my mind and buying them back at $50. (My superiors may have thought I was crazy for doing such things, but they didn't say so.) I didn't have to justify my stock picks at a daily or weekly meeting, or subject myself and my strategy to demoralizing critiques.

Fund managers have enough to worry about in trying to beat the market. We don't need the added burden of conforming to a plan or explaining our strategies every day. As long as we follow the mandate of the fund as described in the prospectus, we ought to be judged once a year on our results. Along the way, nobody should care if we buy Golden Nugget or Horn & Hardart instead of Reynolds Aluminum or Dow Chemical.

By 1981–82, I'd begun to work on Saturdays. I devoted the extra day to cleaning off my desk. I had to peruse a stack of mail, which at one point reached a height of three feet a day. In February and March, I reviewed annual reports. I flipped through my notebooks of corporate contacts, looking for situations in which the stock prices had dropped (I always wrote down the price along with the date whenever I talked to a company) and the fundamentals either had improved or were unchanged. My goal was to see some wood at the end of the afternoon, but I didn't always achieve it.

The first half of 1982 was terrible for the stock market. The prime rate had hit the double digits, as had inflation and unemployment. People who lived in the suburbs were buying gold and shotguns and stocking up on canned soups. Businessmen who hadn't gone fishing in 20 years were oiling their reels and restocking their tackle boxes, preparing for the shutdown of the grocery stores.

Interest rates had gone so high that my biggest position in the fund for several months running was long-term Treasury bonds. Uncle Sam was paying 13–14 percent on these. I didn't buy bonds for defensive purposes because I was afraid of stocks, as many investors do. I bought them because the yields exceeded the returns one could normally expect to get from stocks.

This leads us to Peter's Principle #8, the only exception to the general rule that owning stocks is better than owning bonds:

When yields on long-term government bonds exceed the dividend yield of the S&P 500 by 6 percent or more, sell your stocks and buy bonds.

I couldn't imagine that interest rates could go much higher, or stay at these levels for long, without the economy collapsing and the worst nightmares of the backyard fishermen coming true. If that happened, I'd be out there casting in the surf with the rest of them, and Magellan's portfolio strategy would be the least of my worries. But if it didn't, I'd want to be fully invested in stocks and long-term bonds.

Why investors attempt to prepare for total disaster by bailing out of their best investments is beyond me. If total disaster strikes, cash in the bank will be just as useless as a stock certificate. On the other hand, if total disaster does not strike (a more likely outcome, given the record), the "cautious" types become the reckless ones, selling their valuable assets for a pittance.

In early 1982, I went through my usual scare-proofing drill, concentrating on the Even Bigger Picture, assuming that the worst wouldn't happen, and then asking myself, if it didn't, what then? I figured that interest rates had to come down sooner or later, and when they did, the owners of both stocks and long-term bonds would make big profits.

(In fact, the S&P 500 had a fourfold gain from 1982 to 1990 and 30-year government bonds did slightly better. Then in 1991, when stocks were up another 31 percent, bonds did poorly, proving once again that in the long run stocks will outperform bonds.)

In the gloom and doom of the era, financial commentators continued to harp on slumping auto sales, as if slumping auto sales were a permanent affliction. It seemed to me that recession or no recession, people were going to have to return to the showrooms. If there's anything as certain as death and the collapse of the Red Sox, it's that Americans have to buy cars.

It was this sort of thinking that led me to Chrysler in March 1982. Actually, I stumbled onto Chrysler indirectly. I got interested in Ford as a beneficiary of the rebound in autos, and in talking to Ford I became convinced that Chrysler would benefit even more. As usual, my research into one opportunity led me to another, the way a prospector follows the gold flakes upstream.

Chrysler stock was selling for $2 at the time, because Wall Street expected the number-three automaker to go bankrupt and become the next Penn Central. A quick check of the balance sheet showed me that Chrysler had more than $1 billion in cash—mostly thanks to its sale of a tank division to General Dynamics—so its imminent demise was greatly exaggerated. Chrysler had the capacity to go bankrupt, but not for at least a couple of years. The U.S. government had guaranteed enough loans to Chrysler to ensure its short-term survival.

If auto sales had been robust in general and Chrysler had managed not to sell cars, I would have been more pessimistic about its future. But the entire industry had been in a slump and was due for a rebound. Since Chrysler had reduced its debt and was hovering near the break-even point when sales were slow, it had the potential to do jumbo numbers when sales picked up.

In June I visited corporate headquarters, where I saw the new cars and talked with several top executives in a meeting arranged by investor relations officer Bob Johnson. This was probably the most important day in my 21-year investment career.

The interviews that were supposed to last three hours stretched into seven, and a brief chat with Lee Iacocca turned into another two-hour session. In the end, I was convinced not only that Chrysler had the wherewithal to stay in business for a while, but also that the company was putting some pizzazz into its products.

The Dodge Daytona, Chrysler Laser, and the G-124 Turbo Car were all coming off the assembly lines. The G-124 could accelerate from 0 to 60 faster than a Porsche. There were convertibles for the younger crowd and a sportier New Yorker with front-wheel drive. Mr. Iacocca was most excited about what he called "the first new thing in the auto industry in twenty years," a vehicle that had been given a code name: T-115. This was the Chrysler minivan, which sold over three million copies in the next nine years.

I was more impressed with the cars than with the minivan, but the minivan turned out to be the product that saved the company. No matter how well you think you understand a business, something can always happen that will surprise you. Here was a breakthrough in automotive design and engineering that came not from Japan or Germany or Sweden, but from Detroit. The Chrysler minivan outsold all the Volvos in the U.S. by five to one!

Chrysler was a large company with millions of shares outstanding, which made it possible for Magellan to acquire a large position. The company was so disparaged on Wall Street that the institutions had given up and had stopped following it. In the spring of 1982 and into the summer, I was buying the stock in earnest. By the end of June, it was my number-one holding. By the end of July, 5 percent of Magellan's assets were invested in Chrysler, the maximum percentage allowed by the SEC.

Throughout the fall, Chrysler remained my top position, just ahead of Horn & Hardart, Stop & Shop, IBM, and Ford. If I'd been allowed to, I would have made Chrysler 10 or even 20 percent of my fund. This in spite of the fact that most of my friends and professional colleagues told me I was crazy, and that Chrysler was going bankrupt.

By October, my bond position was whittled down to 5 percent of Magellan's assets. The great bull market had begun in earnest. Interest rates had started to come down, and the economy showed signs of revival. Cyclical stocks were leading the market higher, as they usually do at the end of a recession. I responded by selling some bank and insurance stocks. Eleven percent of the fund was now in the autos, and 10 percent in the retailers.

This shift in allocation was not a policy derived from the headlines, or from remarks made by the chairman of the Federal Reserve Board. My decisions were made on a case-by-case basis, as one company after another told me that business was getting better.

During this period, Genentech came public at $25 and promptly soared to $75 in one day. This was one of the new issues that I bought.

The weekend before Halloween, I made my first appearance on "Wall Street Week." I didn't meet the host, Louis Rukeyser, until about a minute before the cameras rolled. He walked onto the set, leaned over, and said: "Don't worry, you'll do fine, only about eight million people are watching you."

Rukeyser opened the show with a Halloween joke about how politicians scare Wall Street much more than goblins do. Then the three panelists (Dan Dorfman, Carter Randall, and Julia Walsh) did some weekend thinking. As usual there was plenty to be worried about, beginning with the fact that the Dow had fallen 36 points on the prior Friday. The newspapers had made a big deal of this "worst one-day drop since 1929," even though the comparison was absurd. A 36-point drop with the Dow at 990 was not the same thing as a 36-point drop with the Dow at 280, which is where it stood before the Crash.

How frequently today's mountains turn out to be tomorrow's molehills, and vice versa. Asked what might be spooking the market, the three experts mentioned the indictment against automaker John De Lorean, the Tylenol scare, and the large number of members of Congress who might lose their seats in the upcoming election. Mr. Rukeyser read a letter from a viewer who was concerned about a possible bank and S&L crisis that might deplete the resources of the Federal Deposit Insurance Corporation. The panelists thought there was little chance that such a thing could happen. Rukeyser ended the discussion by suggesting that the government could always "print a few more bucks if it had to," a jocularity that may turn out to be prophetic.

For my part of the show, I was ushered in from the wings as I was kindly introduced as the "best mutual-fund stockpicker of the last five years," tops on the Lipper list with a 305 percent gain over that period. I wore a plain brown suit and a blue shirt, the kind you are supposed to wear on television, and I was nervous. Getting on the Rukeyser show was the financial equivalent of opening the envelopes at the Academy Awards.

Rukeyser lobbed me a few easy questions, beginning with the "secret to my success." I said I visited more than 200 companies a year and read 700 annual reports, and that I subscribed to Edison's theory that "investing is ninety-nine percent perspiration"—something I was doing a lot of at the time. "That was Edison's theory of genius, not of investing," Rukeyser corrected. I said nothing. The witty comebacks were trapped in butterflies.

Rukeyser wanted to know more about my modus operandi. What was I going to say? "Well, Lou, I buy what I like"? I didn't. Instead, I said that I divided the Magellan portfolio into two parts: the small-growth and cyclical stocks, and the conservative stocks. "When the market heads lower, I sell the conservative stocks and add to the others. When the market picks up, I sell some of the winners from the growth stocks and cyclical stocks and add to the conservative stocks." Any resemblance between my actual strategy and this attempt to explain it to 8 million viewers on the spur of the moment is purely coincidental.

Asked about my favorite picks, I listed Bassett Furniture, Stop & Shop, and the autos in general, especially Chrysler. The autos had been depressed two straight years, I said, and Chrysler was well positioned to benefit from a comeback. Expressing the popular Wall Street view, Dorfman wondered if Chrysler wasn't too risky. "I'm willing to take risks," I countered.

Things lightened up when somebody asked a question about a technology company. I confessed not only that was I ignorant of technology, but that "I never really understood how electricity works." This got a laugh, and Rukeyser wanted to know if it had ever occurred to me that I was a "very old-fashioned fellow." My brilliant reply to that question was "No, it hasn't."

As jittery as I must have looked, the appearance on Rukeyser's show did wonders for Magellan. The Fidelity sales department got very busy answering phones and taking orders. What had been a $100 million fund after the merger with Salem in 1981 became a $450 million fund by the end of 1982. New money was pouring in at a rate that would have been inconceivable four years earlier: $40 million in October, $71 million in November, $55 million in December. A roaring stock market had a lot to do with this.

Instead of having to sell one stock to buy another, as I'd done in the past, I now had the luxury of maintaining old positions while initiating fresh ones. I wasn't allowed to spend all the money on Chrysler, so I invested some of it in the other autos, in chemical companies, and in retailers. In three months, I bought shares in 166 different companies.

Some of these were large companies, but the majority were not.

One of the many ironies of my career is that when Magellan was a small fund I concentrated on the bigger stocks, and when it became a bigger fund I found myself concentrating on the smaller stocks. This was not a deliberate strategy, but that's the way it worked out.

Magellan's popularity continued to grow into 1983. In February, another $76 million had to be invested, and in March, $100 million. It would have been easier to find stocks to buy in a terrible market, but by early 1983 the Dow had advanced 300 points from the 1982 lows. Many of the technology issues had risen to giddy heights that wouldn't be seen again for six or seven years. These high prices were the cause of great jubilation on Wall Street, but I found them depressing. I was happier with a good 300-point drop that created some bargains.

Bargains are the holy grail of the true stockpicker. The fact that 10–30 percent of our net worth is lost in a market sell-off is of little consequence. We see the latest correction not as a disaster but as an opportunity to acquire more shares at low prices. This is how great fortunes are made over time.

Chrysler was still my biggest holding (5 percent of the fund), and remained so for most of the year. It had doubled in value in eight months. Horn & Hardart, Stop & Shop, and IBM continued to show up in the top five. I dutifully maintained a 3 percent position in IBM (less, it turns out, than IBM's overall weighting in the market of 4 percent of the total value of the S&P 500). Perhaps I was responding to a subliminal message: you aren't really a fund manager unless you have Big Blue in the portfolio.

In April, Magellan hit $1 billion, a milestone which elicited a great ho-hum at the office. Soon afterward, a newsletter writer suggested that Magellan had gotten too big to succeed. This argument would soon gain in popularity.

SIX

MAGELLAN

The Later Years

How much time you spend on researching stocks is directly proportional to how many stocks you own. It takes a few hours a year to keep up with each one. This includes reading the annuals and the quarterlies, and calling the companies for periodic updates. An individual with five stocks can do this work as a hobby. A fund manager of a small- to medium-sized fund can do it as a nine-to-five job. In a larger fund, you're looking at a 60- to 80-hour week.

By mid-1983 there were 450 stocks in the Magellan portfolio, and by fall, the number had doubled to 900. This meant I had to be prepared to tell 900 different stories to my colleagues in 90 seconds or less. To do that, I had to know what the stories were. My able assistants helped me investigate the facts.

John Neff at Vanguard Windsor still had the largest mutual fund in existence, but by the end of 1983 Magellan was running a close second, with $1.6 billion in assets. This latest growth spurt prompted a new group of critics to say that Magellan, like the Roman Empire, had gotten too big to succeed. The theory was that a fund with 900 stocks in it didn't have a chance to beat the market average because it *was* the market average. I was accused of managing the largest closet index fund on the planet.

This theory that a large fund can only be a mediocre fund is still in vogue today, and it's just as misguided as it was a decade ago.

An imaginative fund manager can pick 1,000 stocks, or even 2,000 stocks, in unusual companies, the majority of which will never appear in the standard Wall Street portfolio. This is known as "flying off the radar scope." He or she can own 300 S&Ls and 250 retailers and no oil companies and zero manufacturers, and his results will zig when the rest of the market zags. Conversely, an unimaginative fund manager can limit his portfolio to 50 stocks that are widely held by institutions, and create a miniature S&P 500.

This leads to Peter's Principle #9:

Not all common stocks are equally common.

The size of a fund and the number of stocks it contains tell you nothing about whether or not it can excel. The publicity I received for having bought 900 stocks, or, later, 1,400 stocks, may have caused some investors to shy away from Magellan. This is unfortunate. Of the 900 stocks in the portfolio in 1983, 700 accounted for less than 10 percent of the fund's total assets.

These tiny positions I took for one of two reasons: (1) the companies themselves were quite small, so even if I owned the maximum 10 percent of the shares the dollar value didn't amount to much; or (2) I wasn't convinced they deserved a substantial commitment. Most of the stocks in Magellan fell into this "tune in later" category. It was easier to follow the story when you owned some shares and were put on the mailing list.

An illustration of how an insignificant holding could lead to a great opportunity is Jan Bell Marketing. The executives of this jewelry supplier, a $200 million company and far from the *Fortune* 500, came to Fidelity to meet with our fund managers. I owned the stock, so I hustled over to the conference room to hear the presentation. No other fund managers showed up.

Jan Bell was too small to add much to Magellan's bottom line, but I'm glad I went to the meeting. In describing the business, the executives mentioned that their best customers were the discount clubs (Pace, Warehouse, Wholesale, Costco, etc.) that were ordering a tremendous amount of jewelry—so much, in fact, that Jan Bell had to struggle to keep up with the demand.

That's where I got the idea to invest in the discount clubs. It occurred to me that if they were selling as much jewelry as Jan Bell said they were, then their general sales had to be excellent as well.

I asked Will Danoff, the retail analyst who later took over the Fidelity Contrafund, to do the research.

These stocks were very popular after the initial public offerings, but the euphoria was short-lived. Expectations were so lofty that the results couldn't possibly live up to them, and the stocks sold off. True to form, Wall Street lost interest. Danoff called the big investment houses and found out that not a single analyst was assigned to follow these companies.

The two of us contacted the companies directly. They confirmed what Jan Bell had said—business was terrific. They also told us they'd strengthened their balance sheets by paying off debt. Earnings were on the upswing, the stock prices were still on the downswing—it was a perfect situation. I bought hundreds of thousands of shares of Costco, Wholesale Club, and Pace. All three made money—Costco was a triple.

Employees and shoppers in these stores could have seen the evidence of prosperity with their own eyes, and learned the same details that Danoff and I did. The alert shopper has a chance to get the message about retailers earlier than Wall Street does, and to make back all the money he or she ever spends on merchandise—by buying undervalued stocks.

During the mid-80s, I also scooped up nearly every S&L that came public. Most of them were quite small, so for them to have made a difference to a $1 billion portfolio, I had to buy a passel. Besides, after several financial institutions told me their profits were improving thanks to lower interest rates, I could see that many others would benefit from the same trend. Of the 83 new acquisitions I made in April 1983, 39 were banks or S&Ls. By the end of that year, I'd bought 100 S&Ls, enough to make that group 3 percent of the fund.

The financial press noted my "emphasis" on the S&Ls in enough articles that the casual reader might have gotten the impression that Magellan's fortunes rose and fell with them. It's a good thing it didn't, because when the weakest of the S&Ls collapsed, the prices of the strong ones declined in sympathy. If I'd put 20 percent of Magellan into the S&Ls I might have been forced to retire much earlier.

Banks and S&Ls notwithstanding, it was the autos that get the most credit for Magellan's success during this period. Ford had led me to Chrysler, and Chrysler to Subaru and Volvo. The favorable economic tide that lifted one was lifting them all.

The price of Chrysler stock shot up so fast that for a short period my Chrysler holding exceeded the limit of 5 percent of the fund. Once it got to 5 percent, I wasn't allowed to buy more, though I was allowed to exceed the limit if an increase in a stock's price pushed the value of Magellan's position over the 5 percent limit. At the same time, I was building up Ford and Volvo, until the three together accounted for 8 percent of Magellan's assets, and autos as a group, 10.3 percent.

An individual can pick the most promising auto company and put all his money there, but to get the full benefit from a rebound in autos, the manager of a large fund is forced to make what is known as an "industry bet." There are different ways to make such bets. One way is to tell yourself, "This year, I want to have eight percent in autos," because you have a hunch that autos are going to do well. You can close your eyes and throw darts at a list of auto stocks, and buy a few. Another way is to analyze each company on a case-by-case basis.

In the first instance, the 8 percent weighting in autos is deliberate and the choice of the companies is incidental; in the second, the choice of the companies is deliberate and the weighting is incidental. As you might have guessed, I prefer the latter. Doing the homework takes more effort than throwing darts, but in 1983 the dart throwers were likely to have ended up investing in General Motors.

I never owned much General Motors, even in this favorable period for autos, because I thought that saying it was a miserable company was about the nicest compliment you could give it. Even GM tripled in value from 1982 to 1987, but the fund manager who made the number-one U.S. automaker his number-one investment didn't get the full advantage of the 17-fold profit from Ford, and the nearly 50-bagger from Chrysler.

I have to admit that in my bottoms-up analysis I was right about the rebound in autos, but wrong about the big picture. I was convinced that the Japanese would continue to concentrate on the small-car market, and I never imagined that they would get into the midsize and luxury markets the way they've done. In spite of this miscalculation, I was able to get the maximum benefit out of Ford, Chrysler, and Volvo.

During the entire six-year stretch from 1982 to 1988, at least two of these three auto manufacturers could be found among the top five holdings in Magellan, and sometimes all three appeared at once. Ford and Chrysler stock rose dramatically, and subsequently I made well over $100 million in profits from each, plus $79 million from Volvo. It was huge gains in a few huge positions that led to Magellan's superior results.

Although Magellan was continually described as a growth fund, it was the flexibility to buy any sort of stock that enabled me to take advantage of opportunities such as I found in the autos. Chrysler and Ford would not have appeared in the growth-fund portfolios, yet because these stocks had been beaten so far down, on the rebound they outperformed almost all of the growth stocks.

Another way that a lot of fund managers hemmed themselves in was by worrying about "liquidity." They avoided all the wonderful small companies—a good collection of these could do wonders even for a big portfolio—because the stocks were "thinly traded." They'd get so absorbed in this problem of finding stocks they could get in and out of in five days or less that they'd lose sight of whether these things were worth owning in the first place.

In stocks as in romance, ease of divorce is not a sound basis for commitment. If you've chosen wisely to begin with, you won't want a divorce. And if you haven't, you're in a mess no matter what. All the liquidity in the world isn't going to save you from pain, suffering, and probably a loss of money.

Take Polaroid, which lost 90 percent of its value in a single year, 1973. A lot of fund managers wish they hadn't. Polaroid was a big company and very actively traded, so it was a cinch to sell large blocks of shares at a moment's notice. The stock was in a slow descent for three years, so everybody had a chance to get out, but I know several professionals who didn't. You have to want out to get out, and they didn't notice that the company was falling apart.

They had the chance to get out of Xerox, too, and for some reason they didn't do that, either. So the expert who decided not to invest in something because "it only trades ten thousand shares a day" is looking at things cockeyed. For one thing, 99 percent of all stocks trade fewer than 10,000 shares a day, so fund managers who worry about liquidity are confined to 1 percent of all publicly traded companies. For another thing, if a company is a loser, the fund manager is going to lose money on the stock no matter how many shares it trades, and if it's a winner, he or she will be delighted to unwind a position in the stock leisurely, at a profit.

When Magellan grew into a medium-sized fund, it got harder for me to make a meaningful investment overnight. Once in a while I got the chance to gobble up a huge block of shares from an institutional buyer, which is how I acquired 2 million shares of Owens-Corning in one day. Another time, I bought 2 million shares of BankAmerica in the same fashion. But these were the exceptions to the rule of constant nibbling.

Every time the fund got bigger, which happened almost every day, I had to add to each position to maintain its relative weight versus the other stocks in the fund. With the smaller stocks especially, it sometimes took months to acquire a decent amount. If I bought shares too rapidly, my own buying could cause the price to increase beyond the level at which I would have wanted to start selling.

Throughout 1984, my top 10 positions remained more or less the same, as I stuck to the buy-and-hold strategy, as opposed to my earlier practice of frequent trading. One month, Ford would be number one, followed by Chrysler and then Volvo; another month, Volvo would be number one, followed by Chrysler and then Ford. I also maintained a large position in the Treasury bonds I'd bought in 1983, which continued to increase in value as interest rates declined.

At the climax of my adventure with the carmakers, there were five auto companies in my top 10, including the three regulars plus Subaru and Honda, and for a brief moment even General Motors made the list. As millions of Americans returned to the showrooms, even that mediocre operation was earning lots of money.

Speaking of money, another $1 billion had come into Magellan in 1984. It took me a while to get used to the extra zero on the buy and sell orders I sent to the trading desks. Also, my morning instructions to the traders took longer and longer to relate.

My decisions as to where to go on vacation were based primarily on time zones and the locations of phone booths. Austria was a good spot because it was late afternoon there before our markets opened, giving me the whole day to ski before I phoned the trading desk. My favorite ski place in the U.S. was Balsam's in Dixville Notch, New Hampshire, because it had a phone at the bottom of the lift. I'd ski down, dial the traders, get through a page or so of buys and sells, take the lift up, and contemplate my next move.

In my first five years I didn't travel much, but in the second five I was frequently on the road. Most of the trips were organized around investment seminars held in every region of the country. These were like cram courses in which I could hear from dozens of companies in two or three days.

Montgomery Securities had a conference in San Francisco in September. Hambrecht & Quist had one for smaller technology companies in May. Every April, there was a Robinson-Humphrey conference in Atlanta for companies from the Southeast. Dain, Bosworth had a similar gathering in Minneapolis for companies in the Midwest; Prescott, Ball, and Turben had one in the fall in Cleveland; Alex. Brown had one in Baltimore; and Adams, Harkness, & Hill had one in Boston in August. Howard Weil had two separate conferences in Louisiana, one for energy producers and another for energy service companies. There were theme conferences that dealt exclusively with biotech companies, restaurants, cable companies, and banks.

The investment seminar was the greatest laborsaving device for fund managers ever invented. With two or three presentations going on at once, it was always hard to decide which to attend. Sometimes Fidelity sent a delegation so we had a representative at each meeting. Once in a while, a story would be so good that I'd leave the room before the talk was over to call in a buy order from the lobby.

In my spare time, I'd rent a car or take a cab and drive off to visit companies that weren't involved in the conference, but whose headquarters were located in the area. I got to know cities not by their familiar landmarks, but by who in the *Fortune* 500 had taken up a residence. My tourist attractions were MCI and Fannie Mae in Washington; Chevron and BankAmerica in San Francisco; Litton and Unocal in Los Angeles; Coca-Cola and Turner Broadcasting in Atlanta; TRW, National City Bank, and Eaton in Cleveland.

MY ADVENTURES ABROAD

With the exception of John Templeton, I was the first domestic fund manager to invest heavily in foreign stocks. Templeton's fund was a global version of Magellan. Whereas I might have 10–20 percent of the money invested in foreign stocks, Templeton invested most of his money abroad.

My own global buying began in earnest in 1984. Nobody had devised a system to get reliable, up-to-the-minute quotes of companies traded on many of the foreign exchanges, so every night my traders had to call Stockholm, London, Toyko, and Paris to piece together the information I needed the following day. This ran up the phone bill, but it was worth it. By 1986, we had a foreign department.

With the pile of cash I now had to invest, I was almost forced to turn to foreign stocks, particularly in Europe. With a big fund, I needed to find big companies that would make big moves, and Europe has a higher percentage of big companies than we do. Most of these were not closely followed. The bad news was that foreign firms were not held to the same standards of reporting and accounting as U.S. firms, and therefore were mysterious and harder to analyze. The good news was that if you did your own homework, you'd occasionally come up with a Volvo.

My most successful research trip ever began in mid-September 1985, and ended three weeks and 23 companies later. This was far more exhausting—and useful—than an earlier jaunt I'd taken as a young Fidelity analyst in the fall of 1973, when I visited Dow Chemical plants and was wined and dined across the continent. What I learned then was that if you've seen one Dow Chemical plant you've seen them all.

This time around, I saw three companies in Boston on a Friday, then boarded a plane that same afternoon and arrived in Sweden on Saturday. Things got off to a bad start when the airline lost my luggage. It was Sabena, a stock I decided I was glad I didn't own.

Sweden is a formal country. In two days I was scheduled to meet several of its captains of industry, and I wondered how they'd react when I walked into their offices wearing the same corduroy pants, crumpled sport coat, and sneakers I'd worn in the plane. I began preparing for this cultural disaster as soon as I found out that (1) Sabena had no idea what happened to my suitcase and (2) all the stores in Stockholm were closed.

Resigning myself to the worst, I was picked up at the airport by Birgitta Drogell, the sister of friends of ours, the Sweetlands. I'd made arrangements to stay with her and her family in Sigtuna, a suburb of Stockholm. Miraculously, her Swedish husband, Ingemar, had my exact measurements, right down to the shoe size, and soon I was outfitted in a proper Swedish suit.

With my white hair and my light complexion, all it took was a native costume to convince everybody that I was Swedish. Whenever I walked out onto the street, people would ask me for directions— or at least I assume that's what they were asking. Since I don't speak Swedish, I couldn't be certain.

The luggage was never found, and I'm sure I looked the better for it. On Monday, dressed in my Swedish togs, I went to see the

CEO at Esselte, a company that sells office equipment, including those organizing trays that are found in desk drawers. I also saw ASEA, a high-quality conglomerate that is Sweden's answer to General Electric; and Alfa Laval, which is involved in a curious combination of enterprises—milking machines and biogenetics. That night, I studied for my next day's sessions at Electrolux, a vacuum cleaner and appliance giant whose president was Sweden's answer to Lee Iacocca; and Aga, which makes a profit out of thin air.

In theory, it seems senseless to be investing in a company that sells gases taken from the air, because these are not exactly rare commodities, but I learned from Aga that there is a great demand for oxygen in the steel industry and for nitrogen in the fast-food industry and only a few people have the machinery for mining the atmosphere. Since the raw materials cost zero, these few people (Aga included) are doing very well.

As soon as I'd finished with Aga, I drove over to Ericsson, a telephone equipment company similar to our Western Electric. In the afternoon, I saw Skandia, which sounds like a furniture outlet but actually is a huge insurance firm. George Noble of our Overseas Fund had put me on to Skandia, which nobody else seemed to be following.

With U.S. insurance companies, the rates go up months before the earnings start to show any improvement. These stocks are like cyclicals. If you buy them when the rates first begin to rise, you can make a lot of money. It's not uncommon for an insurance stock to double after a rate increase and double again on the higher earnings that result from the rate increase.

I assumed that this same pattern existed in Sweden. From what I was told, a rate increase already had been approved, which should have boosted the price of Skandia's stock, but it hadn't. Swedish investors ignored the good news that was sure to follow and focused only on the current earnings, which were lousy. This was a stock-picker's dream.

I rubbed my eyes and took a closer look at the company to see if there was something terrible there I was missing. Was there too much debt? Had Skandia invested half its assets in junk bonds or a Campeau real estate deal? Was the company insuring heart bypasses and breast implants, or other risky ventures that could have resulted in millions in unforeseen claims? The answer to all these questions was no. This was a conservative insurer that wrote simple property/

casualty policies and was guaranteed to double its earnings. The stock quadrupled in 18 months.

There was no time to take sauna baths or sail the fjords, because after visiting these seven companies in two days, I had to get to Volvo on the other side of the country. To prepare for the side trip, I sought out the lone Swedish financial analyst, who worked in a brokerage firm founded by one of the Carnegies. The descendants of this Carnegie have been freezing in obscurity in Scandinavia, while the luckier branch of the family got rich in America.

This lone analyst had never visited Volvo, the biggest company in the country and the Swedish equivalent to the entire U.S. auto sector, plus several other businesses thrown in. I made up for his oversight by driving to Göteborg with Carolyn, who by now had joined me on the trip.

In Göteborg, the Volvo people were so excited that an investor would bother to ask for an interview that I got to see the president, the executive vice-president, the head of the truck division, and the treasurer. After that, they gave me the grand tour of the plant.

Volvo was being squeezed by its unions, but that was a distant worry. In the short term, the stock price was $34 and the company had $34 per share in cash, so when you bought this stock you were getting the auto business, the assembly plants, and the many Volvo subsidiaries (food companies, drug companies, energy companies, etc.) for nothing. In the U.S., you might find a giveaway like this in a small company that's been overlooked by analysts, but you could search your whole life and never come across a General Electric or Philip Morris priced this low. That's the reason I'd gone to Europe.

Some people think there's a cultural bias in some foreign markets that causes the stocks there to be overvalued or undervalued forever. Until the recent drop in the Japanese market, we read a great deal about how the Japanese had an inbred tolerance for overpriced equities. Obviously, that wasn't the case. In Sweden, it seemed that investors were underestimating the worth of Volvo, Skandia, and many other firms, but I had no doubt that eventually the true value would become apparent, even to the unimpressed Swedes.

Carolyn and I left Göteborg and drove to Oslo, where I saw Norsk Data and Norsk Hydro. Norsk Data was the Hewlett-Packard of Norway, an exciting company in an exciting industry that had not yet lost its way. Norsk Hydro was an exciting company involved in a variety of unexciting industries—hydroelectric power, magnesium, aluminum, and fertilizer plants. I saw it as a cyclical company and a great energy play at the same time. Its oil and gas fields had more than three times the reserve life of Texaco's reserves, or Exxon's, or the reserves of any other oil giant. Recently, the stock price fell by half, which makes Norsk Hydro a bargain once again.

As I was doing my research, Carolyn was busy playing the currency markets. European finance ministers from the Group of Seven had just readjusted the currency rates and the value of the dollar had dropped 10 percent overnight. The proprietor of a fur store in Oslo must have forgotten to read the newspapers, because the next morning he allowed Carolyn to pay for a fox coat with American Express Travelers Cheques—a 10 percent discount from the price a day earlier.

From Oslo, we took the train to Bergen, passing through beautiful farmland, climbing into the mountains and then down to this charming coastal town. There wasn't much time to take in this charm, because early the following morning we flew to Frankfurt, where I saw the directors of Deutsche Bank, Hoechst, and Dresdner. The next day we went to Düsseldorf, where I saw a German manufacturer, Klöckner-Humboldt-Deutz. I also saw Bayer, the former manufacturer of aspirin, and now a chemical and drug conglomerate.

In a train station somewhere, I handed two marks to a nice German fellow who had volunteered to help with our luggage, thinking he was a porter. He turned out to be a businessman, and I had embarrassed myself by responding to his noble gesture with a tip. With my nose stuck in the balance sheets, I missed some of the cultural nuances and most of the scenery, but I did notice that German men seem to call each other Doctor no matter what, and never their version of Sam or Joe.

We went down the Rhine, which flows from south to north, to reach Cologne, where I visited more companies, and from there we headed to Baden-Baden, where we rented another car just so I could take the wheel on the German autobahn. One of my goals in life besides kissing the Blarney stone was driving the autobahn. Both turned out to be equally terrifying experiences.

To kiss the Blarney stone, you wiggle on your back across what must be a 100-foot drop, and to drive the autobahn you might as well be entered in the Indianapolis 500. I was breezing along at more than 100 mph in my rented car with Carolyn taking a picture of the speedometer to prove it, and then I got my courage up to pass the car in front of me. I moved out into the left lane and sped up to maybe 120, roughly 50 percent faster than I'd traveled in a car in my adult life. Everything was OK until I looked into the rearview mirror. This leads us to Peter's Principle #10:

Never look back when you're driving on the autobahn.

Three inches from my rear bumper and also going 120 mph was the front bumper of somebody else's Mercedes. The two of us were so close that I could see the cuticles on the other driver's fingernails. He had a good manicurist. I figured if I took my foot off the accelerator even for a second, he would be sitting in our front seat with the two of us, so I gritted my teeth and accelerated enough to pass the car to the right of me and escape into the so-called slow lane. There, I proceeded at a reasonable 100 mph.

The next day I was still recovering from this experience. We'd driven to Basel, where Sandoz, the famous Swiss pharmaceutical and chemical company, has its headquarters. Back in the U.S., I'd called Sandoz to set up an interview. Normally, the people in charge of a company understand right away why I might want to see them, but Sandoz was different. I was connected to a vice-president, and when I told him I wanted to visit the company, he asked: "Why?" "I want to learn more about what you do so I can decide whether to buy more shares," I answered. Once again he asked: "Why?" "Well, because I'd like to be fully up to date," I continued. "Why?" he wanted to know. "Because if I buy it and the price goes up, I can make money for the shareholders." "Why?" he asked, and I said good-bye. I never got to see Sandoz, although subsequently I heard it loosened up its visiting rules.

We continued on through the Alps to Italy and got to Milan, where I saw Montedison, another hydroelectric company. In its 300-year-old boardroom there was a fascinating contraption that dripped water in rhythm with the amount that was actually flowing through the dam. Besides Montedison, I saw IFI, another company in the neighborhood, as well as the famous mural *The Last Supper*. I also saw Olivetti. I'm probably one of the few tourists who would list Montedison, IFI, Olivetti, and *The Last Supper* as their favorite northern Italian attractions.

Italy was suffering from high inflation and impossible politics, but the inflation rate was going down and politicians were becoming more businesslike, and the people had started buying their groceries in supermarkets. It occurred to me that Italy in 1985 was a lot like America in the 1940s and 1950s, a place where appliance companies, electric companies, and supermarkets would be the fast growers of the future.

Carolyn went to Venice, where I couldn't find any companies to visit (the Doge's Palace and the Bridge of Sighs are not yet publicly traded), so I headed for Rome, where I saw Stet and SIP. On October 9 we were reunited in Rome and boarded the plane that returned us to Boston on the 10th, where I promptly saw four more companies: Comdisco, A. L. Williams, Citicorp, and Montedison. This was the same Montedison I'd seen a week earlier in Milan.

This whirlwind tour of Europe had caused me to miss Ned Johnson's 25th wedding anniversary, and he was my boss, but the absence was for a good cause. The stocks I bought as a result of my European trip did well, beginning with Volvo, Skandia, and Esselte.

Ten percent of Magellan's assets were now invested in foreign equities, and the many happy returns I got from these stocks helped the fund keep its number-one ranking. My top eleven foreign purchases, Peugeot, Volvo, Skandia, Esselte, Electrolux, Aga, Norsk Hydro, Montedison, IFI, Tobu Railway, and Kinki Nippon Railway, made more than $200 million in profits for the shareholders.

The two Japanese railroad stocks were recommended to me by George Noble of the Overseas Fund. I researched them further on a separate trip to Japan, which was just as hectic as the European foray—I'll spare you the details. Tobu Railway was the biggest gainer of all: 386 percent in five years. Alas, it was a small position, with only .13 percent of Magellan's assets devoted to it.

BEYOND $5 BILLION

In 1984, Magellan had managed a 2 percent gain while the S&L 500 lost 6.27. In 1985, the auto stocks and the foreign stocks contributed to a 43.1 percent gain. My largest positions were still in Treasury bonds and the autos, with IBM thrown in for some reason, which couldn't have been a good one. I was also buying Gillette, Eaton, Reynolds, CBS, the old International Harvester (now Navistar),

Sperry, Kemper, Disney, Sallie Mae, the New York Times Company, and Australian bonds. I bought enough SmithKline Beckman, Bank of New England, Metromedia, and Loews for those companies to appear in the top 10. Among the many stocks I wish I hadn't been buying were One Potato Two, Eastern Airlines, Institutional Networks, Broadview Financial, Vie de France, Ask Computer, Wilton Industries, and United Tote.

Another $1.7 billion had come into the fund in 1985, to add to the $1 billion in 1984 and the same amount in 1983. The net asset value of Magellan now equaled the gross national product of Costa Rica. To absorb this money, I was constantly on the offensive, re-evaluating the portfolio, finding new positions or building up the old ones. This leads us to Peter's Principle #11:

The best stock to buy may be the one you already own.

Fannie Mae is a good example. During the first half of 1985, Fannie Mae was one of my typical minor holdings, but then I rechecked the story (see Chapter 18) and discovered it had improved dramatically. I elevated Fannie Mae to 2.1 percent of the fund. I was still partial to the autos, even though Ford and Chrysler had doubled or tripled in price, because the earnings were on the upswing and all the fundamental signs were favorable. But soon enough, Fannie Mae would take over where Ford and Chrysler left off as the key to Magellan's success.

In February 1986, Magellan passed the $5 billion mark in assets. I had to buy more Ford, Chrysler, and Volvo to maintain their weighting in the fund. I was also buying Middle South Utilities, Dime Savings, Merck, Hospital Corporation of America, Lin Broadcasting, McDonald's, Sterling Drug, Seagram, Upjohn, Dow Chemical, Woolworth, Browning-Ferris, Firestone, Squibb, Coca-Cola Enterprises, Unum, DeBeers, Marui, and Lonrho.

Foreign stocks now made up 20 percent of the portfolio, beginning with Volvo, which for most of the year was the top holding. Besides the autos, others in the top 10 included the Bank of New England, Kemper, Squibb, and Digital Equipment.

A $20 million position, equal to the size of the entire Magellan Fund in 1976, was now insignificant. To move this mass of billions, I had to have some $100 million positions. Every day I would go down the alphabetical list of holdings to decide what to sell and what to buy. The list got longer and longer, and the holdings bigger and bigger. I was aware of this intellectually, but it didn't really sink in until a particularly hectic week in the market, when I happened to be visiting Yosemite National Park.

There I was, standing in a phone booth overlooking a mountain range, giving a day's worth of transactions to the trading desk. After two hours, I'd only gotten from the A's through the L's.

My visits with companies, either at our place or at their places or at investment seminars, also had escalated from 214 in 1980 to 330 in 1982, 489 in 1983, back down to 411 in 1984, 463 in 1985, and 570 in 1986. If this kept up, I figured I'd be seeing an average of two companies a day in person, including Sundays and holidays.

After five years of selling, selling, selling, my trader on the sell side, Carlene DeLuca, left the trading desk to marry Fidelity's former president, Jack O'Brien. On her last day at the office, we decided to let her do a few buys just to see how the other half lived. She wasn't prepared for this strange experience. On the other end of the phone, a prospective seller would offer some shares for, say, $24 apiece, and Carlene would hold out for $24.50.

A TACTICAL SHIFT

Magellan was up 23.8 percent in 1986, and another 39 percent in the first half of 1987. With the market rolling along to an all-time high of 2722.42 on the Dow, and the herds of bulls appearing on the covers of every major magazine in the country, I made a major tactical shift—the first in five years. It seemed to me that we were far into the economic recovery and that people who were going to buy new cars had done so, and the analysts who followed the autos were making optimistic earnings projections that my research told me were unsupportable. I began to deemphasize the autos and to upgrade the financial companies—particularly Fannie Mae, but also the S&Ls.

Magellan became a $10 billion fund in May 1987. This announcement provided more grist for the naysayers who predicted it was too big to beat the market. I can't quantify the contribution that skeptics made to my performance, but I don't doubt it was substantial. They said a billion was too big, then 2 billion, 4, 6, 8, and 10 billion, and all along I was determined to prove them wrong.

Other large funds had closed the door to new shareholders once these funds had reached a certain size, but Magellan was kept open, and even this was perceived as a negative. The critics said it was Fidelity's way of capitalizing on my reputation and attracting more fees.

By 1987, I'd satisfied myself that a fund as big as the GNP of Sweden could outperform the market. I was also exhausted from the effort, and yearning to spend more time with my wife than with Fannie Mae. I might have quit then, three years earlier than my actual departure, but what kept me on was the Great Correction.

I can't pretend I saw it coming. Here the market was wildly over-valued and poised for a 1000-point decline—a situation that is obvious in hindsight—yet with my usual clairvoyance about the Big Picture, I managed to miss it. I entered this treacherous stretch fully invested in stocks, with almost no cash on the sidelines. So much for market timing.

The good news was that in August I cut back on the dozens of S&Ls in which I'd invested 5.6 percent of the fund's assets. It had begun to dawn on me (and on Dave Ellison, our in-house S&L expert) that some of these S&Ls were making very stupid loans. The bad news was that I put the proceeds into other stocks.

Before the Great Correction, Magellan was up 39 percent for the year, and I was mad about it because the S&P 500 was up 41 percent. I remember Carolyn saying, "How can you complain about lagging the market by 2 percent when you've made thirty-nine percent for your shareholders?" As it turned out, she was right and I shouldn't have complained, because by December I was down 11 percent. This brings us to Peter's Principle #12:

A sure cure for taking a stock for granted is a big drop in the price.

My own history of handling stock-market declines begins in a fool's paradise. Within a few months of my having taken over Magellan, the market fell 20 percent, while the stocks in the fund were actually up 7 percent. This short-lived triumph convinced me that I was somehow immune to the setbacks that befall the run-of-the-mill stockpicker. This fantasy lasted only until the next big decline, from September 11 to October 31, 1978.

That decline was a doozie, brought about by a weak dollar, strong inflation, congressional dickering over tax cuts, and a tight-money Fed. Short-term Treasury bills were paying higher rates of interest than long-term bonds, a rare situation known as an inverted yield curve. The stock market fell a long way, and Magellan fell even further. This was the beginning of the real trend that lasted through the rest of my career as a fund manager: whenever the stock market did poorly, Magellan did worse.

During nine major declines, including the big one in 1987, this pattern persisted. The stocks in the fund would lose more than the average stock, and then outperform the market on the rebound. I tried to prepare the shareholders for this wilder ride in Magellan's annual reports. Perhaps there's some poetic justice in the fact that the stocks that take you the farthest in the long run give you the most bumps and bruises along the way.

I was delighted when 1987 was over. It was something of a triumph to bring Magellan back to a 1 percent gain and maintain the string of 10 profitable years. I'd also beaten the average equity mutual fund in each of those years. And once again, Magellan's rebound had outdistanced the market's.

The Great Correction had temporarily solved Magellan's size problem. What was an $11 billion fund in August had become a $7.2 billion fund by October. The GNP of Costa Rica was lost in a week.

In *One Up on Wall Street* I describe how I was golfing in Ireland when the calamity occurred. I had to sell a lot of stock to raise cash to pay off the shareholders who got scared out of their assets. Magellan had $689 million in sales in October and $1.3 billion in redemptions, reversing a five-year trend. The sellers outnumbered the buyers two to one, but the vast majority of Magellan investors stayed put and did nothing. They saw the Great Correction for what it was, and not as the beginning of the end of civilization.

It was the end of civilization for some stockplayers who owned shares on margin—i.e., they borrowed money from brokerage houses to buy them. These people saw their portfolios wiped out when the brokerage houses sold their shares, often at rock-bottom prices, to pay off the loans. It was the first time I truly understood the risks of buying on margin.

My traders came to work on a Sunday to prepare for the sell-off that was predicted for Black Monday. Fidelity had spent all weekend planning what to do. I'd raised my cash position to a relatively high level (20 times the fund's greatest single previous one-day redemption) before I left for Ireland. This was hardly enough. A flood of redemption orders had been called in by phone. I was forced to sell a portion of the fund on Monday and another chunk on Tuesday. So at the very moment I would have preferred to be a buyer, I had to be a seller.

In this sense, shareholders play a major role in a fund's success or failure. If they are steadfast and refuse to panic in the scary situations, the fund manager won't have to liquidate stocks at unfavorable prices in order to pay them back.

After the market stabilized, Ford was still my top position, followed by Fannie Mae and Merck, and then Chrysler and Digital Equipment. The best performers on the immediate rebound were the cyclicals. Chrysler, for instance, rallied from a low of $20 to $29, and Ford from a low of $38¼ to $56⅝. But people who stuck with these cyclicals were soon disappointed. Three years later, in 1990, Chrysler was selling for $10 and Ford for $20, less than half what they'd sold for in 1987.

It's important to get out of a cyclical at the right time. Chrysler is an example of how quickly things can go from good to worse. The company earned $4.66 a share in 1988 and people were looking for another $4 for 1989. Instead, Chrysler earned $1 and change in 1989, 30 cents in 1990, and in 1991 it lost a bundle and fell into the red. All I could see was disappointment down the road. I sold.

Several Wall Street analysts were touting Chrysler throughout its descent. My most bullish estimate for Chrysler's earnings, which I thought might be hopelessly optimistic to begin with, was far below the most bearish estimate on Wall Street. My best guess was $3 a share, while some analysts were predicting $6. When your best-case scenario turns out to look worse than everybody else's worst-case scenario, you have to worry that the stock is floating on a fantasy.

The winning stocks in the post-Correction turned out to be growth stocks, not cyclicals. Fortunately, I was able to take money out of the autos and put it into companies with high-quality operations and strong balance sheets, including Philip Morris, RJR Nabisco, Eastman Kodak, Merck, and Atlantic Richfield. Philip Morris became my biggest position. I also bought enough General Electric to make it 2 percent of the fund.

(Two percent was not enough. The market value of General Electric was 4 percent of the value of the market overall, so by having only 2 percent in Magellan I was in effect betting against a company

I loved and recommended. This anomaly was pointed out to me by my successor, Morris Smith.)

Here is another example of how foolish it is to stereotype companies by putting them into categories. General Electric is widely regarded as a semistodgy blue chip with cyclical elements, and not as a growth company. But look at Figure 6-1. You could easily imagine this could be a tire track left in the road by a steady grower like Johnson & Johnson.

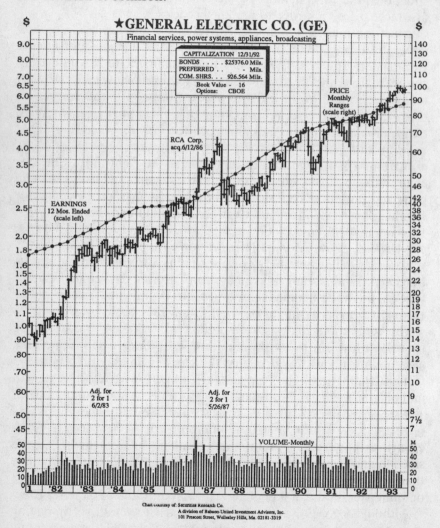

FIGURE 6-1

From the bargain bin, I'd also begun to scoop up the out-of-favor financial-services stocks, including several of the mutual-fund companies, which were pummeled in the market because Wall Street worried about a mass exodus from equity funds.

Magellan had a 22.8 percent gain in 1988 and a 34.6 percent gain in 1989, beating the market again in 1990 when I resigned. It also had beaten the average fund for all 13 years of my tenure.

On my last day at the office, Magellan had $14 billion in assets, of which $1.4 billion was in cash—I'd learned from the last Great Correction, don't leave home without it. I'd built up the holdings in big insurance companies with stable earnings: AFLAC, General Re, Primerica. I'd built up the drug companies, and also defense contractors such as Raytheon, Martin Marietta, and United Technologies. The defense stocks had been pummeled in the market because Wall Street worried that *glasnost* would bring peace on earth, a fear that was highly exaggerated, as usual.

I'd continued to downplay the cyclicals (papers, chemicals, steels), even though some of them appeared to be cheap, because my sources at the various companies told me that business was bad. I had 14 percent of the fund invested in foreign stocks. I'd added to hospital supply, tobacco, and retail, and of course Fannie Mae.

Fannie Mae took over where Ford and Chrysler left off. When 5 percent of a portfolio is invested in a stock that quadruples in two years, this does wonders for a fund's performance. In five years, Magellan made a $500 million profit on Fannie Mae, while all the Fidelity funds combined made more than $1 billion. This may be an all-time record for profits for a single firm from a single stock.

The second-biggest gainer for Magellan was Ford ($199 million from 1985 to 1989), followed by Philip Morris ($111 million), MCI ($92 million), Volvo ($79 million), General Electric ($76 million), General Public Utilities ($69 million), Student Loan Marketing ($65 million), Kemper ($63 million), and Loews ($54 million).

Among these nine all-time winners are two automakers, a cigarette and food company, a tobacco and insurance conglomerate, an electric utility that had an accident, a telephone company, a diversified financial company, an entertainment company, and a company that buys student loans. These weren't all growth stocks, or cyclicals, or value stocks, but together they made $808 million for the fund.

Although I couldn't possibly have bought enough shares in a small company to have it affect Magellan's bottom line, 90 to 100 of them put together could and did make a difference. There were many 5-

Table 6-1. MAGELLAN'S 50 MOST IMPORTANT STOCKS (1977–90)

Alza Corporation	Medco Containment
BankAmerica	Metromedia
Boeing	NBD Bancorp
Cardinal Distribution	Owens-Corning Fiberglas
Chrysler	Pep Boys—Manny, Moe & Jack
Circuit City	Pepsico
Circus Circus	Philip Morris
Coca-Cola	Pic 'N' Save
Comerica	Reebok International
Congoleum	Rogers Communications
Cooper Tire	Royal Dutch
Cracker Barrel Old Country Store	Sbarro
Dunkin' Donuts	Service Corporation International
Envirodyne	Shaw Industries
Federal National Mortgage Association	Skandia
Ford Motor Company	Stop & Shop
General Public Utilities	Stride Rite
Gillette	Student Loan Marketing
Golden Nugget	Taco Bell
Great Atlantic & Pacific	Teléfonos de Mexico
Great Lakes Chemical	Telephone and Data Systems
International Lease Finance	Telerate
King World Productions	Unilever
La Quinta Motor Inns	Volvo
MCI Communications	Zayre

baggers and a few 10-baggers among the smaller stocks, and the ones that did the best in my last five years were Rogers Communications Inc., a 16-bagger; Telephone and Data Systems, an 11-bagger; and Envirodyne Industries, Cherokee Group, and King World Productions, all 10-baggers.

King World is one of those companies whose success was obvious to millions of Americans—everybody who watches TV. It owns the rights to "Wheel of Fortune" and "Jeopardy!" A Wall Street analyst told me about King World in 1987, and soon afterward I took my family to see a taping of "Wheel of Fortune" and to watch Vanna White. There have been a lot of silent movie stars, but Vanna is the only silent TV star I can think of. King World also had rights to a popular talk show hosted by somebody whose name I thought was Winfrah Oprey.

I did some research and learned that game shows generally have

Table 6-2. MAGELLAN'S 50 MOST IMPORTANT
BANK STOCKS (1977–90)

SouthTrust (AL)	Boatmen's Bancshares (MO)
BankAmerica (CA)	Centerre Bancorporation (MO)
Wells Fargo (CA)	Bank of New York (NY)
Wilmington Trust (DE)	First Empire State (NY)
Landmark Banking (FL)	Irving Bank & Trust (NY)
Southwest Florida (FL)	KeyCorp (NY)
First Atlanta (GA)	Marine Midland (NY)
First Railroad & Banking (GA)	NCNB (NC)
SunTrust (GA)	Fifth Third Bank (OH)
Bancorp Hawaii (HI)	Huntington Bank (OH)
West One (ID)	National City (OH)
Harris Bankcorp (IL)	Society Corporation (OH)
Northern Trust (IL)	Continental Bank (Norristown) (PA)
American Fletcher (IN)	CoreStates Financial (PA)
Merchants National (IN)	Dauphin Deposit (PA)
First Kentucky (KY)	Girard Bank & Trust (PA)
First Maryland (MD)	Meridian Bank (PA)
Union Trust (MD)	PNC Financial (PA)
State Street Bank & Trust (MA)	Fleet/Norstar (RI)
Comerica (MI)	South Carolina National (SC)
First of America (MI)	First American (TN)
Manufacturers National (MI)	Third National (TN)
NBD Bancorp (MI)	Signet Bank (VA)
Old Kent Financial (MI)	Sovran Bank (VA)
Norwest Corporation (MN)	Marshall & Ilsley (WI)

a 7- to 10-year run. This is actually a very stable business—a lot more stable than microchips. "Jeopardy!," another King World production, had been around for 25 years, but was only in its 4th year of prime-time syndication. "Wheel of Fortune," the highest-rated show on TV, was in its 5th. Winfrah Oprey was on her way up. So was King World stock.

GOOD MONEY AFTER BAD

There were hundreds of losers in Magellan's portfolio, to go along with the winners I've just described. I've got a list of them that goes on for several pages. Fortunately, they weren't my biggest positions. This is an important aspect of portfolio management—containing your losses.

Table 6-3. MAGELLAN'S 50 MOST IMPORTANT RETAILERS (1977–90)

Pic 'N' Save—discounter	Circuit City—appliances
Dollar General—discounter	The Good Guys—appliances
Service Merchandise— discounter	Sterchi Brothers—furniture
Wal-Mart—discounter	Helig-Myers—furniture
Zayre—discounter	Pier 1 Imports—home furnishings
Family Dollar—discounter	Edison Brothers—diversified
TJX Companies—discounter	Woolworth—diversified
K mart—discounter	Melville—diversified
Michaels Stores—discount crafts	Sterling—jewelry
Del Haize (Food Lion)— supermarkets	Jan Bell Marketing—jewelry
Albertson's—supermarkets	Costco—wholesale club
Stop & Shop—supermarkets and discounter	Pace Membership—wholesale club
Great A&P—supermarkets	House of Fabrics—home sewing
Lucky Stores—supermarkets	Hancock Fabrics—home sewing
American Stores—supermarkets	Transworld Music—records
Gottschalks—department stores	Toys "R" Us—toys
Dillard—department stores	Office Depot—office superstore
J. C. Penney—department stores	Pep Boys—Manny, Moe & Jack—auto supplies
May—department stores	Walgreen—pharmacy
Mercantile Stores—department stores	Home Depot—building supplies
Merry-Go-Round—apparel	CPI Corporation—photo stores
Charming Shoppes—apparel	Pearle Health—eye care
Loehmann's—apparel	Herman's—sporting goods
Children's Place—apparel	Sherwin-Williams—paint, etc.
Gap—apparel	Sunshine, Jr.—convenience

There's no shame in losing money on a stock. Everybody does it. What is shameful is to hold on to a stock, or, worse, to buy more of it, when the fundamentals are deteriorating. That's what I tried to avoid doing. Although I had more stocks that lost money than I had 10-baggers, I didn't keep adding to the losers as they headed for Chapter 11. This leads us to Peter's Principle #13:

Never bet on a comeback while they're playing "Taps."

My top loser of all time was Texas Air: $33 million worth. It could have been worse if I hadn't been selling into the decline. Another stinkeroo was Bank of New England. Obviously, I had overestimated its prospects and underestimated the effects of the New England recession, but when the stock fell by half, from $40 to $20, I started to take my losses. I was completely out at $15.

Meanwhile, people from all over Boston, many of them sophisticated investors, were advising me to buy Bank of New England at the bargain price of $15, and then $10, and when the stock got to $4 they said it was a stupendous opportunity that couldn't be overlooked. I reminded myself that no matter what price you pay for a stock, when it goes to zero you've lost 100 percent of your money.

One of the clues to the bank's deep trouble was the behavior of its bonds. This is often a tip-off to the true dimensions of a calamity. That the value of the Bank of New England's senior debt had fallen from par ($100) to below $20 was a big attention getter.

If a company turns out to be solvent, its bonds will be worth 100 cents on the dollar. So when the bonds sell for only 20 cents, the bond market is trying to tell us something. The bond market is dominated by conservative investors who keep rather close tabs on a company's ability to repay the principal. Since bonds come before stocks in the lineup of claimants on the company's assets, you can be sure that when bonds sell for next to nothing, the stock will be worth even less. Here's a tip from experience: before you invest in a low-priced stock in a shaky company, look at what's been happening to the price of the bonds.

Also near the top of my losers list are First Executive, $24 million; Eastman Kodak, $13 million; IBM, $10 million; Mesa Petroleum, $10 million; and Neiman-Marcus Group, $9 million. I even managed to lose money on Fannie Mae in 1987, a down year for the stock, and on Chrysler in 1988–89, but I'd reduced my Chrysler holdings to less than 1 percent of the fund by then.

Cyclicals are like blackjack: stay in the game too long and it's bound to take back all your profit.

Finally, I note with no particular surprise that my most consistent losers were the technology stocks, including the $25 million I dropped on Digital in 1988, plus slightly lesser amounts on Tandem, Motorola, Texas Instruments, EMC (a computer peripherals supplier), National Semiconductor, Micron Technology, Unisys, and of course that perennial dud in all respectable portfolios, IBM. I never had much flair for technology, but that didn't stop me from occasionally being taken in by it.

SEVEN

ART, SCIENCE, AND LEGWORK

What follows over the next 160 or so pages is a chronicle of the phone calls, speculations, and calculations that led me to the 21 stocks I recommended in the 1992 *Barron's*. The fact that this section is as long as it is is evidence that stockpicking can't be reduced to a simple formula or a recipe that guarantees success if strictly adhered to.

Stockpicking is both an art and a science, but too much of either is a dangerous thing. A person infatuated with measurement, who has his head stuck in the sand of the balance sheets, is not likely to succeed. If you could tell the future from a balance sheet, then mathematicians and accountants would be the richest people in the world by now.

A misguided faith in measurement has proved harmful as far back as Thales, the early Greek philosopher who was so intent on counting stars that he kept falling into potholes in the road.

On the other hand, stockpicking as art can be equally unrewarding. By art, I mean the realm of intuition and passion and right-brain chemistry in which the artistic type prefers to dwell. As far as the artist is concerned, finding a winning investment is a matter of having a knack and following a hunch. People with a knack make money; people without it always lose. To study the subject is futile.

Those who hold this viewpoint tend to prove its validity by neglecting to do research and "playing" the market, which results in more losses, which reinforce the idea that they're lacking in knack. One of their favorite excuses is that "a stock is like a woman—you can never figure one out." This is unfair to women (who wants to be compared to a share of Union Carbide?) and to stocks.

My stockpicking method, which involves elements of art and science plus legwork, hasn't changed in 20 years. I have a Quotron, but not the newfangled work station that many fund managers are using, which reports on what every analyst in the universe is saying about every company, draws elaborate technical charts, and for all I know plays war games with the Pentagon and chess with Bobby Fischer.

Professional investors are missing the point. They're scrambling to buy services like Bridge, Shark, Bloomberg, First Call, Market Watch, and Reuters to find out what all the other professional investors are doing when they ought to be spending more time at the mall. A pile of software isn't worth a damn if you haven't done your basic homework on the companies. Trust me, Warren Buffett doesn't use this stuff.

At earlier *Barron's* panels, my enthusiasm for stocks caused me to go a bit overboard on the recommendations, beginning in 1986, when I recommended more than 100 stocks, a record that stood until the next year, when I recommended 226, causing Alan Abelson to comment: "Maybe we should have asked you what you don't like." At the 1988 panel, the gloomiest on record, I showed some restraint and touted 122, or 129 if you count the seven Baby Bells separately. "You are an equal-opportunity buyer," quipped Abelson. "You're being nondiscriminatory."

In 1989, I showed additional restraint and mentioned only 91 of my favorites, which still was enough to get another rise out of the *Barron's* emcee, who said, "We're once again in the positon of perhaps having to ask you what you don't like—it's a shorter list." In 1990 I reduced the number further, to 73.

I've always believed that searching for companies is like looking for grubs under rocks: if you turn over 10 rocks you'll likely find one grub; if you turn over 20 rocks you'll find two. During the four-year stretch mentioned above, I had to turn over thousands of rocks a year to find enough new grubs to add to Magellan's outsized collection.

The change in my status from full-time to part-time stockpicker caused me to cut back on my recommendations, to 21 companies in

1991 and 21 again in 1992. Since I'd gotten more involved with my family and my charity work, I had time to turn over only a few rocks.

This was OK with me, since the part-time stockpicker doesn't need to find 50 or 100 winning stocks. It only takes a couple of big winners in a decade to make the effort worthwhile. The smallest investor can follow the Rule of Five and limit the portfolio to five issues. If just one of those is a 10-bagger and the other four combined go nowhere, you've still tripled your money.

THE OVERPRICED MARKET

By the time the Roundtable convened in January 1992, stocks in the Dow had enjoyed a great rise to a year-end high of 3200, and optimism abounded. In the festive atmosphere that surrounded a recent 300-point gain in the Dow in three weeks, I was the most depressed person on the panel. I'm always more depressed by an overpriced market in which many stocks are hitting new highs every day than by a beaten-down market in a recession.

Recessions, I figure, will always end sooner or later, and in a beaten-down market there are bargains everywhere you look, but in an overpriced market it's hard to find anything worth buying. Ergo, the devoted stockpicker is happier when the market drops 300 points than when it rises the same amount.

Many of the larger stocks, especially high-profile growth companies such as Philip Morris, Abbott, Wal-Mart, and Bristol-Myers, had risen in price to the point that they'd strayed far above their earnings lines, as shown in Figures 7-1, 7-2, 7-3, and 7-4. This was a bad sign.

Stocks that are priced higher than their earnings lines have a regular habit of moving sideways (a.k.a. "taking a breather") or falling in price until they are brought back to more reasonable valuations. A glance at these charts led me to suspect that the much-ballyhooed growth stocks that were the champions of 1991 would do nothing or go sideways in 1992, even in a good market. In a bad market, they could suffer 30 percent declines. I told the *Barron's* panel that on my list of prayers, Mother Teresa had to be moved down. I was more worried about the growth stocks.

There's no quicker way to tell if a large growth stock is over-

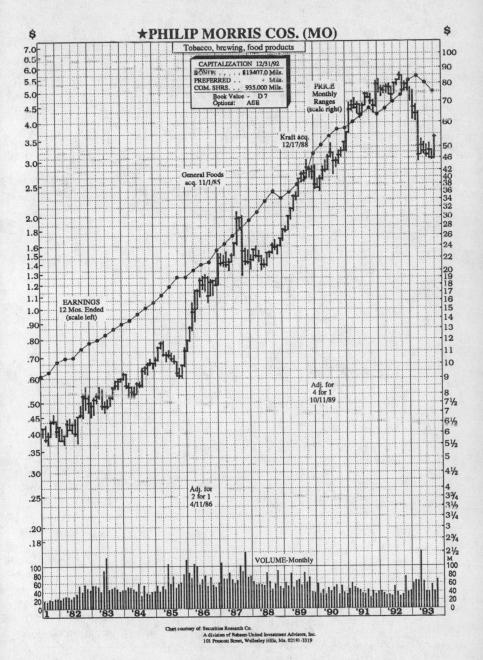

★PHILIP MORRIS COS. (MO)
Tobacco, brewing, food products

CAPITALIZATION 12/31/92
BONDS . . . . . $13407.0 Mils.
PREFERRED . .   * Mils.
COM. SHRS. . . 935.000 Mils.
Book Value -   D 7
Options: ASE

PRICE
Monthly
Ranges
(scale right)

Kraft acq.
12/17/88

General Foods
acq. 11/1/85

EARNINGS
12 Mos. Ended
(scale left)

Adj. for
4 for 1
10/11/89

Adj. for
2 for 1
4/11/86

VOLUME-Monthly

Chart courtesy of: Securities Research Co.
A division of Babson-United Investment Advisors, Inc.
101 Prescott Street, Wellesley Hills, Ma. 02181-3319

FIGURE 7-1

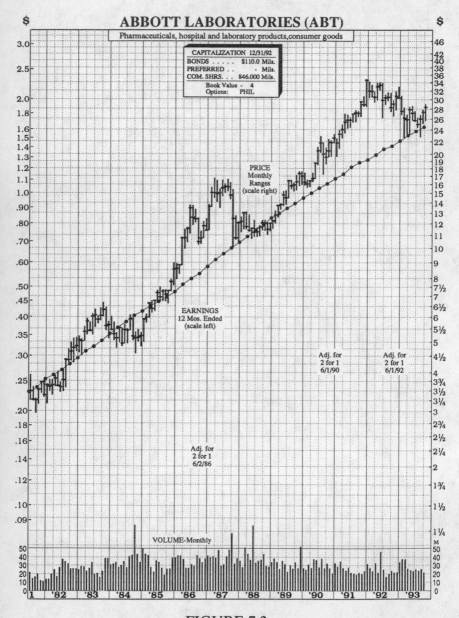

FIGURE 7-2

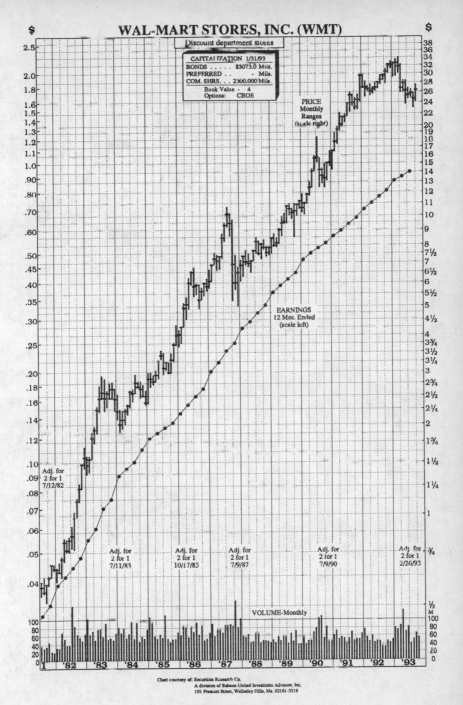

WAL-MART STORES, INC. (WMT)

Discount department stores

CAPITALIZATION 1/31/93
BONDS . . . . . $3073.0 Mils.
PREFERRED . . - Mils.
COM. SHRS. . . 2300.000 Mils.
Book Value - 4
Options: CBOE

PRICE
Monthly
Ranges
(scale right)

EARNINGS
12 Mos. Ended
(scale left)

Adj. for
2 for 1
7/12/82

Adj. for
2 for 1
7/11/83

Adj. for
2 for 1
10/17/85

Adj. for
2 for 1
7/9/87

Adj. for
2 for 1
7/9/90

Adj. for
2 for 1
2/26/93

VOLUME-Monthly

Chart courtesy of: Securities Research Co.
A division of Babson-United Investment Advisors, Inc.
101 Prescott Street, Wellesley Hills, Ma. 02181-3319

FIGURE 7-3

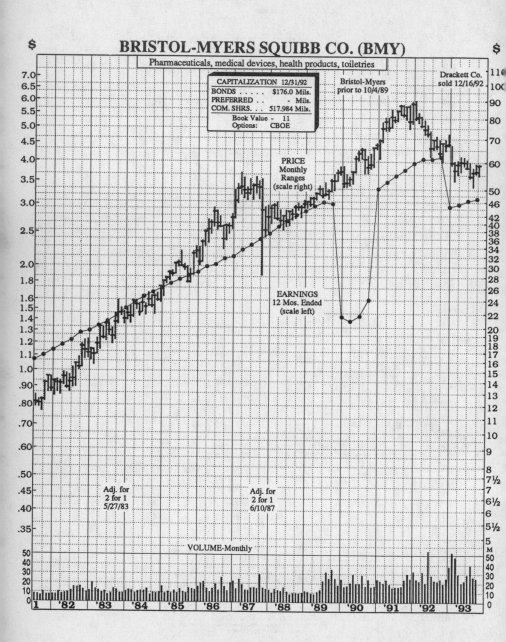

BRISTOL-MYERS SQUIBB CO. (BMY)

Pharmaceuticals, medical devices, health products, toiletries

CAPITALIZATION 12/31/92
BONDS . . . . . $176.0 Mils.
PREFERRED . .   - Mils.
COM. SHRS. . . 517.984 Mils.
Book Value -   11
Options: CBOE

Bristol-Myers
prior to 10/4/89

Drackett Co.
sold 12/16/92

PRICE
Monthly
Ranges
(scale right)

EARNINGS
12 Mos. Ended
(scale left)

Adj. for
2 for 1
5/27/83

Adj. for
2 for 1
6/10/87

VOLUME-Monthly

FIGURE 7-4

valued, undervalued, or fairly priced than by looking at a chart book (available in libraries or a broker's office). Buy shares when the stock price is at or below the earnings line, and not when the price line diverges into the danger zone, way above the earnings line.

The Dow and the S&P 500 had also reached very pricey levels relative to book value, earnings, and other common measures, but many of the smaller stocks had not. In the late fall, which is always when I begin to do my *Barron's* homework, annual tax selling by disheartened investors drives the prices of smaller issues to pathetic lows.

You could make a nice living buying stocks from the low list in November and December during the tax-selling period and then holding them through January, when the prices always seem to rebound. This January effect, as it's called, is especially powerful with smaller companies, which over the last 60 years have risen 6.86 percent in price in that one month, while stocks in general have risen only 1.6 percent.

Small stocks are where I expected to find the bargains in 1992. But before beginning to explore the small-stock universe, I turned my attention to the companies I had recommended to *Barron's* readers in 1991.

Don't pick a new and different company just to give yourself another quote to look up in the newspaper or another symbol to watch on CNBC! Otherwise, you'll end up with too many stocks and you won't remember why you bought any of them.

Getting involved with a manageable number of companies and confining your buying and selling to these is not a bad strategy. Once you've bought a stock, presumably you've learned something about the industry and the company's place within it, how it behaves in recessions, what factors affect the earnings, etc. Inevitably, some gloomy scenario will cause a general retreat in the stock market, your old favorites will once again become bargains, and you can add to your investment.

The more common practice of buying, selling, and forgetting a long string of companies is not likely to succeed. Yet many investors continue to do this. They want to put their old stocks out of their minds, because an old stock evokes a painful memory. If they didn't lose money on it by selling too late, then they lost money on it by selling too soon. Either way, it's something to forget.

With a stock you once owned, especially one that's gone up since you sold it, it's human nature to avoid looking at the quote on the business page, the way you might sneak around the aisle to avoid meeting an old flame in a supermarket. I know people who read the stock tables with their fingers over their eyes, to protect themselves from the emotional shock of seeing that Wal-Mart has doubled since they sold it.

People have to train themselves to overcome this phobia. After running Magellan, I'm forced to get involved with stocks I've owned before, because otherwise there'd be nothing left to buy. Along the way, I've also learned to think of investments not as disconnected events, but as continuing sagas, which need to be rechecked from time to time for new twists and turns in the plots. Unless a company goes bankrupt, the story is never over. A stock you might have owned 10 years ago, or 2 years ago, may be worth buying again.

To keep up with my old favorites I carry a large wire-bound, campus-style notebook, a sort of *Boswell's Life of Johnson & Johnson,* in which I record important details from the quarterly and annual reports, plus the reasons that I bought or sold each stock the last time around. On the way to the office or at home late at night, I thumb through these notebooks, as other people thumb through love letters found in the attic.

This time around, I reviewed the 21 selections I'd made in 1991. It was a mixed bag that did extremely well in a year when the market at large enjoyed a broad-based rally. The S&P rose 30 percent; I think my recommendations rose 50 percent or more. The list included Kemper (insurance and financial services), Household International (financial services), Cedar Fair (amusement parks), EQK Green Acres (shopping center), Reebok (sneakers), Caesars World (casinos), Phelps Dodge (copper), Coca-Cola Enterprises (bottling), Genentech (biotechnology), American Family, now AFLAC (Japanese cancer insurance), K mart (a retailer), Unimar (Indonesian oil), Freddie Mac and Capstead Mortgage (mortgages), SunTrust (a bank), five savings and loans, and Fannie Mae (mortgages), a stock that I touted for six straight years.

I perused my diaries and noted several important changes. Mostly, the prices had gone up. This wasn't necessarily enough of a reason not to repeat a recommendation, but in most cases it meant that the stock had ceased to be a bargain.

One such stock was Cedar Fair, which owns amusement parks in

Ohio and Minnesota. What had brought Cedar Fair to my attention in 1991 was that the stock had a high yield (11 percent). It was selling for less than $12 then. A year later, it was selling for $18, and at that price the yield was reduced to 8.5 percent. It was still a nice yield, but not nice enough to cause me to want to put more money into Cedar Fair. I needed some indication that earnings would improve, and from what I could gather in a chat with the company, there was nothing in the works that would provide such a boost. So I figured there were better opportunities elsewhere.

I went through the same drill with the other 20 companies. EQK Green Acres I rejected because of a passing reference in its latest quarterly report. I've always found it useful to pay attention to the text in these little brochures. What caught my eye was that this company, which owns a Long Island shopping center, was debating whether or not to pay the regular quarterly increase (of one cent) in the dividend as was customary. Green Acres had raised its dividend every quarter since it went public six years earlier, so to break this string to save $100,000 I took as evidence of short-term desperation. When a company that has a tradition of raising the dividend mentions in public that it might discontinue the practice for the sake of a paltry savings, it's a warning that ought to be heeded. (In July 1992, EQK Green Acres not only didn't raise the dividend, it cut it drastically.)

Coca-Cola Enterprises had gone down in price, but this bottler's prospects were gloomier than before, so I rejected it. Fannie Mae had gone up in price, but its prospects were excellent, so I put it back on my list for the seventh year in a row. Just because a stock is cheaper than before is no reason to buy it, and just because it's more expensive is no reason to sell. I also decided to repeat my prior recommendation on Phelps Dodge and two savings and loans, for reasons I'll discuss later.

EIGHT

SHOPPING FOR STOCKS

The Retail Sector

After examining my previous year's selections and finding five that might be worth recommending again, I began my search for new selections in the usual fashion. I headed straight for my favorite source of investment ideas: the Burlington Mall.

The Burlington Mall is located 25 miles from my hometown of Marblehead. It's the huge, covered variety of mall, of which there are only 450 or so in the United States, and a delightful atmosphere in which to study great stocks. Public companies on the way up, on the way down, on the way out, or turning themselves around can be investigated any day of the week by both amateur and professional stock shoppers. As an investment strategy, hanging out at the mall is far superior to taking a stockbroker's advice on faith or combing the financial press for the latest tips.

Many of the biggest gainers of all time come from the places that millions of consumers visit all the time. An investment of $10,000 made in 1986 in each of four popular retail enterprises—Home Depot, the Limited, the Gap, and Wal-Mart Stores—and held for five years was worth more than $500,000 at the end of 1991.

Driving to the Burlington Mall takes me down a memory lane of many other retailers I've bought and sold in the past—beyond Marblehead I pass two Radio Shacks (owned by Tandy—$10,000 invested there in the early 1970s would have resulted in a $1 million payoff, had you gotten out when the stock peaked in 1982); a Toys "R" Us, which went from 25 cents to $36; a Kids "R" Us; an Ames Department Store, a reminder that the lowest a stock can go is zero; and a LensCrafters, a large division whose problems were a drag on U.S. Shoe.

Approaching Burlington from the north on Route 128—the source of many of the famous "go-go" technology stocks of the 1960s, such as Polaroid and EG&G, when this area was America's original Silicon Valley—I exit the thruway. Beyond the exit ramp, I pass a Howard Johnson's, a great growth stock in the 1950s; Taco Bell, a wonderful stock until Pepsi took over the company, and a boost to Pepsi's earnings since; a Chili's (with its charming stock symbol, EAT), which I missed in spite of my children's recommendation because I thought to myself, "Who needs another Chili's-type restaurant?"

The parking lot of the Burlington Mall is roughly the size of the entire town center of Marblehead, and always full of cars. On the far end is a car care center that advertises tires from Goodyear, a stock I bought at $65 and then regretted, although lately it's come back.

The main building is laid out in the form of a giant cross, anchored on the east by Jordan Marsh and on the south by Filene's, both formerly owned by developer Robert Campeau. Campeau bounced into my office one day, full of facts and figures about retailing, and I found his grasp of numbers so impressive that I bought stock in his Campeau Corporation, another mistake. On the north there's Lord & Taylor, now a division of May Department Stores, a great growth company, and on the west a Sears, which hit its high 20 years ago and hasn't approached that summit since.

The inside of the mall reminds me of an old town square, complete with ponds and park benches and large trees and a promenade of lovestruck teenagers and the elderly. Instead of the one movie theater facing the park, there's a fourplex down the corridor; and instead of a drugstore, a hardware store, and a five-and-dime, there are 160 separate enterprises on two floors of commercial space where people can browse.

But I don't think of it as browsing. I think of it as fundamental analysis on the intriguing lineup of potential investments, arranged side by side for the convenience of stock shoppers. Here are more likely prospects than you could uncover in a month of investment conferences.

That the Burlington Mall lacks a brokerage office is too bad, because otherwise it would be possible to sit here all day and check the traffic in and out of the various stores, then shuffle down to the broker to put in buy orders on the ones that are the most crowded. This technique is far from foolproof, but I'd put it far ahead of buying stocks because Uncle Harry likes them, which brings us to Peter's Principle #14:

If you like the store, chances are you'll love the stock.

The very homogeneity of taste in food and fashion that makes for a dull culture also makes fortunes for owners of retail companies and of restaurant companies as well. What sells in one town is almost guaranteed to sell in another, as it has with donuts, soft drinks, hamburgers, videos, nursing-home policies, socks, pants, dresses, gardening tools, yogurt, and funeral arrangements. The stockpicker who got in on the Westward Ho of Home Depot, which began in Atlanta, or the Eastward Ho of Taco Bell, which began in California, or the Southward Ho of Lands' End, which began in Wisconsin, or the Northward Ho of Wal-Mart, which began in Arkansas, or the Coastward Ho of the Gap or the Limited, both of which started in the Midwest, ended up with enough money to be able to travel the world and get away from malls and chain stores!

There were fewer opportunities to make fortunes in retail stocks in the 1950s, a decade famous for mass production and cookie-cutter houses, but still diverse in its shopping and eating habits. When John Steinbeck wrote *Travels with Charley,* he and Charley could tell one place from another, but now if you dropped them off at the Burlington Mall, then transported them blindfolded to a Spokane mall, an Omaha mall, and an Atlanta mall, they'd think they hadn't traveled an inch.

I've been partial to retailers since I was introduced to Levitz Furniture early in its 100-fold rise—an experience I never forgot. These companies don't always succeed, but at least it's easy to monitor their progress, which is another attractive quality they have. You can wait for a chain of stores to prove itself in one area, then take its show on the road and prove itself in several different areas, before you invest.

Employees at the malls have an insiders' edge, since they see what's going on every day, plus they get the word from their colleagues as to which stores are thriving and which are not. The managers of malls have the greatest advantage of all—access to the monthly sales figures that are used to compute the rents. Any store operator who didn't buy shares in the Gap or the Limited, knowing firsthand the success these stores were having month after month, should be swaddled in ticker tape and set on a dunce stool in the window of the local Charles Schwab office. Even Ivan Boesky never got better tips than these—and he cheated.

The Lynch family has no relatives who are mall operators, otherwise I'd be inviting them over for dinner three or four times a week. But we do have shoppers, which is the next best thing. My wife, Carolyn, doesn't do as much research at the register as she once did (although she does have several friends who have their black belts in shopping), but our three daughters have more than made up for her absence. It took me a while to catch on to their excellent analysis.

A couple of years ago, we were sitting around the kitchen table when Annie asked, "Is Clearly Canadian a public company?," which is the kind of question our family has been encouraged to pose. I already knew they liked this new carbonated drink because our refrigerator was full of Clearly Canadian bottles, but instead of taking the hint and doing my homework, I looked it up in the S&P book, didn't see it listed, and promptly forgot about it.

It turned out that Clearly Canadian was listed on the Canadian exchanges and hadn't yet appeared in the S&P book. That I neglected to pursue it was very unfortunate. After Clearly Canadian went public in 1991, the stock price increased from $3 to $26.75, for nearly a nine-bagger in one year, before settling back to the $15 level. This is the kind of return you'd be happy to get in a decade. It certainly outdid all of my 1991 recommendations in *Barron's*.

I'd also ignored their positive reports on Chili's restaurants. The three girls often wore their green Chili's sweatshirts to bed, which reminded me how stupid I was not to take their investment counseling more seriously. How many parents have followed a neighbor's bad advice and bought shares in a gold mining enterprise or a commercial real-estate partnership instead of following their children to the mall, where they would have been led straight to the Gap and its 1,000 percent return from 1986 to 1991? Even if they'd waited until 1991 to follow their children to the Gap, they would have doubled their money in that one year, beating all the major known funds.

As much as we like to think our children are unique, they are also part of an international tribe of shoppers with the same taste in caps, T-shirts, socks, and prewrinkled jeans, so when my oldest daughter, Mary, gets her wardrobe from the Gap, it's a safe assumption that teenagers at all the nation's outlets are doing the same.

Mary had initiated coverage on the Gap in the summer of 1990 by buying some of her school wardrobe from the store on the second floor of the Burlington Mall. (Here's another tip from a veteran mall watcher: in double-decker malls, the most popular retailers are usually found upstairs. The managers arrange it that way so as many customers as possible pass by as many stores as possible on their way to the busiest, and therefore the most profitable, haunts.) When the Gap had been a jeans outlet she had had a poor opinion of it, but like thousands of other teens she was attracted to the colorful new merchandise. Once again, I ignored this powerful buy signal, just as I had with Chili's and Clearly Canadian. I was determined not to repeat the mistake in 1992.

Just before Christmas, I took my three daughters to Burlington for what was billed as a "Christmas present trip" for them, but for me was more of a research trip. I wanted them to lead me to their favorite store, which based on past experience was as infallible a buy signal as you could hope to find. The Gap was crowded, as usual, but that's not where they headed first. They headed to the Body Shop.

The Body Shop sells lotions and bath oil made from bananas, nuts, and berries. It sells beeswax mascara, kiwi-fruit lip balm, carrot moisture cream, orchid-oil cleansing milk, honey-and-oatmeal scrub mask, raspberry ripple lotion, seaweed-and-birch shampoo, and something even more mysterious, called Rhassoul mud shampoo. Rhassoul mud shampoo is not something I'd normally put on my shopping list, but obviously a lot of other people would, because the store was clogged with buyers.

In fact, the Body Shop was one of the three most crowded stores in the entire mall, along with the Gap and the Nature Company, owned by CML, which also owns the popular NordicTracks that now sit in people's living rooms. By my rough calculation, the Body Shop and the Nature Company together occupied 3,000 square feet, but they appeared to be doing as much business as Sears, which has 100,000 square feet of selling space and looked empty.

As I contemplated the bottles of banana bath oil that my children were carrying to the cash register, I remembered that a young analyst at Fidelity, Monica Kalmanson, had recommended the Body Shop at one of our weekly meetings back in 1990. I also remembered that Fidelity's head librarian, Cathy Stephenson, subsequently had left that well-paying and demanding job (she ran a department of 30 people) to open a Body Shop franchise with her own money.

I asked one of the clerks if Ms. Stephenson was the owner of this particular Body Shop, and it turned out she was, although she wasn't in the store the day of our visit. I left a message that I was eager to speak to her.

The store appeared to be well managed, with a young and enthusiastic sales force of at least a dozen people. We left with several bags of shampoos and body soaps, the ingredients of which would have made an impressive salad.

Back at the office, I looked up the Body Shop on my master printout of stocks that Magellan owned on the day of my departure— a printout that was twice as long as my hometown telephone directory. There, to my chagrin, I saw that I'd bought shares in this company in 1989 and somehow had forgotten the fact. The Body Shop was one of the many "tune in later" stocks that I'd purchased in order to keep track of future developments, which in this case I'd obviously neglected to do. Before I'd seen it in the mall, you could have told me the Body Shop was an auto repair franchise and I would have believed it. A certain amount of amnesia is bound to set in when you're trying to follow 1,400 companies.

Through the analysts' reports from a couple of brokerage firms, I got caught up on the story. This was a British company started by an ambitious housewife, Anita Roddick, whose husband was frequently out of town on business. Instead of watching the soap operas or taking aerobics classes, she began tinkering with potions in her garage. Her potions were so popular that she began to sell them in the neighborhood, and this backyard enterprise soon developed into a serious business that went public in 1984, for 5 pence (roughly 10 cents) a share.

From its modest beginning, the Body Shop was soon transformed into an international network of franchises devoted to applying fruits and salads to the skin. In spite of two big bobbles (the stock lost half its value in the Great Correction and again in the Saddam Sell-off), in six years the 5-pence issue had turned into 362 pence, more than a 70-fold return on investment for the lucky friends of the founders who bought in on the initial offering. The Body Shop trades on the London Stock Exchange, but it can also be bought and sold through most U.S. brokers.

This is a socially conscious enterprise like Celestial Seasonings or Ben & Jerry's ice cream. It relies on natural ingredients (including some that are extracted from the rain forest by Kayapó Indians who if they didn't have this job might be cutting down the trees to make a living), shuns advertising, gives all employees one day of paid leave per week for community service activities, promotes health instead of beauty (after all, how many of us will ever be beautiful?), recycles its shopping bags, and pays a 25 cent reward for each little lotion bottle that's returned for a refill.

The Body Shop's commitment to something other than money has not inhibited the franchises from making plenty of it. Cathy Stephenson told me that a franchise owner could expect to turn a profit in the first year. She'd done so well with the Burlington store that she was preparing to open a second store in Harvard Square, and this in the midst of a recession.

In spite of the recession, Body Shops worldwide reported an increase in same-store sales in 1991. (Same-store sales is one of the two or three key factors in analyzing a retail operation.) Body Shop products are priced above the shampoos and lotions sold in discount stores, but below those sold in specialty and department stores. This gives the company a "price niche."

The best part of the story was that the expansion was in its early stages and the idea seemed to have worldwide appeal. The country with the most Body Shops per capita was Canada, with 92 outlets open for business. Already, the Body Shop had become the most profitable of all Canadian retailers, in sales per square foot.

There was only 1 Body Shop in Japan, 1 in Germany, and 70 in the U.S. It seemed to me that if Canada, with one tenth the U.S. population, could support 92 Body Shops, the U.S. could support at least 920.

With years of growth ahead of it, the company was proceeding carefully and expanding with caution. You want to avoid the retailers that expand too fast, especially if they're doing it on borrowed money. Since the Body Shop was a franchise operation, it was able to expand on the franchisees' money.

It was from Cathy Stephenson that I learned of the company's cautious, deliberate approach. She already had proven her ability to run a successful Body Shop in Burlington, but before she was permitted to buy a second franchise in Harvard Square, the chairman of the board flew over from England to inspect the site and to review her performance. This wouldn't have been so remarkable if the Body Shop had been investing its own money, but this was Ms. Stephenson's money at stake and still her second store wasn't automatically approved.

It was a lucky coincidence that I knew the owner of a Body Shop, but millions of shoppers worldwide could get the same feel for the business from visiting one of the outlets, and the same facts and figures from reading the annual and quarterly reports. I mentioned to a poker buddy that I'd gone to a Body Shop, and he told me that his wife and daughter both loved the place. When a 45-year-old and a 13-year-old are enthusiastic about the same store, it's time to launch the investigation.

Same-store sales were OK, the expansion plans seemed realistic, the balance sheet was strong, and the company was growing at 20–30 percent a year. What was wrong with this story? The p/e ratio of 42, based on the S&P estimate of 1992 earnings.

Any growth stock that sells for 40 times its earnings for the upcoming year is dangerously high-priced, and in most cases extravagant. As a rule of thumb, a stock should sell at or below its growth rate—that is, the rate at which it increases its earnings every year. Even the fastest-growing companies can rarely achieve more than a 25 percent growth rate, and a 40 percent growth rate is a rarity. Such frenetic progress cannot long be sustained, and companies that grow too fast tend to self-destruct.

Two analysts who follow the Body Shop were predicting that the company would continue to grow at a 30 percent rate in the next couple of years. So here was a possible 30 percent grower selling at 40 times earnings. In the abstract these were not attractive numbers, but from the perspective of the current stock market they didn't look quite as bad.

At the time I was researching this company, the p/e ratio of the entire S&P 500 was 23, and Coca-Cola had a p/e of 30. If it came down to a choice between owning Coca-Cola, a 15 percent grower selling at 30 times earnings, and the Body Shop, a 30 percent grower selling at 40 times earnings, I preferred the latter. A company with a high p/e that's growing at a fast rate will eventually outperform one with a lower p/e that's growing at a slower rate.

The key question was whether the Body Shop could actually keep up a 25–30 percent growth rate long enough for the stock to "catch up" to its lofty current price. This is easier said than done, but I was impressed with the company's proven ability to move into new markets, and its worldwide popularity. This was an international enterprise almost from the start. The company had installed itself on six continents and had hardly scratched the surface of any of them. If all goes according to plan, we could eventually see thousands of Body Shops, and the stock might increase another 7,000 percent.

It was the unique global aspect of this company that inspired me to support it publicly in *Barron's*. I wouldn't have touted it as the only stock a person should own, and I was aware that the high price relative to earnings left little room for error. The best way to handle a situation in which you love the company but not the current price is to make a small commitment and then increase it in the next sell-off.

The most fascinating part of any of these fast-growth retailing stories, whether it's the Body Shop, Wal-Mart, or Toys "R" Us, is how much time you have to catch on to them. You can afford to wait for things to clarify themselves before you invest. You don't have to rush in and buy shares while the inventor of the Body Shop lotions is still testing the original potions in her garage. You don't have to buy shares when 100 Body Shops have been opened in England, or even when 300 or 400 have been opened worldwide. Eight years after the public offering, when my daughters led me into the Burlington store, it was still not too late to capitalize on an idea that clearly had not yet run its course.

If anybody ever tells you that a stock that's already gone up 10-fold or 50-fold cannot possibly go higher, show that person the Wal-Mart chart. Twenty-three years ago, in 1970, Wal-Mart went public with 38 stores, most of them in Arkansas. Five years after the initial offering, in 1975, Wal-Mart had 104 stores and the stock price had quadrupled. Ten years after the initial offering, in 1980, Wal-Mart had 276 stores, and the stock was up nearly 20-fold.

Many lucky residents of Bentonville, Arkansas, the hometown of Wal-Mart's founder, the recently deceased Sam Walton, invested at the earliest opportunity and made 20 times their money in the first decade. Was it time to sell and not be greedy and put the money into computers? Not if they believed in making a profit. A stock doesn't care who owns it, and questions of greed are best resolved in church or in the psychiatrist's office, not in the retirement account.

The important issue to analyze was not whether Wal-Mart stock would punish the greed of its shareholders, but whether the company had saturated its market. The answer was simple: even in the 1970s, after all the gains in the stock and in the earnings, there were Wal-Mart stores in only 15 percent of the country. That left 85 percent in which the company could still grow.

You could have bought Wal-Mart stock in 1980, a decade after it came public, after the 20-fold gain was already achieved, and after Sam Walton had become famous as the billionaire who drove a pickup truck. If you held the stock from 1980 through 1990, you would have made a 30-fold gain, and in 1991 you would have made another 60 percent on your money in Wal-Mart, giving you a 50-bagger in 11 years. The patient original shareholders have that to feel greedy about, on top of the original 20-fold gain. They also have no problem paying their psychiatrists.

In a retail company or a restaurant chain, the growth that propels earnings and the stock price comes mainly from expansion. As long as the same-store sales are on the increase (these numbers are shown in annual and quarterly reports), the company is not crippled by excessive debt, and it is following its expansion plans as described to shareholders in its reports, it usually pays to stick with the stock.

Stock Symbol	Company	1/13/92 Price
BOSU[1]	Body Shop	325p

*Traded on London Stock Exchange

NINE

PROSPECTING IN BAD NEWS

*How the "Collapse" in Real Estate Led Me to
Pier 1, Sunbelt Nursery, and General Host*

Digging where the surroundings are tranquil and pleasurable may
prove to be as unrewarding as doing detective work from a stuffed
chair. You've got to go into places where other investors and especially fund managers fear to tread, or, more to the point, to invest.
As 1991 came to a close, the most fearsome places were all connected
to housing and real estate.

Real estate had been the principal national scare for more than
two years. The famous collapse of commercial real estate was ru-
mored to be spreading into residential real estate—house prices
were said to be plummeting so fast that the sellers would soon be
giving their deeds away.

I saw this despair in my own neighborhood in Marblehead, where
so many for-sale signs had sprouted that you would have thought
the for-sale sign was the new state flower of Massachusetts. The
signs eventually disappeared as the frustrated sellers got tired of
waiting for decent offers. People complained that the indecent offers
they did get were 30–40 percent below what they could have gotten
two or three years earlier. There was plenty of circumstantial evi-

dence, if you lived in a fat-cat environment, that the great boom in real estate had gone bust.

Since the owners of fat-cat houses included newspaper editors, TV commentators, and Wall Street money managers, it's not hard to figure out why the collapse in real estate got so much attention on the front pages and the nightly news. Many of these stories had to do with the collapse in commercial real estate, but the word "commercial" was left out of the headlines, giving the impression that all real estate would soon be worthless.

What caught my eye on the back pages one day was a tidbit from the National Association of Realtors: the price of the median house was going up. It had gone up in 1989, in 1990, and again in 1991, as it had every year since the organization started publishing this statistic in 1968.

The price of the median house is only one of the many quiet facts that can be a great source of strength and consolation for investors willing to explore the scariest areas of the market. Other useful quiet facts are the "affordability index" from the National Association of Home Builders and the percentage of mortgage loans in default.

I've found that on several occasions over the years, the quiet facts told a much different story than the ones being trumpeted. A technique that works repeatedly is to wait until the prevailing opinion about a certain industry is that things have gone from bad to worse, and then buy shares in the strongest companies in the group.

(This technique isn't foolproof. In the oil and gas drilling industries, people were saying things couldn't get any worse in 1984, and they've been getting worse ever since. It's senseless to invest in a downtrodden enterprise unless the quiet facts tell you that conditions will improve.)

The news about the price of the median house having gone up in 1990 and again in 1991 was so poorly disseminated that when I brought it up at the *Barron's* panel nobody seemed to believe me. Moreover, the decline in interest rates had made houses more affordable than they'd been in more than a decade. The affordability index was so favorable that unless the recession was going to last forever, a better housing market seemed inevitable.

Yet while the quiet facts pointed in a positive direction, many influential people were still worrying about the collapse in real estate, and the prices of stocks in any enterprise remotely related to home building and home finance reflected their pessimistic view. In October 1991 I looked up Toll Brothers, a well-known building company that has appeared from time to time in my portfolio and in my diaries. Sure enough, Toll Brothers stock had dropped from $12⅝ to $2⅜—a five-bagger in reverse. A lot of the sellers must have owned fat-cat houses.

I chose Toll Brothers for further study because I remembered it as a strong company with the financial wherewithal to survive hard times. Ken Heebner, a fine fund manager who'd recommended Toll Brothers to me years earlier, had told me what a classy operation this was. Alan Leifer, a Fidelity colleague, also had mentioned it to me in an elevator.

Toll was strictly a home builder and not a developer, so it wasn't risking its own money by speculating in real estate. With many of its poorly capitalized competitors going out of business, I figured Toll Brothers would end up capturing more of the home-building market after the recession. In the long run, the latest slump would be good for Toll.

So what was wrong with this picture that would have justified a fivefold decrease in the value of Toll Brothers shares? I read the recent reports to find out. Debt had fallen by $28 million, and cash was up $22 million, so the balance sheet had improved during these hard times. So had the order book. Toll Brothers had a two-year backlog of orders for new homes. If anything, the company had too much business.

The company had expanded into several new markets and was well positioned to benefit from a recovery. You didn't need a terrific housing market for Toll to post record earnings.

You can imagine my excitement at finding a company with very little debt and enough new orders to keep it busy for two years, its competitors dropping by the wayside, and its stock selling for one fifth its 1991 high.

I put Toll Brothers at the top of my *Barron's* list in October, expecting to recommend it at the panel in January, but in the meantime the stock quadrupled to $8. (By the time the panel convened, it had reached $12 again.) Here's a tip from the prospectors of year-end anomalies: act quickly! It doesn't take long for bargain hunters to find the bargains in the stock market these days, and by the time they're finished buying, the stocks aren't bargains anymore.

More than once I've identified a likely winner that's been beaten down by the tax sellers in the fall, only to see it soar in price before I could get its name published in *Barron's* two months later. In 1991, the price of the Good Guys, a chain of appliance and electronics stores, rose dramatically between January 14, the day of the *Barron's* meeting at which I recommended the stock, and January 21, the day the magazine was scheduled to hit the stands. On January 19, the editors and I had a conversation about this predicament, and we decided to delete the Good Guys from the text.

Obviously, I wasn't the only investor who discovered the Toll Brothers bargain in the fall of 1991. Frustrated that others were screaming their Eurekas before I had a chance to mention it in print, I turned my attention to other companies that I imagined would benefit in subtler ways from the overblown crisis in real estate. The first that came to mind was Pier 1.

PIER 1

It didn't take a clairvoyant to figure out that people who moved into the houses they bought, new or used, were going to need lamps and room dividers, place mats and dish racks, rugs and shades and knickknacks and maybe a few rattan couches and chairs. Pier 1 sold all of these items at prices that customers on a budget could afford.

Naturally, I'd owned Pier 1 in Magellan. It was spun out of Tandy in 1966, and the virtues of this home furnishings outlet with a Far East flavor were pointed out to me by my wife, Carolyn, who enjoyed browsing through the Pier 1 located on the outskirts of the North Shore Shopping Center. This was a great growth stock in the 70s that ran out of steam, then had another great run in the 80s. Investors who'd bought these shares during Pier 1's latest renaissance were well rewarded until the Great Correction of 1987, when the stock price dropped from $14 to $4. After that, it bounced back to the $12 level, where it remained until the Saddam Sell-off, when it was struck down once again—to $3.

When it came to my attention for the third time, the stock had rallied all the way to $10 and then faded to $7. At $7, I figured it might be undervalued, especially in light of a probable recovery in housing. I opened up my Pier 1 file to refresh my memory. The company had had 12 years of record earnings before it got hurt in the recession. At one point, a conglomerate called Intermark had owned 58 percent of the stock and prized it so highly it allegedly rejected an outside offer to sell these shares for $16 apiece. The story on Wall Street was that Intermark was holding out for $20, but later, when Intermark was strapped for cash, it was forced to sell all its Pier 1 shares for $7. Subsequently, Intermark went bankrupt.

Getting the huge overhang of Intermark shares out of the way was a promising development. I talked to Pier 1's CEO, Clark Johnson, in late September 1991 and again on January 8, 1992. He brought up several favorable factors: (1) the company had made money in 1991 in a very difficult environment; (2) it was expanding at a rate of 25–40 new stores a year; and (3) with only 500 stores in the U.S., it was nowhere close to saturating the market. The company also had managed to reduce expenses, in spite of having added the 25 new stores in 1991. Thanks to Pier 1's devotion to cost-cutting, the profit margins had continued to improve.

As for the old reliable indicator, same-store sales, Mr. Johnson reported that in the regions hardest hit by the recession sales were down 9 percent, but in the rest of the country they had increased. In a recession, it's not unusual for same-store sales to decline, so I took this report as a modest positive. I'd be more worried if the same-store sales had declined in a period of general prosperity for retailers, which this was not.

Whenever I'm evaluating a retail enterprise, in addition to the factors we've already discussed I always try to look at inventories. When inventories increase beyond normal levels, it is a warning sign that management may be trying to cover up the problem of poor sales. Eventually, the company will be forced to mark down this unsold merchandise and admit to its problem. At Pier 1, the inventories had increased, but only because the company had to fill the shelves in 25 new stores. Otherwise, they stood at acceptable levels.

Here was a fast grower with plenty of room to grow more. It was cutting costs, improving its profit margins, and making money in a bad year; it had raised its dividend five years in a row, and was perfectly positioned in a part of the market that was bound to get better: housing. Plus, a lot of Carolyn's friends are very fond of Pier 1. The bonus in the story was Sunbelt Nursery.

In 1991, Pier 1 sold 50.5 percent of its Sunbelt Nursery chain in a public offering. Of the proceeds of $31 million, $21 million was used to reduce the company's debt and the other $10 million was returned to Sunbelt to help finance Sunbelt's renovation and expansion. Overall, Pier 1's debt was reduced by $80 million in 1991, to about $100 million. A stronger balance sheet made it very unlikely that Pier 1 would be going out of business anytime soon, which is what frequently happens to more heavily indebted retailers during recessions.

The $31 million that Pier 1 received for selling half of Sunbelt was $6 million more than it had paid to acquire all of Sunbelt in 1990. You had to figure that the other half of Sunbelt retained by Pier 1 was also worth $31 million, which represented a valuable hidden asset to the company.

At the time I was looking into all this, Pier 1 stock was selling for $7 with a p/e ratio of 10, based on earnings estimates of 70 cents a share for 1992. With the company growing at a 15 percent annual rate, the p/e of 10 was a promising number. When I flew to New York in January to meet with the panel, the stock price had risen to $7.75. Still, I regarded it as a good buy, both of its own merit and because of the Sunbelt "kicker."

Every month, a few more of Pier 1's biggest competitors in home furnishings, mostly local mom-and-pops, were closing their doors and going out of business. Major department stores were dropping their home furnishing sections to concentrate on clothes and fashion accessories. When the economy turns around, Pier 1 will have a huge share of a market in which nobody else seems to want to compete.

Perhaps I'm a frustrated matchmaker. Whenever I get interested in a company, I try to imagine what other company might want to acquire it. In my daydreams, I imagine that Pier 1 would be a logical acquisition for K mart, which was moderately pleased with its earlier acquisitions of a drug chain, a book chain, and an office supply chain, and is always looking for new ways to expand.

SUNBELT NURSERY

About 10 seconds after I put away the Pier 1 file, I pulled out Sunbelt Nursery. Often one stock leads to another and the devoted stockpicker is sent off on a new path, the way the trained hound follows his nose and picks up a new scent.

Sunbelt is in the retail lawn and garden business. It occurred to me that the lawn and garden business would benefit from a rebound in housing just as much as the lampshade and dish rack business. Every new dwelling was going to need trees, shrubs, window box flowers, etc., to enhance its appearance.

It also occurred to me, as I pondered this further, that the nursery business was one of the last of the mom-and-pop enterprises that had not been supplanted by franchises or chain stores. In theory, there was a great opportunity for a well-managed regional or national nursery chain to do for flower beds what Dunkin' Donuts had done for the donut.

Could Sunbelt become that national chain? Operating as Wolfe Nursery in Texas and Oklahoma, Nurseryland Garden Centers in California, and Tip Top Nursery in the Arizona region, Sunbelt already had established itself in 6 of the 11 largest lawn and garden markets in the U.S. According to a Smith Barney research report that found its way to my desk, the company was trying to cater to "the upscale, quality-conscious lawn and garden customer seeking a broader range and quality of plants and supplies as well as a higher level of service than is generally associated with discount-oriented retailers."

Originally, Sunbelt was spun out of Tandy, along with Pier 1. My first introduction to the independent entity came in August 1991 when Sunbelt management visited Boston in a road show to sell some of the 3.2 million shares that Pier 1 was putting into the market. At this meeting, I picked up a copy of the prospectus, alias the red herring, which gets its nickname from the bright red lines used to highlight the dire warnings that are sprinkled throughout. Reading a prospectus is like reading the fine print on the back of an airline ticket. Most of it is boring, except for the exciting parts that make you never want to get on an airplane or buy a single share of stock again.

Since initial public offerings are often sold out, you have to figure a lot of investors are ignoring the highlighted paragraphs. But in addition to those, there's useful information in a prospectus that shouldn't be overlooked.

The initial offering for Sunbelt went off successfully at $8.50 per share. Thanks to these proceeds, the company began its independent life with a strong balance sheet—no debt and $2 a share in cash. The plan was to use the cash to remodel the best of its 98 lawn and garden centers, thereby improving their profitability, and to shut down a few of the duds.

These stores had not been remodeled since the Vietnam War, so there was plenty of room for improvement. The most important renovation was enclosing a portion of the nursery space so that plants and flowers could survive into the colder months and wouldn't be left to freeze to death and be reincarnated as mulch.

Pier 1 was still the major Sunbelt shareholder with its 49 percent stake, a factor that I viewed as very favorable. I already knew that Pier 1 knew how to run a retailing business, so it wasn't like an insurance company having a majority interest in a paper company. Moreover, Pier 1 had already done its own remodeling, and I thought Sunbelt could benefit from Pier 1's experience. The management of both operations owned a lot of shares, which gave them a substantial incentive to make Sunbelt a success.

By the time I got around to considering Sunbelt as a possible *Barron's* selection, the year-end tax selling had dropped the stock price to a tantalizing $5 a share. After a single disappointing quarter, mainly caused by a string of natural lawn and garden calamities (premature frost in Arizona, 14 inches of rain in Texas), Sunbelt had lost half of its market value.

What a bonanza for the investors who had the courage to buy more! This was the same company that had come public at $8.50 two months earlier. It still had the same $2 in cash, and its renovation plans were still intact. At $5 a share, Sunbelt was selling for less than its book value of $5.70, and with 1992 earnings estimated at 50–60 cents, its p/e ratio was slightly less than 10. This was a 15 percent grower. Other lawn and garden retailers were selling at twice book value and had p/e ratios of 20.

One way to estimate the actual worth of a company is to use the home buyer's technique of comparing it to similar properties that recently have been sold in the neighborhood. Multiplying the $5 share price by the number of Sunbelt shares, 6.2 million, I arrived at the conclusion that the market value for the entire company and its 98 lawn and garden centers was $31 million. (Normally in this exercise you have to subtract the debt, but since Sunbelt had no debt, I could ignore this step.)

Checking other publicly owned nursery companies, I discovered that Calloway's, which operates 13 Sunbelt-type stores in the Southeast, had 4 million shares outstanding and its stock was selling for $10. That gave Calloway's a market value of $40 million.

If Calloway's with 13 stores was worth $40 million, how could Sunbelt with 98 stores be worth only $31 million? Even if Calloway's was a superior operation that made more money per store than Sunbelt—which it was—Sunbelt had seven times the number of outlets and five times Calloway's total sales. All things being remotely equal, Sunbelt should have been worth as much as $200 million, or more than $30 a share. Or all things not being equal—for instance, if Calloway's was overpriced and Sunbelt was a mediocre operation—Sunbelt was still cheap.

By the time my Sunbelt tip got into print, the stock had bounced back up to $6.50.

GENERAL HOST

Though I didn't plan it this way, 1992 was the year that Lynch specialized in greenery. The same way Pier 1 led me to Sunbelt, Sunbelt led me to General Host.

You'd never guess that General Host had anything to do with plants. This once was a rather eccentric conglomerate that owned anything and everything—which may explain the name. At one time or another, it had owned Hot Sam's Pretzels and Hickory Farms stores and kiosks and American Salt. It owned All-American Gourmet TV dinners, Van De Kamp's frozen fish, and Frank's Nursery & Crafts. It had owned Calloway's Nursery before Calloway's was spun off in the public stock sale mentioned above.

Lately, General Host had divested itself of the pretzels, the salt, the TV dinners, the farm stores, and the frozen fish in order to concentrate on 280 Frank's Nursery outlets located in 17 states. What impressed me from the outset was the fact that the company had a long-term program to buy back its own shares. Recently, it had bought some back for $10 per share, which tells you that in the company's own expert opinion General Host must be worth more than $10 per share—otherwise, why would it waste all this money on itself?

When a company buys back shares that once paid a dividend and borrows the money to do it, it enjoys a double advantage. The interest on the loan is tax-deductible, and the company is reducing its outlay for dividend checks, which it had to pay in after tax dollars. A few years ago, Exxon's stock was so depressed that it was yielding 8–9 percent. At the time, Exxon was able to borrow money at 8–9 percent to buy back millions of these dividend-paying shares. Since the interest on the loan was tax-deductible, Exxon was really paying only about 5 percent to save 8–9 percent on dividends. This simple maneuver increased the company's earnings without its having to refine an extra drop of oil.

I was impressed by the fact that General Host's stock price had fallen far below the price at which the company had recently bought back shares. When you or I can buy part of a company for less than the company itself has paid, it's a deal worth examining. It's also a good sign when the "insiders," executives and so forth, have paid more than the current price. Insiders are hardly infallible (those at numerous Texas and New England banks were madly acquiring more shares all the way down) but there are smart people in business who often know what they're doing and aren't inclined to squander money on a fool's errand. They are also willing to work extra hard to make their own investments pay off. This leads us to Peter's Principle #15:

When insiders are buying, it's a good sign—unless they happen to be New England bankers.

So in reviewing the latest proxy statement for General Host, I took it as a good sign that Harris J. Ashton, the CEO and owner of a million shares, had not parted with a single one of them during the recent price drop. Another tempting detail was that the book value of General Host was $9 a share, which exceeded the price of this $7 stock. In other words, the buyer of the stock was getting $9 worth of assets for $7. This was my idea of money well spent.

Whenever book value comes up, I ask myself the same question we all ask about the movies: is this based on a true story or is it fictional? The book value of any company can be one or the other. To find out which, I turn to the balance sheet.

Let's take a closer look at General Host's balance sheet, to illustrate my three-minute balance sheet drill. Normally, there's a right side and a left side to a balance sheet. The right side shows the company's liabilities (that is, how much money it owes), and the left side the assets (that is, what it owns). Here, we've printed a portion of the left side on page 171 and the right on page 172. The difference between the two sides, all the assets minus all the liabilities, is what belongs to the shareholders. This is called the shareholders' equity. Shareholders' equity is shown as $148 million. Was this a reliable number?

Of the equity, $65 million was cash, so that part certainly was reliable. Cash is cash. Whether the remaining $83 million in equity was a reliable number depended on the nature of the assets.

The left side of a balance sheet, which lists the assets, can be a murky proposition. It includes such things as real estate, machinery and other equipment, and inventory, which may or may not be worth what the company claims. A steel plant might be listed at $40 million, but if the equipment is outdated, it might fetch zero in a garage sale. Or the real estate, carried on the books at the original purchase price, may have declined in value—although the reverse is more likely.

With a retailer, the merchandise is also counted as an asset, and the reliability of this number depends on the kind of merchandise that it sells. It could be miniskirts that have gone out of style and are now worthless, or it could be white socks that can always attract a buyer. General Host's inventory consisted of trees, flowers, and shrubs, which I assumed had a decent resale value.

A company's acquisitions of other companies are reflected in the category marked "Goodwill" (or, in this case, "Intangibles"), shown here as $22.9 million. The goodwill is the amount that has been paid for an acquisition above and beyond the book value of the actual assets. Coca-Cola, for instance, is worth far more than the value of the bottling plants, the trucks, and the syrup. If General Host bought Coca-Cola, it would have to pay billions for the Coca-Cola name, the trademark, and other intangibles. This part of the purchase price would appear on the balance sheet as goodwill.

Of course, General Host is too small to buy Coca-Cola, but I'm just using this as an example. The balance sheet indicates it has acquired other businesses in the past. Whether it can ever recover these goodwill expenditures is open to speculation, and in the meantime it gradually has to write off the goodwill with part of its earnings.

I can't be certain that General Host's $22.9 million in goodwill is really worth that much. If half of General Host's total assets con-

Table 9-1. CONSOLIDATED BALANCE SHEET—GENERAL HOST CORPORATION

January 27, 1991, and January 28, 1990

(Dollars in thousands)

	1990	1989
Assets		
Current assets:		
Cash and cash equivalents	$ 65,471	$110,321
Other marketable securities	119	117
Accounts and notes receivable	4,447	2,588
Federal income tax receivable	4,265	13,504
Merchandise inventory	**77,816**	83,813
Prepaid expenses	7,517	7,107
Total current assets	159,635	217,450
Property, plant and equipment, less accumulated depreciation of $77,819 and $61,366	245,212	246,315
Intangibles, less accumulated amortization of $5,209 and $4,207	**22,987**	23,989
Other assets and deferred charges	17,901	18,138
	$445,735	$505,893

Liabilities and Shareholders' Equity

Current liabilities:

Accounts payable	**$ 47,944**	$ 63,405
Accrued expenses	41,631	38,625
Current portion of long-term debt	9,820	24,939
Total current liabilities	99,395	126,969

Long-term debt:

Senior debt	119,504	146,369
Subordinated debt, less original issue discount	48,419	50,067
Total long-term debt	**167,923**	196,436

Deferred income taxes	20,153	16,473
Other liabilities and deferred credits	9,632	12,337

Commitments and contingencies

Shareholders' equity:

Common stock $1.00 par value, 100,000,000 shares authorized, 31,752,450 shares issued	31,752	31,752
Capital in excess of par value	89,819	89,855
Retained earnings	158,913	160,985
	280,484	282,592
Net unrealized loss on noncurrent marketable equity securities		(2,491)
Cost of 13,866,517 and 12,754,767 shares of common stock in treasury	(131,738)	(125,545)
Notes receivable from exercise of stock options	(114)	(878)
Total shareholders' equity	**148,632**	153,678
	$445,735	$505,893

sisted of goodwill, I would have no confidence in its book value or in its shareholders' equity. As it turns out, $22.9 million in goodwill out of $148 million in total assets is not a troublesome percentage.

We can assume, then, that General Host's book value did approximate the $9 per share that was claimed.

Turning to the other side of the balance sheet, the liabilities, we see that the company had $167 million in debt to go along with the $148 million in equity. This *was* troublesome. What you want to see on a balance sheet is at least twice as much equity as debt, and the more equity and the less debt the better.

A high debt ratio like this would in some cases be enough to cause me to take the company off the buy list, but there was a mitigating factor: much of this debt was not due for several years, and it was not owed to banks. In a highly leveraged company, bank debt is dangerous, because if the company runs into problems the bank will ask for its money back. This can turn a manageable situation into a potentially fatal one.

Back on the left side, I circled merchandise inventory, which is always something to worry about with retailers. You don't want a company to have too much inventory. If it does, it may mean that management is deferring losses by not marking down the unsold items and getting rid of them quickly. When inventories are allowed to build, this overstates a company's earnings. General Host's inventories had decreased from previous levels, as shown in table 9–1.

A hefty accounts payable is OK. It shows that General Host was paying its bills slowly and keeping the cash working in its favor until the last minute.

In the text of its annual report, General Host described how it was engaged in a vigorous campaign to cut costs in order to become more competitive and more profitable—like everybody else in America. Although most companies make such claims, the proof is in the S, G, and A category (selling, general, and administrative expenses) on the income statement (see Table 9–2). You'll note here that General Host's S, G, and A expenses were declining, a trend that continued into 1991.

It turns out that General Host was taking several steps—both on earth and in outer space—to improve its fortunes. On the terrestrial level, the company was adding new scanning devices to automate its checkout system. The record of each transaction would then be beamed up to a satellite and then down to a central computer. This

Fiscal Years Ended January 27, 1991, January 28, 1990, and January 29, 1989

(In thousands, except per share amounts)

	1990	1989	1988
Revenues:			
Sales	$515,470	$495,767	$466,809
Other income	4,103	13,179	11,661
	519,573	508,946	478,470
Costs and Expenses:			
Cost of sales, including buying and occupancy	355,391	333,216	317,860
Selling, general and administrative	**145,194**	**156,804**	147,321
Interest and debt expense	21,752	26,813	21,013
	522,337	516,833	486,194
Loss from continuing operations before income taxes	**(2,764)**	**(7,887)**	(7,724)
Income tax benefit	(6,609)	(8,768)	(3,140)
Income (loss) from continuing operations	3,845	881	(4,584)
Loss from discontinued operations		(3,424)	(12,200)
Income (loss) before extraordinary losses	3,845	(2,543)	(16,784)
Extraordinary losses			(4,500)
Net income (loss)	$ 3,845	$ (2,543)	$(21,284)
Earnings per share:			
Income (loss) from continuing operations	$ .21	$ .05	$ (.23)
Loss from discontinued operations		(.18)	(.61)
Income (loss) before extraordinary losses	.21	(.13)	(.84)
Extraordinary losses			(.23)
Net income (loss)	$ .21	$ (.13)	$ (1.07)
Average shares outstanding	18,478	19,362	19,921

satellite system, when put into place, was expected to keep track of all the sales in all the nurseries, to help management know when to restock the poinsettias and whether to transfer, say, some hibiscus bushes from the Fort Lauderdale branch to the Jacksonville branch.

In addition, credit card authorizations were being speeded up from 25 seconds per sale to about 3 seconds, to make the lines at the cash register move faster and add to customer satisfaction.

Following the same course as Sunbelt Nursery, General Host was planning to enclose a section of each of its Frank's Nursery outlets to extend the selling season. In addition, it was installing Christmas kiosks in shopping malls during the holidays. This wasn't just a harebrained scheme—General Host had experience in the kiosk business from having deployed more than 1,000 of them to sell its Hickory Farm products.

This is a cheap way for a retailer to add selling space. Already, General Host had installed more than 100 Frank's Nursery kiosks— stocked with gift wrapping, Christmas trees, wreaths, and boughs— in shopping malls in 1991, and the company planned to increase the number to 150 kiosks by Christmas 1992. It was also taking steps to enclose the kiosks and make them more permanent.

Meanwhile, General Host was opening new Frank's Nursery outlets at a steady and careful pace. The goal was to create 150 new Frank's by 1995, bringing the total to 430. The company also launched a new private-label line of fertilizers and seeds.

Every company in existence likes to tell its shareholders that business is going to get better, but what made General Host's assertion believable was that management had a plan. The company wasn't waiting for begonia sales to improve, it was taking concrete steps (the kiosks, the remodeled nurseries, the satellite system) to boost its earnings. When a business as old-fashioned as Frank's is modernizing on all fronts and expanding at the same time, there are several chances for the earnings to improve.

A final reassuring detail was the Calloway's transaction. In 1991, General Host had sold off the Calloway's nursery chain in Texas, and it used the proceeds to reduce its debt, thus strengthening its balance sheet.

Since General Host was now confined to the nursery business, the same as Calloway's, the Calloway's sale gives us another chance to compare two similar enterprises. Once again, I took out my most sophisticated investment tool, a 15-year-old hand-held calculator, to do the following math:

Calloway's, with 13 stores, was valued at $40 million—or roughly $3 million per store. General Host owned 280 Frank's Nursery outlets, or 21 times as many stores as Calloway's. The Frank's outlets were older, smaller, and less profitable than the Calloway's stores, but even if we assume they were half as valuable ($1.5 million per store), the 280 Frank's stores ought to have been worth $420 million.

So General Host had a $420 million asset here. Subtracting the company's $167 million in debt leaves you with an enterprise worth $253 million.

With 17.9 million shares outstanding, this means that General Host's shares ought to be selling for $14, or twice the price at the time I made the calculation. Clearly, the company was undervalued.

Stock Symbol	Company	1/13/92 Price
GH	General Host	$7.75
PIR	Pier 1 Imports	$8.00
SBN	Sunbelt Nursery	$6.25

TEN

MY CLOSE SHAVE AT SUPERCUTS

In December 1991, I got my hair cut at Supercuts, which had recently come public and goes by the symbol CUTS. If a prospectus for this haircutting venture hadn't found its way to the top of a pile on my desk, I would never have cheated on my regular barber, Vinnie DiVincenzo, who offers a $10 haircut with pleasant conversation thrown in as a bonus at his place of business in Marblehead, Massachusetts.

We talk about the kids and whether my rusty old '77 AMC Concord might qualify as an "antique" or a "classic." I hope that Vinnie, who's not yet gone public, will excuse this one absence for the sake of my research.

The Supercuts I visited was located at 829 Boylston Street, Boston, on the second floor of a brownstone. Downstairs, a stand-alone placard advertised the prices, which I dutifully recorded on another indispensable investment tool, the yellow legal pad. The regular Supercut was $8.95; a Supercut with shampoo, $12; a shampoo by itself, $4.

These prices were in line with what Vinnie would have charged, and substantially less than the going rate at the beauty salons and unisex outlets where my wife and my daughters get their trims and where you might as well take out a bank loan to finance a henna treatment or a permanent wave.

As I walked into Supercuts and was greeted by the maître d', three customers were getting haircuts, while four others were waiting in the anteroom. They were all male. Eventually, some women showed up, although in later conversations with the company I learned that men make up more than 80 percent of the clientele, while 95 percent of the stylists (they no longer call these people barbers, it seems) are female. I put my name on the waiting list and made a mental note: a lot of people must think a Supercuts haircut is worth waiting for.

I sat down and began to study the prospectus and the brochure that I'd brought along from my office. There's no more useful way to spend an afternoon than researching a company in its own habitat.

In October 1991, Supercuts made its stock-market debut at an initial offering price of $11 a share. It was a franchise operation, the McTrim of barbershops, with more than 650 stores already established. The founders had been bought out and the new management had embarked on a vigorous expansion campaign. They'd coaxed Ed Faber, the former head of Computerland, out of retirement to oversee the project.

I remembered that Faber was an ex-marine who'd done wonders for Computerland in its most prosperous fast-growth phase, before Computerland fell apart. He left, the company foundered, and then he came back. It was a surprise to find an ex-marine involved in hairstyling, but it didn't really matter what the company did. Faber's expertise was in "rolling out" a franchise operation from its original few locations into a nationwide network.

The theory behind Supercuts is that hair care is a $15–$40 billion industry dominated by independent barbers like Vinnie and locally owned unisex hair salons. Barbers are a vanishing breed (in New York State, for example, the number of licensed haircutters dropped in half in the last decade). Hair grows half an inch a month, and with the Vinnies of the world disappearing, somebody was going to have to cut it. This was a perfect opportunity for a well-managed, efficient nationwide franchise to come in and capture the market.

This was the same sort of situation I encountered years earlier when Service Corporation International began to take over the mom-and-pop mortuaries. People were dying at a regular rate, somebody was going to have to bury them, and the industry was made up of hundreds of inefficient small operators whose children wanted to go to law school.

According to the Supercuts brochure, each stylist is trained to perform quick and efficient snipping with no dawdling or nonsense, which fits nicely into the no-dawdling, no-nonsense ethic of the 1990s. Armed with small scissors and a "revolutionary comb," the Supercuts stylist can snip through an average of 2.8 heads per hour, and the cut you get in Albuquerque should be the same as the cut you get in Miami.

There's always something new to learn on these forays—did you know that haircutters have to be licensed? I didn't, but they do, and that's more than you can say for fund managers. There are no requirements for managing billions of dollars, but before somebody can trim your sideburns, he or she has to pass some sort of a test. Given the record of the average fund manager over the last decade, maybe it should be the other way around.

A Supercuts stylist is paid $5–$7 an hour, which isn't much of a salary, but it's augmented with medical benefits, and at 2.8 heads per hour, she (I say "she" because of the preponderance of females who work there) can double her wages with tips.

Meanwhile, each stylist is bringing in $30 an hour in revenues for the franchise, which is why it's been so profitable to own a Supercuts. This isn't like the aluminum industry, in which half the earnings are eaten up in improvements to the plant and equipment. Other than the rent for the retail space, the biggest ongoing expenditures in a hair salon are for scissors and combs.

As I also read in the prospectus, the average owner of a Supercuts franchise invests $100,000 at the outset—this money pays for the franchise fee, the sinks, the barber chairs, the decorations, the shampoo, etc. In merely two years of operation, that store is expected to generate a 50 percent pretax return on equity, which beats almost any return any of us could get elsewhere and explains why the company has an easy time recruiting future franchisees.

What's good for the owner is also good for the shareholders—this is the part where I got interested. The company receives 5 percent of the gross revenues and 4 percent of the sales of the Nexxus products displayed in each franchise. (I could see these on shelves against the far wall.) The administrative costs are minimal. The biggest expense is in training the stylists. Supercuts hires a new trainer (at $40,000 a year) for each 10 new shops, but then these 10 new shops should contribute $300,000 a year to the annual revenues.

One of the first things you need to know about a retail operation, as mentioned earlier, is whether it can afford to expand. A glance at this balance sheet showed me that debt was 31 percent of total capital, a disturbing number that required further explanation. I made a note of it.

At this point in my deliberations (the employees who saw me looking around and taking notes may have pegged me as a spy from the barbers' union) my name was called and I was ushered past the reclining chairs and into the room with the shampoo sinks. A comely young specialist washed my hair in short order and then directed me back to the cutting area, where she wrapped me in a sheet and proceeded to snip off everything, including my sideburns. This happened so quickly I had no time to object. I felt like the privet hedge in the movie *Edward Scissorhands*.

Since in normal circumstances I'm never sure if I look good or bad, even when I saw myself in the Supercuts mirror I didn't protest, preferring to await the verdict that really counts—from my family. For all I knew, the shorn look was in.

When I got home and was greeted with a "What happened to you?" from Carolyn and my daughters, I realized that the shorn look was not in, at least not when applied to a 48-year-old with Warhol-like white hair. Several acquaintances said I looked "young," but only, I sensed, because they were struggling to be positive without lying too much, and "young" was the best they could do. When people tell me I look young, I begin to realize they once must have thought I looked old and neglected to tell me.

Here is an exception to the rule that you have to like the store before you buy the stock. After being sheared at Supercuts, I found myself liking the stock (or at least its prospects on paper) far more than I liked the store. I promised myself never again to stray from Vinnie DiVincenzo and his regular $10 haircut.

The privet hedge problem I brought up with Supercuts' senior vice-president and chief financial officer, Steven J. Thompson, in a phone call to California. He commiserated with me for my lost sideburns and then said, "The good news is that hair grows back at the rate of a half inch per month." I'd already taken hope from this fact when I read it in the brochure.

We discussed the idea that Supercuts stylists are all licensed professionals who have to take a refresher course every seven months, and that the medical benefits and the tips will attract good people. What I worried about here was high turnover and poor hedgemanship among poorly qualified and/or disgruntled employees. I asked about the turnover rate, which Mr. Thompson said had been low so far.

Most of the news was positive. The debt level that I'd noted earlier as a potential problem turned out not to be as much of one as I thought. Supercuts had $5.4 million in annual free cash flow, and most of that, Mr. Thompson said, would be used to pay off debt. By 1993, the company expected to have no debt at all, and the interest expense of $2.1 million in 1991 would disappear.

Since this was a franchise operation, the money to set up the new Supercuts would come from the franchisees. This was another big plus: Supercuts could expand rapidly without using its own capital and without excessive borrowing.

The biggest plus of all was that 250 million Americans needed haircuts every month, and with the mom-and-pop haircutters closing their doors, no dominant chain store had emerged to fill the void. Supercuts' major competitors included Regis Corporation, which operates Mastercuts in malls, where the rents are much higher and the clientele is mostly women; Fantastic Sam's, which has twice as many locations as Supercuts but most are franchise operations that produce less than half the revenue of a Supercuts shop; and J. C. Penney, whose unisex salons are confined to J. C. Penney stores.

Supercuts had the additional advantage of being open on Sundays and in the evenings. The company was working on a national advertising campaign to give it a brand recognition that none of its competitors enjoyed. This was a 20 percent grower at the initial stages of its takeoff, selling for 16 times earnings at the time I recommended it.

In the end, the excellent numbers won out over the lost sideburns, and I touted Supercuts in *Barron's*. "I got a haircut there, I tried it out," I told the rest of the panel. "Is this your current haircut?" asked Mario Gabelli, and I had to admit it was. "We won't advertise that," said Abelson.

Stock Symbol	Company	1/13/92 Price
CUTS	Supercuts	$11.33

ELEVEN

BLOSSOMS IN THE DESERT

Great Companies in Lousy Industries

SUN TELEVISION & APPLIANCES

I'm always on the lookout for great companies in lousy industries. A great industry that's growing fast, such as computers or medical technology, attracts too much attention and too many competitors. As Yogi Berra once said about a famous Miami Beach restaurant, "It's so popular, nobody goes there anymore." When an industry gets too popular, nobody makes money there anymore.

As a place to invest, I'll take a lousy industry over a great industry anytime. In a lousy industry, one that's growing slowly if at all, the weak drop out and the survivors get a bigger share of the market. A company that can capture an ever-increasing share of a stagnant market is a lot better off than one that has to struggle to protect a dwindling share of an exciting market. This leads us to Peter's Principle #16:

> **In business, competition is never as healthy as total domination.**

The greatest companies in lousy industries share certain characteristics. They are low-cost operators, and penny-pinchers in the executive suite. They avoid going into debt. They reject the corporate caste system that creates white-collar Brahmins and blue-collar untouchables. Their workers are well paid and have a stake in the companies' future. They find niches, parts of the market that bigger companies have overlooked. They grow fast—faster than many companies in the fashionable fast-growth industries.

Pompous boardrooms, overblown executive salaries, demoralized rank and file, excessive indebtedness, and mediocre performance go hand in hand. This also works in reverse. Modest boardrooms, reasonable executive salaries, a motivated rank and file, and small debts equals superior performance most of the time.

I called John Weiss, an analyst from Montgomery Securities in California who'd written reports on several discount appliance store chains. I wanted his opinion about the Good Guys, a stock I'd been following since 1991. Weiss said that competition from Circuit City was hurting the Good Guys' earnings. When I asked him what else he liked in this lousy industry, he mentioned Sun Television & Appliances.

Weiss's version of the Sun TV story was so compelling that as soon as I'd hung up with him I called corporate headquarters in Ohio to talk to the source.

When you can get the CEO on the line without delay and you've never met this person, you know the company doesn't suffer from excessive hierarchy. I was connected to Bob Oyster, an amiable chap. We rhapsodized on the merits of Ohio golf courses before we got around to the purpose of the call.

Sun TV is central Ohio's lone high-volume discount outlet for small appliances as well as refrigerators, washers, and dryers. Oyster said there were seven Sun TV stores in Columbus alone. The company's most profitable outlet is located in Chillicothe, Ohio, a name that my fellow *Barron's* panelists later congratulated me for being able to pronounce. It also has a dominant position in the Pittsburgh area.

Trivia buffs and shareholders of Sun Television & Appliances will be happy to know that 50 percent of the U.S. population lives within 500 miles of Columbus. In fact, Columbus is the only major city east of the Mississippi and north of the Mason-Dixon line that increased its population from 1950 to 1990.

The population growth in this part of Ohio, the news of which has yet to reach the East Coast, augurs well for the future of Sun TV. The company was engaged in a vigorous expansion program

(7 new stores in 1991, 5 more in 1992), which would bring the total to 22. It had less than $10 million in debt. With the stock selling for $18, its p/e ratio was 15. Here was a 25–30 percent grower with a 15 p/e. Several of its competitors were struggling to stay in business.

Sun TV made money in the 1990–91 recession when the economy was terrible, home sales were sluggish, and people weren't buying new appliances. The company's earnings actually increased in 1991. I had no reason to doubt it would do even better in 1992.

Nevertheless, Sun TV has a lot to prove before it makes my all-star team of great companies in lousy industries. A what-if portfolio of this Magnificent Seven (plus Green Tree, which is a provisional member) would have given you the results shown in Table 11-1. Most of these stocks had recent run-ups, which caused me to omit them from my 1992 list of recommendations. But every one is worth tuning in later.

SOUTHWEST AIRLINES

In the 1980s, what business was worse than the airline business? Eastern, Pan Am, Braniff, Continental, and Midway went bankrupt, and several others were on the verge of doing so, yet in this disastrous 10-year stretch the stock in Southwest Airlines rose from $2.40 to $24. Why? Mostly because of all the things Southwest Airlines didn't do.

It didn't fly to Paris, it didn't serve fancy meals, it didn't borrow too much money to buy too many airplanes, it didn't overpay its

Table 11-1. Magnificent Seven Portfolio (+ One)

Company	Total Return, 1990–91
Southwest Airlines	115%
Bandag	46
Cooper Tire	222
Green Tree Financial	188
Dillard	75
Crown Cork & Seal	69
Nucor	50
Shaw Industries	17
Portfolio Average	87%
S&P 500	26%

executives, and it didn't give its workers a good reason to resent the company.

Southwest Airlines (symbol LUV) was the lowest-cost operator in the industry. How do we know this? The telling statistic is "operating cost per seat mile." Southwest's ranged from 5 to 7 cents during a period when the industry average was 7 to 9 cents.

One way to judge a company's commitment to frugality is by visiting the headquarters. "The fact that a company you put your money in has a big building doesn't mean that the people in it are smart, but it does mean that you've helped pay for the building," says investment adviser William Donoghue. In my experience, he's right. At Golden West Financial in California, a champion of productive penny-pinching and the lowest-cost operator in the S&L business, the role of the receptionist was taken over by an old-fashioned black telephone and a sign that said, "Pick up." Southwest Airlines operated for 18 years out of a home office at Love Field in Dallas that resembled a barracks. The nicest thing you could say about it was that it was "antiquated." In 1990, the company splurged and built a new three-story high rise. A decorator was hired to beautify the interior, but he made the mistake of trying to replace the employee award plaques and photographs of company picnics with expensive art. When CEO Herb Kelleher got wind of this, he fired the decorator and spent the weekend rehanging the plaques and the photographs.

Kelleher set the tone for Southwest's wacky esprit. His office was decorated with turkeys. The annual get-together was a chili cookout. Pay raises for the higher-ups were limited to the same percentage increase the work force got. One day a month, all the big shots from Kelleher on down served as counter agents or baggage handlers.

Southwest's stewardesses were outfitted in blue jeans, T-shirts, and sneakers. Meals were limited to peanuts and cocktails. Prizes were awarded to the passengers with the biggest holes in their socks, and the safety information was delivered as a rap song.

While other airlines were flying their widebodies over the same routes to Los Angeles, New York, and Europe, Southwest found a niche: the short hop. It called itself "the only high-frequency, short-distance, low-fare airline." As the others killed themselves off, Southwest grew from a four-plane operation in 1978 to the eighth-largest carrier in the country. It was the only U.S. airline to have made money every year since 1973. For return on capital, Southwest has yet to be outdone.

As its competitors falter, Southwest is fully prepared to take advantage, which is what usually happens to a great company in a lousy industry. It recently expanded into routes abandoned by USAir and America West, both of which were forced to cut back on service because of financial problems.

Shareholders who saw their Southwest holdings increase 10-fold from 1980 to 1985 had their patience tested from 1985 to 1990, when the stock price went sideways. It could have been worse—they could have been invested in Pan Am or Eastern. After 1990, patience was rewarded, as Southwest doubled again.

BANDAG

What could be less exciting than a company that makes retread tires in Muscatine, Iowa? I've never been to Muscatine, but I've looked it up on a map. It's a small node on the Mississippi River southwest of Davenport and southeast of Moscow, Atalissa, and West Liberty.

Whatever is up to date in Kansas City probably hasn't gotten to Muscatine, which may be to Muscatine's advantage. Wall Street hasn't spent much time in Muscatine either. Only three analysts have followed Bandag on its rise from $2 to $60 in 15 years.

Bandag's CEO, Martin Carver, returns the favor by staying away from New York. He holds the world speed record for a diesel truck. You won't see him sipping champagne in the courtyard at the Trump Plaza Hotel, but on the other hand, Carver is solvent.

This is the Southwest Airlines of retreads: earthy management (in the 1988 annual report, Carver thanked his family), devoted penny-pinching, and an unusual niche in what otherwise is a cutthroat business. Every year in the U.S., 12 million worn-out truck and bus tires are replaced with retreads. About five million of these replacements are Bandag's.

Bandag has increased its dividend every year since 1975. Its earnings have grown at a 17 percent clip since 1977. Its balance sheet is a bit weak, primarily because Bandag has invested in overseas expansion (it now has 10 percent of the foreign retread market) and has bought back 2.5 million of its own shares.

While the earnings continued to grow, Bandag's stock price dropped sharply in the Great Correction and again in the Saddam

Sell-off. This overreaction on Wall Street's part was a perfect opportunity to buy more shares. Both times, the stock recovered all its lost ground and then some.

COOPER TIRE

Cooper Tire is another version of Bandag. It has found its own niche in the replacement tire market. As the industry giants carry on a money-losing battle to equip new cars with new tires, Cooper stays out of their way and equips old cars with new tires. It's a low-cost producer, which is why independent tire dealers like to buy from Cooper.

In the late 1980s, when the big three (Michelin, Goodyear, and Bridgestone) were ruining one another's business, Cooper was making money. Its earnings increased every year from 1985 and hit another record in 1991. The stock price tripled from the 1987 low to $10 a share before the Saddam Sell-off, when it lost much of those gains and fell to $6. Investors ignored the fundamentals to focus on the sad future for tires after the world came to an end. When that didn't happen, the stock rose fivefold to $30.

GREEN TREE FINANCIAL

This company belongs in the Enchanted Forest Portfolio along with Cedar Fair, Oak Industries, EQK Green Acres, Maple Leaf Foods, and Pinelands, Inc. Green Tree has tremendous debt and a CEO who is higher paid, even, than some second basemen, so it doesn't qualify as one of our great companies in a lousy industry. I include it here to show that even an OK company in a lousy industry can do well.

The lousy industry I'm talking about is mortgage loans for mobile homes. Green Tree specializes in such loans, and the business has been getting lousier. Every year since 1985, mobile-home sales have declined. In 1990, buyers were so scarce that only 200,000 new units were sold.

To make matters worse, record numbers of mobile-home owners were defaulting on their loans and abandoning their property, leaving notes for the lenders: our trailer is your trailer. There's not a lot of resale value in a 10-year-old double-wide.

The industry's disaster was a boon for Green Tree, because its major competitors gave up. Valley Federal, a hapless California S&L, made $1 billion in mobile-home loans, lost money, and fled the business. So did Financial Services Corporation, a subsidiary of an insurance company in Michigan. So did Citicorp, the biggest mobile-home lender of all. Green Tree was left to take advantage of all the action—if and when the action resumed.

There were enough doubters that it ever would resume that the stock fell to a low of $8 at the end of 1990. *Forbes* magazine had published a negative article in May of that year. The headline itself, "Are the Tree's Roots Withering?," was enough to make you want to sell your Green Tree shares. The reporter did a thorough job of recounting every woe: the slump in mobile-home buying, the loan troubles, a nasty lawsuit overhanging Green Tree's assets. "Even at just seven times earnings, Green Tree doesn't look like much of a bargain," *Forbes* concluded.

Investors shrugged off this bad review and the stock rose to $36 in nine months. How could something so terrible have turned out so well? With no competitors, Green Tree had the mobile-home loan business to itself. This resulted in a sharp increase in loan volume. The company had also begun to package its loans and sell them in the secondary market, the way Fannie Mae does with mortgages on houses. It was also making lucrative home improvement loans and used-mobile-home loans, and was moving into the motorcycle financing market.

If you had bought Green Tree as soon as you read the *Forbes* article, you would have tripled your money in less than nine months. I'm not out to chide a good magazine—I've missed plenty of Green Trees in my career. The point is that a survivor in a lousy industry can reverse its fortunes very quickly once the competitors have disappeared. (This company recently changed its name from Green Tree Acceptance.)

DILLARD

Here's another folksy bunch of managers with a tight grip on corporate purse strings. The Dillard family (principally 77-year-old William and his son William II) own 8 percent of this department-store company and almost all of the voting stock. They run it out of Little Rock.

With Scroogian intensity, they search the books looking for new ways to cut costs, but not at the expense of employees. Dillard employees are relatively well paid. One place where Dillard does scrimp is on debt. There's little of that on the balance sheet.

The Dillards caught on to computers very early, not only to keep track of the money, but also to manage the merchandise. If a shirt is selling well in any Dillard store in the country, the store's computer notices it and automatically sends a reorder message to the warehouse computer. The warehouse computer then passes the order along to the vendor. Store managers and front-office types always know what is selling where, and the company doesn't have to support an army of wandering experts to tell it what to buy.

Dillard has stayed away from the glamour markets where the larger retail chains stumble over one another. Dillard stores are found in small towns and cities like Wichita and Memphis. As the glamour chains (Federated, Allied, Macy) restructure or go bankrupt, Dillard expands by buying some of their discarded divisions and hooking them up to the Dillard computers. Among others, it bought Joske's out of Allied and J.B. Ivey out of B.A.T. Industries.

A $10,000 investment in Dillard stock in 1980 has turned into $600,000 today.

CROWN CORK & SEAL

Crown Cork & Seal reminds me of New England Wire & Cable, the company Danny DeVito tried to acquire in *Other People's Money*. The executive suite at New England Wire was a messy room over the factory, decorated with muffler-shop calendars. The executive suite at Crown Cork & Seal amounts to an open loft above the assembly lines. New England Wire made wire, Crown Cork & Seal makes soda cans, beer cans, paint cans, pet food containers, jugs for antifreeze, bottle caps, bottle washers, bottle rinsers, bottle crowners, and can warmers.

In both cases, the CEO was a businessman with old-fashioned ideas. The difference is that New England Wire & Cable was about to go bankrupt, whereas Crown Cork & Seal is the world's most successful can maker.

I probably don't need to tell you that can making is a lousy industry with a thin profit margin, or that Crown Cork & Seal is a low-cost producer. Its ratio of expenses to sales is 2.5 percent, which is more than a couple of notches below the industry average of 15 percent.

This piddling level of expenditure, bordering on the monastic, was inspired by John Connelly, the CEO, who recently died. Connelly's hostility to extravagance brings us to Peter's Principle #17:

All else being equal, invest in the company with the fewest color photographs in the annual report.

Connelly's annual report had zero photographs. Where he didn't mind spending money was on the new can-making technologies that enabled CC&S to maintain its status as the lowest-cost producer.

Profits that weren't reinvested in improving the can-making operation were used to buy back shares. This boosted the earnings for the remaining shares, which boosted the share price for the lucky shareholders who hadn't sold. You'd almost have thought that Mr. Connelly was working for the shareholders, which at many companies is an eccentric thing to do.

Since Mr. Connelly's death, the company has changed tactics. It now uses its sizable cash flow to buy out its rivals and grow via that familiar method. Capital spending has increased and so has the debt level, but to date the new tactic has been as profitable as the old one. The price of Crown Cork & Seal moved up from $54 to $92 in 1991.

NUCOR

Nobody wants to be in the steel business these days, with all the competition from the Japanese and the billions invested in equipment that may soon be outmoded. The big-name producers, U.S. Steel (alias USX) and Bethlehem Steel, once symbols of American prowess, have tested their shareholders' patience for 12 years. Bethlehem fell to $5 a share in 1986 and has come a long way back from there, but at the current price of $13 it still has a long way to go to return to its high of $32 in 1981. USX has also yet to return to its 1981 high.

Meanwhile, if you'd invested in Nucor in 1981, your $6 stock would be worth $75 today, and you'd think the steel business is a great business after all. Or if you'd gotten into Nucor for $1 a share in 1971, you'd now be convinced that steel is one of the greatest businesses of all time. You wouldn't think so if you'd bought Bethlehem for $24 a share in 1971, because now you'd have $13, the sort of result that gives investing in Treasury bills a good name.

Here again we have a penurious maverick with a vision, F. Kenneth Iverson, who's not above taking fancy corporate clients to lunch at Phil's Deli across from corporate headquarters in Charlotte, North Carolina. There is no executive dining room at Nucor, there are no limos in the parking lot, there is no corporate jet at the airport, and there are no special privileges for wearing a suit—when profits decline, the people in the suits and the people in the overalls both take home less pay. When profits increase (as they usually do), everybody gets a bonus.

Nucor's 5,500 employees don't belong to a union, but they fare better than their colleagues at other steel plants who do. They share in the profits and they can't be laid off. Their children get college scholarships. If the economy slows down and production is cut, the entire work force puts in a shorter week, so the suffering of the layoff is shared.

Nucor has had two niches in its history. In the 1970s it specialized in turning scrap metal into construction-grade steel. Lately, as other companies have caught on to this process, Nucor has kept a step ahead of them by learning to produce a high-grade, flat-rolled steel. These flat-rolled sheets can be used for auto bodies and appliances. With this new "thin-slab casting" technique, Nucor can now compete directly with the Bethlehems and the USXs.

SHAW INDUSTRIES

A search of a magazine data base for articles about this company produced two listings. There was a paragraph in *Textile World* and a sentence in an obscure technology journal called *Datamation*. I also found two feature articles in *The Wall Street Journal* and one from the PR Newswire. Apparently, very little has been written about this $1 billion enterprise, soon to be a $2 billion enterprise, that has captured 20 percent of the carpet business in the U.S.

In keeping with our Great Opportunities in Out-of-the-Way Places theme, Shaw's headquarters are in Dalton, Georgia, located on a southern hump of the Blue Ridge Mountains and at least two hours from a major airport. Historically, Dalton is famous for moonshine, clog dancing, and the fact that in 1895 a young girl from the area figured out a way to make tufted bedspreads. This new tufted bedspread technology led to a boom in bedspreads, which led to a boom in carpets—but Shaw wasn't around back then.

Shaw didn't get started until 1961. The founder, Robert Shaw, now 58, is still the president and CEO and his brother, J.C., is still the chairman. In the sketchy news accounts, Robert Shaw is described as a person of few words, most of them serious. Behind the president's desk hangs a banner with this catchy motto: "Maintain sufficient market share to allow full utilization of our production facilities."

One time he made people laugh was when he announced that Shaw Industries would become a billion-dollar company. The guffaws could be heard all the way to the offices of West Point–Pepperell, a giant in the industry that sold twice as many carpets as Shaw. They stopped the day Shaw bought out West Point–Pepperell's carpet operations.

There hasn't been a worse business in contemporary America. In the 1960s, when the Shaw brothers got into it, so did everybody else who had $10,000 to invest in a carpet factory. The area around Dalton was stippled with small mills, as 350 new carpet makers revved up their looms to meet the nation's demand for a carpet on every floor. Demand was great, but supply was greater, and soon enough the carpet makers responded by cutting prices. This ensured that neither they nor their rivals would make money.

Then in 1982, homeowners rediscovered the wood floor and the carpet boom came to an end. Half the top 25 manufacturers were out of business by mid-decade. Carpet has been a nongrowth industry ever since, and Shaw has thrived as the low-cost producer. With every competitor that fails, it picks up more business.

Shaw pumps every available dollar into improving operations and cutting costs even further. Tired of paying a high price for yarn, it acquired a yarn-making facility and eliminated the middleman. It has its own distribution network with its own fleet of trucks. In its never-ending quest for economy, Shaw opted not to maintain an expensive trade showroom in Atlanta. It sends a bus to Atlanta and transports its customers to Dalton.

During the worst of times for carpets, Shaw has managed to keep up its 20 percent annual growth rate. The stock price has followed along dutifully, up 50-fold since 1980. It lagged a bit in 1990–91 and doubled again in 1992. Who would have believed we'd see a 50-bagger in carpets?

In May 1992, Shaw purchased Salem Carpet Mills, further strengthening its grip on the industry. Shaw now predicts that by the end of this century three or four huge companies will dominate carpet making worldwide. Competitors worry that a single huge company will dominate carpet making, and they already know which one.

Stock Symbol	Company	1/13/92 Price
SNTV	Sun Television & Appliances	$18.50

TWELVE

IT'S A WONDERFUL BUY

Savings and loans are the latest untouchables among equities. Mention the term and people grab for their wallets. They think about the $500 billion S&L bailout bill we all have to pay, the 675 bankrupt institutions closed since 1989, the lavish spending by their officers and directors, the 10,000 bank fraud cases pending with the FBI. The word "thrift" once reminded us of Jimmy Stewart in *It's a Wonderful Life*. Now it's Charles Keating in handcuffs.

Since 1988, it's been impossible to pick up a newspaper and not read some story about an S&L bankruptcy or a civil lawsuit or a prosecution or Congress's struggle with the bailout bill. At least five books have been written on the sorry subject, and not one has been called *How to Make a Fortune on S&L Stocks*.

Yet for the scores of S&Ls that have stayed out of trouble or survived it, it still is a wonderful life. Based on equity-to-assets ratio, the most fundamental measure of financial strength, more than 100 S&Ls are stronger today than the nation's strongest bank, J. P. Morgan. People's Savings Financial of New Britain, Connecticut, to name just one, has an equity-to-assets ratio of 12.5, while J. P. Morgan's is 5.17.

Other factors combine to make J. P. Morgan the preeminent bank that it is, so the comparison with People's Savings Financial is somewhat fanciful. The essential point is that many S&Ls are in terrific financial shape, which is the opposite of what we've been hearing.

There are also plenty of S&Ls in lousy financial shape, which is why it's important to make distinctions. I've identified three basic types: the bad guys that perpetrated the fraud, the greedy guys that ruined a good thing, and the Jimmy Stewarts. Let's take these one at a time:

1. THE BAD GUYS

The tried-and-true scheme, which was quickly duplicated by connivers across the nation, worked as follows. A bunch of people got together, let's say 10 for simplicity's sake, and put up, let's say, $100,000 apiece to buy the In God We Trust S&L on Main Street. With their $1 million in equity, they could take in $19 million in deposits and make approximately $20 million worth of new loans.

To acquire the $19 million, they offered an exceptionally high rate of interest to attract certificates of deposit, and hired brokers such as Merrill Lynch and Shearson to raise the cash. A few years back, you probably saw the ads in the papers: "In God We Trust offers a 13 percent jumbo CD, guaranteed by the FSLIC." With the government standing behind it, In God We Trust had no trouble selling CDs as fast as it could print them. The brokers were delighted with the rich commissions.

Soon enough, the owners and directors of In God We Trust were lending the $20 million proceeds from the CDs to friends, relatives, and associates for a variety of construction projects of dubious merit. This created a building boom in a lot of places that didn't need buildings. Meanwhile, the S&L looked very profitable on paper because of the enormous up-front fees it skimmed off the top of these loans.

These "profits" were added to the S&L's equity, and for every dollar the equity was increased, the owners and directors could make another $20 worth of loans. The system fed on itself, which is how small-town S&Ls such as Vernon in Texas got to be billion-dollar operations. As the loans grew, the equity grew, until soon there was enough money to pay kickbacks to accountants and auditors and tributes to representatives and senators on the powerful banking committees, with enough left over for Lear Jets and parties with hookers and imported elephants.

With some notable exceptions, such as Charles Keating's, the vast majority of the fraudulent S&Ls were privately owned. The owners and directors involved in the dirty tricks couldn't have tolerated the scrutiny of a publicly held company.

2. THE GREEDY GUYS

You didn't have to be a crook or a con man to sink an S&L. All you had to be was greedy. The trouble begins when the directors of First Backwater Savings look around and see their competitors at In God We Trust and elsewhere getting rich on fees from the big commercial loans they've advanced to their cronies. As other institutions make millions overnight and brag about it at cocktail parties, First Backwater plods along, making old-fashioned residential mortgage loans.

These First Backwater directors hire a Wall Street expert, Mr. Suspenders, to advise them on how to maximize profits. Mr. Suspenders always has the same idea: borrow as much money as the rules allow, directly from the Federal Home Loan Bank, and put it into a few of those wonderful commercial deals that the other S&Ls are making.

So First Backwater borrows money from the Federal Home Loan Bank, and also sells CDs, and its ads appear in the papers alongside the ones from In God We Trust. It takes the cash and gives it to developers who want to build office parks, condos, and shopping centers. First Backwater may even become a partner in some of these projects, to make more profits. Then the recession hits and the would-be tenants for the office parks and condos and shopping centers disappear, and the developers default on the loans. The net worth of First Backwater, which had been built up for 50 years, evaporates in less than 5.

Essentially, this is the In God We Trust story all over again, except the directors at First Backwater didn't lend the money to their friends, and didn't take kickbacks under the table.

3. THE JIMMY STEWARTS

The Jimmy Stewart S&Ls are my favorites. They've quietly been making a profit all along. These are the no-frills, low-cost operators who take in deposits from the neighborhood and are content to make old-fashioned residential mortgage loans. They can be found in small cities and towns across America and in certain urban areas the commercial banks have overlooked. Many have big branches with enormous deposit bases, which are much more profitable than having a lot of tiny branches.

By sticking to its simple function, a Jimmy Stewart S&L can avoid hiring the high-priced loan analysts and other expensive mucka-mucks employed by big banks. Likewise, it can avoid spending money on a Greek temple for the main office, Queen Anne furniture for the lobby, blimps, billboards, celebrity sponsors, and original artwork for the walls. Travel posters will suffice.

A money-center bank such as Citicorp routinely spends the equivalent of 2½ to 3 percentage points of its entire loan portfolio just to cover its overhead and related expenses. Therefore, it must make a "spread" of at least 2½ percent between what it pays for deposits and what it receives from its loans in order to break even.

A Jimmy Stewart S&L can survive on a much narrower spread. Its break-even point is 1½ percent. Theoretically, it could make a profit without making any mortgage loans at all. If it pays 4 percent in interest to passbook savers, it could invest the proceeds in 6 percent Treasury bonds and still earn money. When it writes 8 or 9 percent mortgages, it becomes highly profitable for the shareholders.

For years, the inspiration for all the Jimmy Stewart S&Ls has been Golden West, based in Oakland, California. Golden West owns and operates three S&L subsidiaries, all of them run by a delightful couple, Herb and Marion Sandler. They have the equanimity of Ozzie and Harriet and the smarts of Warren Buffett, which is the perfect combination to run a successful business. Like Ozzie and Harriet, they've managed to avoid a lot of unnecessary excitement. They avoided the excitement of investing in junk bonds that defaulted and commercial real-estate ventures that defaulted, both of which enabled them to avoid the excitement of getting taken over by the Resolution Trust Corporation.

The Sandlers have always been reluctant to waste money on foolishness. Their distrust for the newfangled caused them never to install automated teller machines. They never lured depositors with toaster ovens or ice buckets. They missed the great boom in misguided construction loans. They stuck to residential mortgages, which still make up 96 percent of Golden West's portfolio.

When it comes to economizing in the front office, the Sandlers are champions. I visited their headquarters, not in San Francisco where most of the fancier banks are located, but in a lower-rent district in Oakland. Visitors to the corporate suite announced themselves by picking up a black telephone in the reception area.

The Sandlers don't mind spending money in the branches, where the goal is to make customers as happy and as comfortable as possible. Teams of covert "shoppers," as the Sandlers call them, are sent out periodically to investigate the service.

In a famous incident in the mid-1980s, Marion Sandler was addressing her peers at an S&L conference in West Virginia on one of her favorite topics, "productivity and expense control." The subject was so captivating to the other S&L directors in the audience that a third of them walked out. They'd packed the house to hear about exciting new computer systems and counting machines, but not to hear Ms. Sandler talk about cutting costs. Perhaps if they'd stayed for her lecture and taken good notes, more of them would still be in business today.

Prior to the 1980s, Golden West was one of the few S&Ls that was a public company. Then in a rash of stock offerings in mid-decade, hundreds of the formerly private thrifts, operating as "mutual savings banks," went public more or less simultaneously. I acquired many of these for the Magellan Fund. I was so selective in my purchases during this period that anything that had the word "first" or "trust" in it, I bought. Once, I confessed to the *Barron's* panel that I'd invested in 135 of the 145 thrifts whose prospectuses had landed on my desk. The response from Abelson was typical: "What happened to the others?"

There are two explanations for my indiscriminate and sometimes fatal attraction for S&Ls. The first is that my fund was so big and they were so small that to get enough nourishment out of them I had to consume large quantities, like the whales who are forced to survive on plankton. The second is the unique way that S&Ls came public, which made them an automatic bargain from the start. (To learn how you, too, can get something for nothing, turn to page 215.)

The experts at SNL Securities in Charlottesville, Virginia, who keep tabs on all the thrifts in existence, recently provided me with an update on what happened to the 464 S&Ls that came public after 1982. Ninety-nine of these were subsequently taken over by bigger banks and S&Ls, usually at a large profit to the shareholders. (The watershed example is the Morris County [New Jersey] Savings Bank. The initial offering price in 1983 was $10.75 a share, and Morris was bought out three years later for $65.) Sixty-five of the publicly traded S&Ls have failed, usually at a total loss to the shareholders. (I know this from personal experience because I owned several in this category.) That leaves 300 still in business.

HOW TO RATE AN S&L

Whenever I get the urge to invest in an S&L, I always think of Golden West, but after it doubled in price in 1991 I decided to search for better prospects. As I went down the S&L list in preparation for *Barron's* 1992, I found several. You couldn't have invented a better atmosphere for creating bargains.

The S&L-fraud story had drifted off the front pages, only to be replaced by the collapse-of-the-housing-market story. This had been a popular scare for two years running: the housing market was going to crash and take the banking system down with it. People remembered that when the housing market collapsed in Texas in the early 1980s, several banks and S&Ls collapsed in sympathy, and they expected that the same fate would befall S&Ls in the Northeast and California, where fat-cat houses were already suffering a correction.

The latest quiet facts put out by the National Association of Home Builders, that the median price of a home had increased in 1990 and again in 1991, convinced me that the collapse of the housing market was largely a figment of the fat-cat imagination. I knew that the best of the Jimmy Stewart S&Ls had a limited involvement in expensive houses, commercial real estate, or construction loans. For the most part, their portfolios were concentrated in $100,000 residential mortgages. They had good earnings growth, a solid base of loyal depositors, and more equity than J. P. Morgan.

Yet the virtues of the Jimmy Stewart S&Ls were lost in the funk. Wall Street was down on these stocks, and so was the average investor. Fidelity's own Select S&L Fund had dwindled in size from $66 million in February 1987 to a low of only $3 million in October 1990. Brokerage houses had reduced their coverage of the thrift industry, and some had stopped covering it at all.

There used to be two full-time analysts at Fidelity assigned to

S&Ls: Dave Ellison for the larger thrifts and Alec Murray for the smaller ones. Murray left for Dartmouth graduate school and wasn't replaced. Ellison was given other large companies to follow, including Fannie Mae, General Electric, and Westinghouse, so for him the S&Ls had become a part-time job.

There are nearly 50 analysts in the country who track Wal-Mart and another 46 analysts who track Philip Morris, but only a few devote themselves to keeping up with the publicly traded S&Ls. This leads to Peter's Principle #18:

When even the analysts are bored, it's time to start buying.

Intrigued by the cheap prices at which many S&L stocks were selling, I immersed myself in a copy of *The Thrift Digest*—my idea of the perfect bedside thriller. It's published by SNL Securities, a company I mentioned above, and it's edited by Reid Nagle, who does an outstanding job. *The Thrift Digest* is as thick as the Boston metropolitan telephone directory, and it costs $700 a year to get the monthly updates. I mention the price so you won't run out and order the thing, only to discover you could have bought two round-trip tickets to Hawaii instead.

If you decide to pursue the subject of undervalued S&Ls—which to me is much more exciting than any trip to Hawaii—you'd be well advised to seek out the latest copy of *The Thrift Digest* at the local library or to borrow one from your broker. I borrowed mine from Fidelity.

I spent so much time with my nose in this book before dinner, during dinner, and after dinner that Carolyn began to refer to it as the Old Testament. The Old Testament in hand, I devised my own S&L scorecard, listing 145 of the strongest institutions by state and jotting down the following key details. This, in a nutshell, is everything you need to know about an S&L:

Current Price

Self-explanatory.

Initial Offering Price

When an S&L is selling below the price at which it came public, it's a sign that the stock may be undervalued. Other factors, of course, must be considered.

Equity-to-Assets Ratio

The most important number of all. Measures financial strength and "survivability." The higher the E/A, the better. E/As have an incredible range, from as low as 1 or 2 (candidates for the scrap heap) to as high as 20 (four times stronger than J. P. Morgan). An E/A of 5.5 to 6 is average, but below 5, you're in the danger zone of ailing thrifts.

Before I invest in any S&L, I like to see that its E/A ratio is at least 7.5. This is not only for disaster protection, but also because an S&L with a high E/A ratio makes an attractive takeover candidate. This excess equity gives it excess lending capacity that a larger bank or S&L might want to put to use.

Dividend

Many S&Ls pay better-than-average dividends. When one of them meets all the other criteria and also has a high yield, it's a plus.

Book Value

Most of the assets of a bank or an S&L are in its loans. Once you assure yourself that an S&L has avoided high-risk lending (see below), you can begin to have confidence that its book value, as reported in the financial statements, is an accurate reflection of the institution's real worth. A lot of the most profitable Jimmy Stewarts are selling at well below book value today.

Price-Earnings Ratio

As with any stock, the lower this number, the better. Some S&Ls with annual growth rates of 15 percent a year have p/e ratios of 7 or 8, based on the prior 12 months' earnings. This is very promising, especially in light of the fact that the overall p/e of the S&P 500 was 23 when I did this research.

High-Risk Real-Estate Assets

These are the common problem areas, especially commercial loans and construction loans, that have been the ruination of so many S&Ls. When high-risk assets exceed 5–10 percent, I begin to get nervous. All else being equal, I prefer to invest in an S&L that has a small percentage of its assets in the high-risk category. Since it's impossible for the casual investor to analyze a commercial lending portfolio from afar, the safest course is to avoid investing in S&Ls that make such loans.

Even without *The Thrift Digest,* it's possible to do your own calulation of high-risk assets. Check the annual report for the dollar value of all construction and commercial real estate lending, listed under "Assets." Then find the dollar value of all outstanding loans. Divide the latter into the former, and you'll arrive at a good approximation of the high-risk percentage.

90-Day Nonperforming Assets

These are the loans that have already defaulted. What you want to see here is a very low number, preferably less than 2 percent of the S&L's total assets. Also, you'd like this number to be falling and not rising. An extra couple of percentage points' worth of bad loans can wipe out an S&L's entire equity.

Real Estate Owned

This is property on which the S&L has already foreclosed. The REO category, as it's called, is an index of yesterday's problems, because whatever shows up here has been written off as a loss on the books.

Since this financial "hit" has already been taken, a high percentage of real estate owned isn't as worrisome as a high percentage of nonperforming assets. But it's worrisome when REO is on the rise. S&Ls aren't in the real-estate business, and the last thing they want is to repossess more condos or office parks that are expensive to maintain and hard to sell. In fact, where there's a lot of REO, you have to assume that the S&L is having trouble getting rid of it.

• • •

I ended up choosing seven S&Ls to recommend in *Barron's,* which tells you how much I liked the group. Five of these were strong Jimmy Stewart-type thrifts, and two were long shots—I call these the born-agains—which have come back from the edge of Chapter 11. Two of the five strong thrifts, Germantown Savings and Glacier Bancorp, were repeat recommendations from 1991.

The five Jimmy Stewarts got excellent marks in several categories: book value (four sold at a discount), equity-to-assets ratio (all 6.0 or better), high-risk loans (under 10 percent), 90-day delinquencies (2 percent or less), real estate owned (less than 1 percent), and p/e ratio (below 11). That two of them had been buying back their own shares in recent months was another positive. For Glacier and Germantown, the percentage of commercial lending was a bit high, but this was less bothersome after I heard the bankers' explanations.

With the two born-agains, many of the numbers are quite dismal—everything a conservative investor should try to avoid. I picked them as long shots because they still maintained high equity-to-assets ratios in spite of their problems. Having this equity cushion gave them a little leeway to work out of their troubles. The region in which these two S&Ls do business, near the Massachusetts–New Hampshire border, was beginning to show signs of stability.

I couldn't guarantee that these born-agains would survive, but their stock prices had fallen so low (in the case of Lawrence Savings, from $13 to 75 cents) that I knew the bottom fishers would make a lot of money if they did.

Dozens of S&Ls around the country are as strong as or stronger than my top five. You might find one or more of them in your own neighborhood. A lot of investors are going to be very pleased that they've concentrated on this group. The Jimmy Stewarts will either continue to prosper on their own or be taken over by larger institutions at prices far above the current levels.

An S&L with excess equity, excess lending capacity, and a loyal depositor base is a prize that commercial banks covet. Commercial banks can take in deposits only in their home states (this rule is changing, to some degree), but they can lend money anywhere. This is what makes taking over an S&L a very tempting proposition.

If I were the Bank of Boston, for instance, I'd be sending love notes to Home Port Bancorp of Nantucket, Massachusetts. Home

Port has a 20 percent equity-to-assets ratio, making it perhaps the strongest financial institution in the modern world. It also has a captive island market with crusty New England depositors, who aren't about to change their banking habits and run off to a new-fangled money-market fund.

Maybe the Bank of Boston doesn't want to make loans on Nantucket, but once it acquires Home Port's equity and its deposit base, it can use the excess lending capacity to make loans in Boston, or anywhere else around the country.

During 1987–90, a terrible period for S&Ls, more tha 100 were acquired by larger institutions that saw the same sort of potential the Bank of Boston ought to see in Home Port. Banks and thrifts will continue to consolidate at a rapid rate, and with good reason. Currently, the U.S. has more than 7,000 banks, thrifts, and other assorted deposit takers—which is about 6,500 too many.

There are 6 different deposit takers in my little town of Marblehead, half the number there are in all of England.

Table 12-1.

Name	Price Third Quarter 1991	Initial Public Offering Price	Equity/ Assets	Dividend	Book Value	90-Day Nonper- forming Assets	Real Estate Owned	Commercial Real Estate and Other Commercial Loans
				Strong Thrifts				
Germantown	$14+	$ 9+	7.5	40¢	$26 ⅛	0.5%	0.0%	7.0%
Glacier	$12	$ 8+	11.0	40¢	$11 ½	0.9%	0.2%	9.2%
People's	$11	$10+	13.0	68¢	$18 ⅝	2.0%	0.9%	2.7%
Eagle	$12	$11+	9.7	60¢	$19 ⅛	1.8%	0.7%	2.9%
Sovereign	$ 9+	$ 4+	6.0	16¢	$10 ¼	0.9%	0.4%	3.9%
				Born-Agains				
First Essex	$ 2	$ 8	9.0	—	$ 7 ⅞	10.0%	3.5%	13.0%
Lawrence	75¢	$13+	7.8	—	$ 6 ½	9.6%	7.5%	21.0%

Source: SNL Quarterly Thrift Digest

THIRTEEN

A CLOSER LOOK AT THE S&Ls

The casual stockpicker could stop here, pick five S&Ls that fit the Jimmy Stewart profile, invest an equal amount in each of them, and await the favorable returns. One S&L would do better than expected, three OK, and one worse, and the overall result would be superior to having invested in an overpriced Coca-Cola or a Merck.

But being an inquisitive sort, and not wishing to rely entirely on secondhand information, I usually try to improve my odds by calling companies before spending money on them. This increases the phone bill, but in the long run it pays off.

Usually I get to talk to the president or the CEO or some other top official. Either I'm trying to find out something specific or I'm fishing around for surprises that haven't yet come to the attention of Wall Street analysts. Glacier Bancorp, for instance, had done more commercial lending than I like to see from a strong thrift. I wouldn't have bought the stock, or recommended it, without exploring this matter with the company.

You don't have to be an expert to talk to an S&L, but you do have to have a basic idea of how the business works. An S&L needs loyal depositors to keep money in their savings and checking accounts. It needs to make money on that money by lending it out—but not to borrowers who default. And it needs low operating expenses in order to maximize its profits. Bankers like to live on threes and sixes: borrow money at 3, lend money at 6, play golf at 3.

Anyway, I made six phone calls to six S&Ls (four strong ones and the two born-agains) to gather relevant details. Eagle Financial I didn't bother to call. Because Eagle was on a September–September fiscal year, the annual report arrived on my desk in time for me to see the details in print. It read like a bank examiner's dream. The annuals for the other S&Ls wouldn't arrive until February or March. Here's what I discovered from my conversations:

GLACIER BANCORP

I talked to Glacier the day after Christmas. I'd come into my office in Boston wearing plaid pants and a sweatshirt. The building was empty except for me and the security guard.

Holidays are an excellent time to do this sort of work. I'm always impressed when I find executives who are sitting at their desks on December 26.

Above the debris on mine, I'd opened my Glacier Bancorp file. The stock was selling for $12 a share, a 60 percent gain over the year before. This was a 12–15 percent grower selling at 10 times earnings—not a spectacular bargain, but there wasn't much risk in it either.

Glacier Bancorp used to be called the First Federal Savings and Loan of Kalispell, and I wish they'd kept the old name. It sounded antiquated and parochial, which to me is always reassuring. I'd rather have antiquated and parochial than trendy and sophisticated, which usually means a company is desperate to improve its image.

I like companies that stick to business and let the images take care of themselves. There is this unfortunate tendency among financial institutions to take the "bank" out of their names and replace it with "bancorp." I know what a bank is, but "bancorp" makes me nervous.

Anyway, whoever answered the phone at Glacier Bancorp in Kalispell told me they were having a retirement party for one of the officers, but they'd inform chairman Charles Mercord that I called. They must have dragged him out of the party, because a few minutes later Mercord called me back.

Asking a president or a CEO about a company's earnings is a ticklish proposition. You're not going to get anywhere by blurting out, "What are you going to earn next year?" First you have to establish rapport. We chatted about the mountains. I said that the entire Lynch family had been to all the Western states to see the national parks, and that we loved Montana. We chatted about the timber industry, the spotted owl, the Big Mountain ski area, and the big copper smelter owned by Anaconda, a company I often visited as an analyst.

Then I began to slip in more serious investment-type questions, such as "What's the population out there?" and "what's the elevation of the town?," leading up to the more substantive "Are you adding any new branches or standing pat with what you've got?" I was trying to get a sense of the mood at Glacier.

"Anything unusual in the third quarter?" I continued. "You made thirty-eight cents, I see." It's best to pepper these inquiries with bits of information, so that your source thinks you've done your homework.

The mood at Glacier Bancorp was upbeat. Nonperforming loans were almost nonexistent. In all of 1991, this bancorp had had to write off only $16,000 in bad loans. It had raised its dividend for the 15th year in a row. It had just bought out two other thrifts with wonderful names: the First National Banks of Whitefish and Eureka, respectively.

This is how many of the stronger S&Ls are going to speed up their growth in the next few years. They are acquiring the valuable deposits of troubled and defunct S&Ls. Glacier can fold the First National of Whitefish into its own system and make more loans with the additional Whitefish deposits. It can also do some administrative cost-cutting, since two S&Ls together can live more cheaply than one.

"You're building up a nice asset here," I said, introducing the Whitefish subject. "I'm sure it's a good move, accountingwise." My only worry was that Glacier may have overpaid for its acquisition, a topic I approached obliquely. "I assume you had to pay way over book value for this," I said, inviting Glacier's president to admit the worst. But no, Glacier hadn't overpaid.

We talked about Glacier's 9.2 percent of commercial loans, the sole troubling statistic I'd gleaned from *The Thrift Digest.* If this had been a New England thrift, that high number would have scared me away, but Montana wasn't Massachusetts. The Glacier president assured me that his S&L wasn't loaning money to developers of empty office towers or unsalable vacation condos. Glacier's commercial loans were mostly in multifamily housing, which was in great demand. Montana's population was growing. Every year, thousands of escapees from California smog and taxes were taking up residence in the Big Sky, small government state.

I never hang up on a source without asking: what other companies do you most admire? It doesn't mean much when the CEO of Bethlehem Steel tells me he admires Microsoft, but when the head of one S&L says he admires another S&L, it usually means that other S&L is doing something right. I've found many good stocks this way. So when Mercord mentioned United Savings and Security Federal, I cradled the phone in my neck and opened my handy S&P stock guide to get the symbols, UBMT and SFBM, and punched them up on the Quotron as he was describing them. Both were Montana thrifts with impressive equity-to-assets ratios (20 percent at Security Federal!). I put them on my "tune in later" list.

GERMANTOWN SAVINGS

I called Germantown in January, the day before I flew to New York to meet with the Roundtable. This was another of my recommendations from the prior year. The stock was $10 then, $14 now. Germantown was earning $2 a share, giving it a p/e of less than 7. It had a book value of $26, equity-to-assets ratio of 7.5, and less than 1 percent nonperforming loans.

Germantown was located in the suburbs of Philadelphia. It had $1.4 billion in assets and a wonderful record, yet not a single brokerage firm bothered to cover the story. I prepared for my phone call by reading the latest annual report. Deposits were up, which meant the customers were keeping their money here, but loans were down. There was a decline on the asset side of the balance sheet. That meant the bankers were being conservative and holding back on making loans.

I found more evidence of the bankers' prudence in the "investment securities" category, which had increased by $50 million from the year before. Investment securities include Treasury bills, bonds, stocks, and cash. An S&L that's worried about the economy or the creditworthiness of borrowers parks its assets in bonds, just as individual investors do. When the economy improves and it's safe to lend money, Germantown will sell its investment securities and make more loans, and this will cause a surge in the earnings.

On that subject, I examined the earnings report to see if any unusual factors might be giving investors a false impression. You don't want to be fooled into buying a stock after a company reports a gain in earnings, only to discover that the gain was an aberration, caused by some onetime event such as the sale of investment securities. Here I found the reverse—Germantown had taken a small loss from the sale of some of its securities, which had depressed its regular earnings, but not enough to make much difference.

"We have a very boring story," said the CEO, Martin Kleppe, when I reached him by phone. This was just the kind of story he must have known I liked. "We also have a fortress balance sheet. When we get in trouble, other guys are walking the plank."

Loan losses and defaults were scarce to begin with, and getting scarcer by the month. Nevertheless, Germantown had protected itself by adding to its loan-loss reserves, which punishes earnings in the short term but will boost earnings later, when the unused reserves are returned to the corporate kitty.

The area around Germantown is not what you'd call brimming with prosperity, but the people there have always been savers and loyal depositors. Germantown Savings was not going to fritter away this money. I figured this prudent S&L would outlive many of its wilder competitors and make big profits somewhere down the line.

SOVEREIGN BANCORP

In the November 25, 1991, issue of *Barron's,* I came across an article entitled "Hometown Lender to the Well-Heeled." It described how Sovereign Bancorp serves a wealthy element in southeastern Pennsylvania from its headquarters in Reading. I liked the part about how a bell goes off in a Sovereign branch every time a mortgage loan is approved.

This was not the only time in my career I was introduced to a stock by a weekly magazine. I checked the annual and the quarterlies. In every important category, Sovereign got good marks. Nonperforming loans were 1 percent of assets. Commercial and construction lending was 4 percent. Sovereign had set aside sufficient reserves to cover 100 percent of its nonperformers.

Sovereign had acquired two New Jersey thrifts from the Resolution Trust Corporation, which boosted its deposits and eventually would boost its earnings. To review some of the details, I called Jay Sidhu, Sovereign's Indian-born president. We chatted about Bombay and Madras, which I'd visited the year before on a charity trip.

When we got around to serious subjects, Mr. Sidhu said that management was determined to "grow" the business by at least 12 percent a year. Meanwhile, based on the latest analysts' estimates for 1992, the stock was selling at a p/e ratio of 8.

The only negative detail was that Sovereign had sold an additional 2.5 million shares in 1991. We've already discussed how it's usually a good thing when a company buys back its shares, as long as it can afford to do so. Conversely, it's a bad thing when a company increases the number of shares. This has the same result as a government printing more money: it cheapens the currency.

At least Sovereign wasn't squandering the proceeds from its stock sale. It was using the proceeds to buy more troubled thrifts from the Resolution Trust.

Mr. Sidhu's model for success, I was pleased to discover, was Golden West. Basically, he wanted to copy the penurious Sandlers by increasing loan originations and cutting expenses. With the payroll that Sovereign inherited from its recent acquisitions, the overhead was 2.25 percent, much higher than Golden West's 1 percent, but Mr. Sidhu seemed devoted to bringing that down. The fact that he owned 4 percent of the stock gave him a considerable incentive to carry out this plan.

Instead of holding on to the mortgages as many thrifts do, Sovereign had decided to specialize in making loans and then selling them to packagers such as Fannie Mae or Freddie Mac. This strategy enabled Sovereign to get its money back quickly and plow it into new mortgages, profiting from the points and other up-front fees. The risk of owning the mortgages was transferred to others.

Even so, Sovereign was being very conservative in the kinds of loans it would approve. It was devoted to residential mortgages. It hadn't made a single commercial loan since 1989. Its average residential loan didn't exceed 69 percent of the value of the property on which the loan was made. The few bad loans were thoroughly investigated so that Sovereign could learn who or what went wrong and not repeat its mistakes.

As often happens in my conversations with companies, I learned something new from Sidhu. He described a sneaky method by which unscrupulous banks and S&Ls camouflage their problem loans. If a developer, say, asks to borrow $1 million for a commercial project, the bank offers him $1.2 million on the basis of an inflated appraisal. The extra $200,000 is held in reserve by the bank. If the developer defaults on the loan, the bank can use this extra money to cover the developer's payments. That way, what has turned into a bad loan can still be carried on the books as a good loan—at least temporarily.

I don't know how widespread this practice has become, but if Sidhu is right, it's another reason to avoid investing in banks and S&Ls with large portfolios of commercial real estate.

PEOPLE'S SAVINGS FINANCIAL

I phoned CFO John G. Medvec at corporate headquarters in New Britain, Connecticut, near Hartford. Mr. Medvec said a lot of weak banks had failed in the area, which strengthened People's position as a safe place to keep money. People's had capitalized on the situation with advertising: the gist was that this was a secure institution with an equity-to-assets ratio of 13. As a result of the advertising, People's deposits of $220 million in 1990 had grown to $242 million in 1991.

People's equity-to-assets ratio would have been even higher if it hadn't used some of its equity to buy back stock. In two phases, this Connecticut S&L had retired 16 percent of its shares and spent $4.4 million in the process. If it continues to buy back shares in this manner, someday they will be very scarce and very valuable. With fewer shares outstanding, the earnings per share will increase even when business is flat. When business is good, the share price can skyrocket.

Corporate managers often pay lip service to "enhancing shareholder value" and then go out and squander the money on fanciful acquisitions, ignoring the simplest and most direct way to reward shareholders—buying back shares. Mundane businesses like International Dairy Queen and Crown Cork & Seal have been spectacular performers in the stock market because their management was committed to buying back shares. That's how Teledyne became a 100-bagger.

When People's Savings Financial first went public in 1986, its shares sold for $10.25. Here it was five years later, a bigger and more profitable operation with fewer shares outstanding, and selling for $11. What was depressing this stock, I suspected, was that the company had to operate in a depressed state. I don't mean emotionally. I mean Connecticut.

All things considered, I'd rather invest in an S&L that's proven it can survive in a depressed state than in one that thrives in a booming economy and has never been tested in bad times.

From my *Thrift Digest,* I'd noted that nonperforming loans were a relatively modest 2 percent, but I wanted to check into this further. Medvec said that most of this 2 percent problem was caused by a single construction loan, and that People's wasn't making any new loans of this type.

People's had already taken its "hit" against earnings when these nonperformers were written off. The next step was to foreclose on the property. Medvec reiterated what I'd heard elsewhere, that the foreclosure process is drawn-out and expensive. It may take two years to oust a borrower who has defaulted. This isn't like Scrooge firing Bob Cratchit, forcing him and Tiny Tim out onto the street, because most of the defaults at People's Savings have been of the commercial variety, or in fat-cat houses that deadbeats can occupy for months free of charge, until their legal remedies are exhausted.

Eventually, a foreclosed property enters the category called "real estate owned," and from there the aggrieved lender can attempt to sell it and get something back for its long-lost loan. In some cases, the lender gets back more than was expected, so there's a potential upside here.

Medvec and I also discussed business conditions in the area. You worry about such things when you're talking about Connecticut in 1992. He said that hardware manufacturers used to be the biggest employers in New Britain, but Stanley Works is the only one left. Central Connecticut State University and the New Britain General Hospital have taken up some of the slack, but unemployment is still high.

Before we hung up, I asked the usual parting question: name your most impressive competitor. Medvec mentioned American Savings Bank of New Britain, with a 12 percent equity-to-assets ratio, which hadn't yet gone public. I was tempted to drive down there and open an account so I could get in on the first stage of the eventual public offering. If you turn to page 215 you'll find out why.

FIRST ESSEX

This was the first of my two born-agains. Here's a case in which it didn't make sense for the company to buy back its own shares. First Essex came public in 1987, with 8 million shares sold for $8 apiece, and two years later, after the stock had done nothing, the management bought back 2 million of those shares at the same $8 price. If management had only waited until 1991, it could have gotten a 75 percent discount, because by then the stock had fallen to $2.

There were some frightening numbers in my First Essex file—10 percent nonperforming assets, 3.5 percent real estate owned, and 13 percent commercial and construction loans. This tiny S&L in Lawrence, Massachusetts, had lost $11 million in 1989 and another $28 million in 1990, a victim of zealous lending to condo developers and real-estate magnates who perished in the recession. Lawrence is located just across the border from New Hampshire, in one of the most depressed spots in all New England.

"Bottom fishing with a six-hundred-foot line" is the way First Essex CEO Leonard Wilson described his predicament when I got him on the phone. For three terrible years, this S&L had faced a procession of foreclosures, each one requiring a "hit" on earnings, each one causing First Essex to own another piece of real estate, until the S&L was cash poor and rich in unoccupied buildings nobody wanted to buy. It was a top absentee landlord in the region—absent of tenants.

Still, First Essex had a book value of $7⅞ and enough equity remained to give it an equity-to-assets ratio of 9. And this was a $2 stock.

Here's the gamble with S&Ls such as First Essex that have fallen on hard times. If the commercial real estate market stabilizes and the foreclosures stop, the institution will survive, and eventually recoup its losses. This could easily become a $10 stock. The problem is, it's impossible to know when or if the commercial market will stabilize or how deep the recession will be.

I could see from the annual report that First Essex had a total of $46 million in commercial loans at the end of 1991. It also had $46 million in equity. This one-to-one ratio between equity and commercial lending was somewhat reassuring. If 50 percent of the remaining commercial loans went bad, then First Essex would lose 50 percent of its equity, but it would still survive.

LAWRENCE SAVINGS

Lawrence is another long shot that comes from the same area in the Merrimack valley. It has the same problem as First Essex—a lousy local economy. Their stories are also the same: profitable S&L gets caught up in heady commercial lending, loses millions of dollars, and the stock price collapses.

According to the 1990 annual report, Lawrence still had a 7.8 equity-to-assets ratio, but as I analyzed it, the situation here was riskier than at First Essex. At Lawrence, commercial real-estate loans made up 21 percent of the loan portfolio, whereas at First Essex they made up 13 percent. Lawrence had made more commercial loans ($55 million worth) and had less raw equity ($27 million) than First Essex. This was a much thinner margin for error. If half of Lawrence's remaining commercial loans go bad, it's a goner.

This is the way you look at a long-shot S&L: find out what the equity is and compare that to the commercial loans outstanding. Assume the worst.

Stock Symbol	Company	1/13/92 Price
EAG	Eagle Financial	$12.06
FESX	First Essex Bancorp	$ 2.13
GSBK	Germantown Savings	$14.50
GBCI	Glacier Bancorp	$11.14
LSBX	Lawrence Savings Bank	$ 1.00
PBNB	People's Savings	$11.00
SVRN	Sovereign Bancorp	$ 6.95

THE CAN'T-LOSE PROPOSITION (ALMOST) THAT CHARLES GIVENS MISSED

Imagine buying a house and then discovering that the former owners have cashed your check for the down payment and left the money in an envelope in a kitchen drawer, along with a note that reads: "Keep this, it belonged to you in the first place." You've got the house and it hasn't cost you a thing.

This is the sort of pleasant surprise that awaits investors who buy shares in any S&L that goes public for the first time. And since 1,178 S&Ls have yet to take this step, there will be many more chances for investors to be surprised.

I learned about the hidden cash-in-the-drawer rebate early in my career at Magellan. This explains why I bought shares in almost every S&L and mutual savings bank (another name for the same sort of institution) that appeared on my Quotron.

Traditionally, the local S&L or mutual savings bank has no shareholders. It is owned cooperatively by all the depositors, in the same way that rural electric utilities are organized as co-ops and owned by all the customers. The net worth of a mutual savings bank, which may have been built up over 100 years, belongs to everyone who has a savings account or a checking account in one of the branches.

As long as the mutual form of ownership is maintained, the thousands of depositors get nothing for their stake in the enterprise. That and $1.50 will get them a glass of mineral water.

When the mutual savings bank comes to Wall Street and sells stock in a public offering, a fascinating thing happens. First of all, the S&L directors who put the deal together and the buyers of the stock are on the same side of the table. The directors themselves will buy shares. You can find out how many in the offering circular that accompanies the deal.

How do directors price a stock that they themselves are going to buy? Low.

Depositors as well as directors will be given the opportunity to buy shares at the initial offering price. The interesting thing about this is that every dollar that's raised in the offering, minus the underwriting fees, will end up back in the S&L's vault.

This is not what happens when other kinds of companies go public. In those cases, a sizable chunk of the money is carted away by the founders and original shareholders, who then become millionaires and buy palazzi in Italy or castles in Spain. But in this case, since the mutual savings bank is owned by the depositors, it would be inconvenient to divvy up the proceeds from a stock sale to thousands of sellers who also happen to be buyers. Instead, the money is returned to the institution, in toto, to become part of the S&L's equity.

Say your local thrift had $10 million in book value before it went public. Then it sold $10 million worth of stock in the offering—1 million shares at $10 apiece. When this $10 million from the stock sale returns to the vault, the book value of this company has just doubled. A company with a $20 book value is now selling for $10 a share.

This doesn't guarantee that what you're getting for free will necessarily turn out to be a good thing. You could be getting a Jimmy Stewart S&L, or it could be a lemon S&L with inept management that's losing money and eventually will lose all its equity and go bankrupt. Even in this can't-lose situation, you ought to investigate the S&L before you invest in it.

The next time you pass a mutual savings bank or an S&L that's still cooperatively owned, think about stopping in and establishing an account. That way, you'll be guaranteed a chance to buy shares at the initial offering price. Of course, you can always wait until after the offering to buy your shares on the open market, and you'll still be getting a bargain.

But don't wait too long. Wall Street seems to be catching on to the cash-in-the-drawer trick, and the increase in stock prices of mutual savings banks and savings and loans that have converted to public ownership since 1991 is nothing short of remarkable. It's been a bonanza almost anywhere you look, from one end of the country to the other.

In 1991, 16 mutual thrifts and savings banks came public. Two were taken over at more than four times the offering price, and of the remaining 14, the worst is up 87 percent in value. All the rest have doubled or better, and there are four triples, one 7-bagger, and one 10-bagger. Imagine making 10 times your money in 32 months by investing in Magna Bancorp, Inc., of Hattiesburg, Mississippi.

In 1992, another 42 mutual thrifts came public. The only loser in this group has been First FS&LA of San Bernardino, and it's down a modest 7.5 percent. All the rest have advanced—38 of them by

Table 13-1. MUTUAL THRIFT AND SAVINGS BANK
IPOs COMPLETED IN 1991†

Ticker	Name	City	State	IPO Date	Offering Price ($)*	Price as of 9/30/93 ($)	Change from Offering Price (%)
MGNL	Magna Bancorp, Inc.	Hattiesburg	MS	3/8/91	3.542	37.750	965.78
CRGN	Cragin Financial Corp.	Chicago	IL	6/6/91	6.667	36.375	445.60
FFSB	FF Bancorp, Inc.	New Smyrna Beach	FL	7/2/91	3.333	13.625	308.79
COOP	Cooperative Bank for Savings	Wilmington	NC	8/16/91	5.333	20.00	275.02
KOKO	Central Indiana Bancorp	Kokomo	IN	7/1/91	7.500	27.000	260.00
AMBS	Amity Bancshares	Tinley Park	IL	12/16/91	10.000	34.000	240.00
AFFC	AmeriFed Financial Corp.	Joliet	IL	10/10/91	10.000	33.750	237.50
FCVG	FirstFed Northern Kentucky Bancorp, Inc.	Covington	KY	12/3/91	10.000	30.000	200.00
UFBI	UF Bancorp, Inc.	Evansville	IN	10/18/91	10.000	27.750	177.50
LBCI	Liberty Bancorp	Chicago	IL	12/24/91	10.000	26.250	162.50
CRCL	Circle Financial Corp.	Shelbyville	OH	8/6/91	11.000	27.250	147.73
CENF	CENFED Financial Corp.	Pasadena	CA	10/25/91	6.667	16.250	143.74
KFSB	Kirksville Bancshares	Kirksville	MO	10/1/91	10.000	21.000	110.00
BELL	Bell Bancorp	Chicago	IL	12/23/91	25.000	46.750	87.00
FFBS	FedFirst Bancshares	Lumberton	NC	3/27/91	10.000	**	
DKBC	Dakota Bancorp, Inc.	Watertown	SD	4/16/91	8.000	***	

Sixteen mutual thrifts and savings banks came public in 1991. Two have been acquired. All of the remaining 14 have gone up: 13 of the 14 have increased more than 100 percent in value.

*Split adjusted.

†Two banks from the original lists have recently been acquired:

**FedFirst Bancshares was acquired by Southern National on January 29, 1993, at $48.00.

***Dakota Bancorp, Inc., was acquired by South Dakota Financial on July 30, 1993, at approximately $36.00.

Note: Kirksville Bancshares, Inc., is no longer followed by SNL Securities. The company reports that the stock is thinly traded.

Source: SNL Securities, L.P.

Table 13-2. THE 10 BEST AND 10 WORST RESULTS:
MUTUAL THRIFT AND SAVINGS BANK IPOs COMPLETED IN 1992

Ticker	Name	City	State	IPO Date	Offering Price ($)*	Price as of 9/30/93 ($)	Change from Offering Price (%)
UPBI	United Postal Bancorp	St. Louis	MO	3/11/92	5.000	28.750	475.00
MSBK	Mutual Savings Bank	Bay City	MI	7/17/92	4.375	23.750	442.86
LGFB	LGF Bancorp, Inc.	La Grange	IL	6/18/92	10.000	27.250	172.50
RESB	Reliable Financial Corp.	Bridgeville	PA	3/30/92	10.000	27.000	170.00
CTZN	CitFed Bancorp, Inc.	Dayton	OH	1/10/92	9.000	24.000	166.67
HFBS	Heritage Federal Bancshares†	Kingsport	TN	4/8/92	7.667	20.000	160.86
HFFC	HF Financial Corp.	Sioux Falls	SD	4/8/92	10.000	24.750	147.50
ABCW	Anchor Bancorp Wisconsin	Madison	WI	7/16/92	10.000	24.750	147.50
AADV	Advantage Bancorp, Inc.	Kenosha	WI	3/23/92	11.500	28.000	143.48
AMFF	AMFED Financial, Inc.	Reno	NV	11/20/92	10.455	25.125	140.32
CNIT	CENIT Bancorp, Inc.	Norfolk	VA	8/5/92	11.500	20.500	78.26
ABCI	Allied Bank Capital, Inc.	Sanford	NC	7/9/92	11.500	19.500	69.57
PVSB	Park View Federal SB	Bedford Heights	OH	12/30/92	10.000	16.750	67.50
KNKB	Kankakee Bancorp, Inc.	Kankakee	IL	12/30/92	9.875	16.500	67.09
BASF	Brentwood Financial Corp.	Cincinnati	OH	12/29/92	10.000	16.250	62.50
MIFC	Mid-Iowa Financial Corp.	Newton	IA	10/13/92	10.000	16.000	60.00
FDNSC	Financial Security Corp.	Chicago	IL	12/29/92	10.000	14.750	47.50
COLB	Columbia Banking System†	Bellevue	WA	6/23/92	8.875	12.000	35.21
FFML	First Family Federal S&LA	Eustis	FL	10/9/92	6.5000	7.500	15.38
FSSB	First FS&LA of San Bernardino	San Bernardino	CA	12/30/92	10.000	9.250	−7.50

*Split adjusted.
†Not on the original list.
Source: SNL Securities, L.P.

Table 13-3. THE 10 BEST AND 10 WORST PERFORMING
MUTUAL THRIFT AND SAVINGS BANK IPOs COMPLETED IN 1993 THROUGH 9/30/93

Ticker	Name	City	State	IPO Date	Offering Price ($)*	Price as of 9/30/93 ($)	Change from Offering Price (%)
WAYN	Wayne Savings & Loan Co. MHC	Wooster	OH	6/23/93	10.000	19.875	98.75
FSOU	First Southern Bancorp	Asheboro	NC	2/24/93	10.000	18.500	85.00
JSBA	Jefferson Savings Bancorp	Baldwin	MD	4/8/93	10.000	17.000	70.00
MARN	Marion Capital Holdings	Marion	IN	3/18/93	10.000	17.000	70.00
CGFC	Coral Gables Fedcorp, Inc.	Coral Gables	FL	3/31/93	10.000	16.750	67.50
HFSB	Hamilton Bancorp. Inc.	Brooklyn	NY	4/1/93	10.800	17.500	62.04
CASH	First Midwest Financial	Storm Lake	IA	9/10/93	10.000	15.750	57.50
FDEF	First Federal Savings & Loan of Defiance	Defiance	OH	7/21/93	10.000	15.250	52.50
MORG	Morgan Financial Corp.	Fort Morgan	CO	1/8/93	10.000	15.000	50.00
LFCT	Leader Financial Corp.	Memphis	TN	9/30/93	10.000	14.875	48.75
FFWD	Wood Bancorp, Inc.	Bowling Green	OH	8/31/93	10.000	13.250	32.50
FFEF	FFE Financial Corp.	Englewood	FL	8/26/93	10.000	13.250	32.50
ROSE	TR Financial Corp.	Garden City	NY	6/29/93	9.000	11.500	27.78
KSBK	KSB Bancorp, Inc.	Kingfield	ME	6/23/93	10.000	12.750	27.50
FBHC	Fort Bend Holding Corp.	Rosenberg	TX	6/30/93	10.000	12.500	25.00
SCBN	Suburban Bancorporation	Cincinnati	OH	9/30/93	10.000	12.500	25.00
TRIC	Tri-County Bancorp	Torrington	WY	9/28/93	10.000	12.250	22.50
COSB	CSB Financial Corp.	Lynchburg	VA	9/24/93	10.000	13.125	21.25
ALBC	Albion Banc Corp.	Albion	NY	7/23/93	10.000	11.250	12.50
HAVN	Haven Bancorp	Woodhaven	NY	9/23/93	10.000	10.500	5.00

*Split Adjusted

Source: SNL Securities, L. P.

50 percent or more, and 23 by 100 percent or more. These gains have come in 20 months!

There are two quadruples in the group—Mutual Savings Bank of Bay City, Michigan, and United Postal Bancorp in St. Louis. A portfolio of the five top performers taken together has produced a 285 percent return. Even a person who was unlucky enough to have chosen the five worst-performing thrifts that came public in 1992 has made 31 percent on his money through September 1993. Investing in the five worst has beaten the S&P 500 and most of the equity mutual funds.

Through the first nine months of 1993, another 34 mutual thrifts have come public, and in this shorter period the worst is up 5 percent, 26 are up 30 percent or better, 20 are up 40 percent or better, and 9 are up 50 percent or better. (All the above numbers were provided by the skillful crunchers at SNL Securities.)

From Asheboro, North Carolina, to Ipswich, Massachusetts, on the East Coast; from Pasadena, California, to Everett, Washington, on the West; from Stillwater, Oklahoma, to Kankakee, Illinois, to Rosenberg, Texas, in the middle, neighborhood S&Ls have been the best investments that hundreds of thousands of people have ever made. This is the ultimate example of how individual investors can succeed by ignoring companies that are widely held by institutions and by investigating what's close to home. What could be closer to home than the local thrift where you keep your safety deposit box and your checking account?

An account in any one of these thrifts or savings banks entitles you to participate in the IPO if and when it happens, but you certainly aren't required to do so. You can go to the meeting where the deal is explained to potential shareholders, see whether the insiders are buying the shares, read the prospectus to find out the book value, the p/e ratio, what the earnings are, the percentage of nonperforming assets, the quality of the loan portfolio, etc., and thus get all the information you need to make an informed decision. It's an opportunity to take a close look at a local company—and it's free. If you don't like the deal, the organization, or the management, you simply don't invest.

There are still 1,372 mutual savings banks that have not yet come public. Check to see whether any of these are located in your area. By opening a savings account in any of them, you'll have the right to participate in the IPO when it happens. Sit back and await developments.

FOURTEEN

MASTER LIMITED PARTNERSHIPS

A Deal with a Yield

Here's another group of companies whose benefits are being ignored by Wall Street. The very name "limited partnership" brings back memories of the suffering of thousands of investors who were lured into heavily promoted tax-shelter boondoggles—oil and gas partnerships, real-estate partnerships, movie partnerships, farming partnerships, and gravesite partnerships—in which the losses far exceeded the amount of taxes they had hoped to avoid.

As a result of bad publicity from the boondoggle partnerships, the good ones that are publicly traded (the so-called master limited partnerships) continue to suffer from guilt by association. These are ongoing enterprises whose purpose is to make money, not to lose it in order to outsmart the IRS. More than 100 MLPs trade on the various stock exchanges. Every year, I find a bargain or two in this group.

The shareholder in an MLP has to do some extra paperwork. Special tax forms have to be prepared. This is less of a nuisance than it used to be, because the investor relations department of the partnership fills in all the blanks. Once a year, you get a letter asking you to confirm how many shares you own and whether or not you bought additional shares.

But this is nuisance enough to dissuade many investors, particularly fund managers, from investing in these stocks. I'd answer questionnaires that were written in Sanskrit if I thought it would help master limited partnerships become less popular than they already are, because this lack of popularity keeps the prices down and helps create the bargains that are often found in this group of companies.

Another appealing feature of the MLP group is that these companies tend to be involved in down-to-earth activities, like playing basketball (the Boston Celtics is an MLP) or pumping oil and gas. ServiceMaster runs a janitorial and cleaning service, Sun Distributors sells auto parts, Cedar Fair runs an amusement park, and EQK Green Acres owns a shopping center on Long Island.

Even the names of the master limited partnerships seem antiquated and out of sync with our high-tech culture. *Cedar Fair* could easily have been written by William Makepeace Thackeray and *Green Acres* by Jane Austen, and I wouldn't be surprised to see Tenera show up on Dartmoor with the other characters from Thomas Hardy.

This all adds up to a bunch of companies with strangely romantic names, engaged in mundane activities, and organized in a complicated manner that requires extra paperwork. It takes an imaginative person to be attracted to the idea of owning shares in a limited partnership, and then he or she runs into the paperwork requirement, which most imaginative people can't stand. A small minority of imaginative people with retentive tendencies is left to reap the rewards.

The biggest difference between an MLP and a regular corporation is that the MLP distributes all its earnings to the shareholders, either as dividends or as a return of capital. The dividends, as a rule, are unusually high. The return of capital feature allows a certain percentage of the annual distribution to be exempt from federal tax.

The first of these publicly traded partnerships came onto the scene in 1981. The majority appeared in 1986, after changes in the tax laws made this form of organization even more advantageous than before. Whereas the real estate and natural resource partnerships can continue to exist indefinitely, all the others must be closed out in 1997–98. They lose their tax benefits at that time. An MLP that's earning $1.80 today might only be earning $1.20 in 1998. This is something to worry about in three or four years, but not today.

Most of my favorite MLPs are listed on the New York Stock Exchange. At the 1991 *Barron's* panel I recommended EQK Green Acres and Cedar Fair, and a year later I chose Sun Distributors and Tenera. What follows is a rundown on why I was attracted to each of these.

EQK GREEN ACRES

EQK Green Acres got my attention after the Saddam Sell-off. (The EQ comes from the Equitable Life Assurance Society, a partner in this enterprise. K stands for Kravco.) The company came public at $10 four years earlier and once had hit a high of $13.75, but in the summer of 1990, when investors were fretting about the demise of shopping centers along with the rest of retailing, the price dropped to $9.75. At that price, EQK Green Acres had a 13.5 percent yield, as good as the yield on some junk bonds, and I thought it was more secure than some junk bonds. The company's principal asset was its huge enclosed mall on Long Island.

Not only did the stock have a chance to appreciate in value, but the management owned a bundle of the shares, and the dividend had been raised every quarter since the company went public.

I remembered some of these details because of course I'd bought some EQK Green Acres for Magellan. Originally, I heard about it from a fund manager at Fidelity, Stuart Williams, but 750,000 insiders on Long Island got essentially the same tip. That's how many people live within five miles of the Green Acres mall, situated in the middle of densely populated Nassau County.

This is the kind of story I've always favored, the kind that can be reviewed at the mall. I visited Green Acres and bought a pair of shoes there—this is a popular place. There are only 450 such enclosed malls in the entire country, and contrary to popular impression, not many new ones are being built. If you wanted to put up a rival mall of similar magnitude, you'd have zoning problems and it wouldn't be easy to find 92 empty acres to pave over for a parking lot.

Strip malls are going up in every neighborhood, but enclosed malls have what amounts to a niche. If you believe in the value of this niche and you want to invest in a mall, Green Acres is the only public company I know that's devoted exclusively to running one.

The bugaboo of any mall owner is vacancies. That was the first thing I checked when I read the annual report. Malls in general had a 4 percent average vacancy rate at the time; Green Acres' was lower. A true insider (that is, a resident of Nassau County who shops at Green Acres) has the advantage of checking for vacancies every week, but I was satisfied that vacancies were no problem.

Moreover, a Waldbaum's supermarket and a Pergament Home Center were moving into the mall, and both of these together were certain to increase the revenues from rent. One third of the stores in the mall were subject to large rent increases in 1992–93. This augured well for the future earnings.

The worrisome elements were a highly leveraged balance sheet (the company must pay back all its debts in 1997), a high p/e ratio, and the vulnerability of any mall to a recession. These were over-ridden, in the short term at least, by the excellent dividend and the fact that the stock price already was depressed. A high p/e ratio is a common characteristic of master limited partnerships.

When I got around to making my 1992 selections, Green Acres stock was $11. When you added in the yield, the total return for 1991 exceeded 20 percent. This was a nice gain, but in rechecking the story I found more cause for concern. A lousy holiday season for retailers had depressed the rents, which are based in part on a percentage of sales. If a store does poorly, the mall gets less.

Presumably, all malls and all retailers were facing the same pre-dicament, so it wasn't as if Green Acres was doing any worse than the rest. I find general gloom in an industry far less bothersome than if a specific company struggles while its competitors thrive. Nonetheless, in a telling paragraph in its third-quarter report for 1991, Green Acres admitted it might forgo a penny a year increase in its dividends.

This apparently innocuous action was an attention-getter, as I mentioned in Chapter 2. If a company has raised its dividend 13 quarters in a row, as Green Acres had, it has powerful built-in incentive to continue the string. To break it for the sake of a penny, or a grand total of $100,000, I suspected was symptomatic of deeper troubles.

Another factor in my decision not to recommend Green Acres a second time was the terrific news on the horizon. The company had announced it was negotiating with two large potential tenants, Sears and J. C. Penney, to lease space in the expansion of the second floor of the mall. This wasn't the same as a signature on a contract. If the company had announced a signed agreement with Sears and J. C. Penney, I would have bought as many shares as I could get my hands on. A potential agreement was too iffy.

The popular prescription "Buy at the sound of cannons, sell at the sound of trumpets" can be misguided advice. Buying on the bad news can be a very costly strategy, especially since bad news has a habit of getting worse. How many people lost substantial amounts of investment capital when they bought on the bad news coming out of the Bank of New England after the stock had already dropped from $40 to $20, or from $20 to $10, or from $10 to $5, or from $5 to $1, only to see it sink to zero and wipe out 100 percent of their investment?

Buying on the good news is healthier in the long run, and you improve your odds considerably by waiting for the proof. Maybe you lose a dollar a share or so by waiting for the announcement of a signed contract between Sears and Green Acres, as opposed to buying the rumor, but if there's a real deal it will add many more dollars to the stock price in the future. And if there isn't a real deal, you've protected yourself by waiting. I deferred further commitments and made a note to watch for the expected announcement.

CEDAR FAIR

This was the second of the master limited partnerships I recommended back in 1991. Cedar Fair is the permanent county fair for Middle America. It owns and operates two amusement parks, one, Cedar Point, on the Ohio shore of Lake Erie, and the other, Valley Fair, in Minnesota. These are open from May to Labor Day, and on weekends in the fall.

Cedar Point has 10 different roller coasters, including the one with the highest drop in the world, Magnum, and the highest wooden roller coaster in the world, Mean Streak. There's a large framed poster of Mean Streak on the far wall facing my desk. That and the photograph of the Fannie Mae headquarters in Washington are the only corporate mementos that share space with my children's artwork and all the photographs of my family.

Cedar Point is in its 120th year, and it's had roller coasters for 100. Seven U.S. presidents have visited this park, and Knute Rockne had summer jobs at Cedar Point. During one of his summers here, Rockne apparently invented the forward pass. A historic plaque commemorates the fact.

Next week, somebody might come up with a new AIDS drug and the companies that make the competing AIDS drugs will lose half their value overnight, but nobody is going to sneak up and install $500 million worth of rides on the shores of Lake Erie.

One of the side benefits of owning shares in an amusement park, as opposed, say, to an oil company, is that an annual visit, complete with test rides on the Ferris wheel and fundamental analysis on the roller coaster, could be construed as research for investment purposes. This gives grown-ups who love amusement parks a great excuse to frequent them.

It also occurred to me that in a recession the 6 million or so people who live within a three hours' drive of Cedar Point might decide to forgo the summer trip to France in favor of staying at the Cedar Point Hotel and taking a few flings on the world's highest roller coaster. This was a company that could benefit from an economic downturn.

In 1991, Cedar Fair stock rose from $11.50 to $18, which together with the dividend gave shareholders a one-year return of more than 60 percent. At the outset of 1992, I asked myself, is this stock still a buy? The yield was 8.5 percent, still a nice return, but no matter how good the dividend, a company will not prosper in the long run unless its earnings continue to improve.

This is a useful year-end review for any stockpicker: go over your portfolio company by company and try to find a reason that the next year will be better than the last. If you can't find such a reason, the next question is: why do I own this stock?

With that in mind, I called the company directly and spoke to the president, Dick Kinzel. If Joe Oddlot can't always speak to the president, he can get the information from the investor relations department. Having the ear of management will not necessarily make you a better investor, any more than having the ear of the owner of a racehorse will make you a better handicapper. Owners can always give you a reason their horses will win, and they are wrong 90 percent of the time.

In keeping with my low-key technique, I didn't ask Kinzel "How are the earnings going to improve?" straightaway. I asked about the weather in Ohio. I asked about the condition of the Ohio golf courses, the economy in Cleveland and Detroit, and whether it had been hard getting summer help this year. Only after I'd warmed up my source did I pop the important questions.

When I'd called Cedar Fair in previous years, there was always some new attraction—a new roller coaster, a loop-de-loop, etc.— that would add to the earnings. In 1991, the opening of the highest wooden roller coaster was a definite plus for earnings, but in 1992, there were no major exciting developments at the amusement parks, beyond the expansion of a hotel. Attendance at Cedar Fair usually drops the year after a new ride has been introduced.

At the end of our conversation, I didn't see the potential for another big move in Cedar Fair's earnings in 1992. I liked Sun Distributors better.

SUN DISTRIBUTORS

Sun Distributors has nothing to do with solar energy. This company, spun out of Sun Oil in 1986, sells auto glass, sheet glass, insulated glass, cables, mirrors, windshield glass, fasteners, ball bearings, and hydraulic systems to builders and to auto repair shops. These are activities that put graduates of our business schools to sleep. Financial analysts would rather count the ceiling tiles than follow a company that sells auto parts.

In fact, a lone analyst, Karen Payne of Wheat First Securities, had been covering the company, but her April 1990 report apparently was her last. Even Sun's president, Don Marshall, whom I called on December 23, 1991, didn't seem to know what had become of her.

This was point one in Sun's favor: Wall Street was ignoring it.

I'd owned the stock in Magellan (of course), and its poor showing by the end of 1991 had once again brought it to my attention. Actually, there were two kinds of shares, the Class A shares, which got a big dividend, and the Class B shares, which didn't. Both were traded on the New York Stock Exchange. This was a further complication from the normal complication of a master limited partnership: two classes of stock, and extra paperwork to boot. "Sun Distributors is a simple, well-run business hiding in a complicated financial structure" is the way Ms. Payne put it in her final communication on the subject.

Except for the dividend, the Class A shares offered very little upside—eventually, the company will buy these shares back for $10 apiece, and they were selling for $10 already. All the action was going to be in the Class B shares. The price of these had fallen in half, from $4 to $2, in 1991.

From Ms. Payne's last report, I found out that Shearson Lehman owned 52 percent of these B shares, and that the management of Sun Distributors had an option to buy up to half of Shearson Lehman's half at a fixed price. This gave the managers a powerful incentive to boost the value of those shares by making the company succeed. That the president was in his office taking phone calls on December 23, two days before Christmas, I took as powerful evidence that management was serious about its mission.

Marshall is an unassuming sort whose life story has not been told in *Vanity Fair* magazine, but can be found in a book called *The Service Edge*. In his frugal regime, executives get no bonuses unless the company does well in a particular year. Success and not status is the basis for rewards.

The gist of my investigation was the same as with every company whose shares have taken a beating in the market. Will Sun Distributors survive? Did it do anything to deserve this punishment, or was it simply the victim of the annual tax-loss selling that creates bargains year after year?

Obviously it was still making money, because it still had earnings. Sun Distributors had made money every year since 1986, when it got its independence. It even made money in 1991, in spite of the fact that the glass business was terrible in general and so was the electrical parts business, and they weren't whooping it up over at the fluid power division, either. But this was another case in which the low-cost operator was a survivor and bad times eventually worked to its benefit, as competitors faltered and disappeared.

How did I know this was a low-cost operator? I could figure it out with information I found on the income statement (see Table 14-1). By dividing the cost of sales by net sales, I arrive at Sun's gross margin, or its return on sales. This had held steady over two years, at roughly 60 percent. Meanwhile, Sun had increased its sales, and its overall profits were also increasing. A company with a 60 percent gross margin is making a $40 profit on every $100 worth of stuff that it sells. This was tops among all the distributors of glass, fasteners, etc.

This business requires very little capital spending, another plus on the checklist. Capital spending has been the undoing of many a major manufacturer, such as a steel company, that might make $1 billion a year but have to spend $950 million to do it. A regional grocery store for windshields and spare parts doesn't have this problem. I could see on page two of the annual report that Sun Distributors' outlay for capital expenses was only $3–$4 million a year. Compared to its revenues, this was peanuts.

As a tightfisted operation in a nongrowth industry, capturing a bigger and bigger share of the market as its free-spending competitors fell by the wayside, Sun Distributors deserved to be included in my "blossoms in the desert" category. If it hadn't been a master limited partnership, I would have put it there.

More important, even, than the earnings was the cash flow. I focus on the cash flow situation with any company that makes a lot of acquisitions. Since 1986, Sun had bought no less than 36 related

Table 14-1. SUN DISTRIBUTORS L.P. AND SUBSIDIARY—
CONSOLIDATED STATEMENTS OF INCOME
(dollars in thousands, except for partnership interest amounts)

	1990	1989	1988
Net sales	$594,649	$561,948	$484,376
Cost of sales	357,561	340,785	294,640
Gross profit	237,088	221,163	189,736
Operating expenses:			
Selling, general and			
administrative expenses	187,762	175,989	151,784
Management fee to general			
partner	3,330	3,330	3,330
Depreciation	5,899	6,410	7,024
Amortization	4,022	3,920	3,282
Total operating expenses	201,013	189,649	165,420
Income from operations	36,075	31,514	24,316
Interest income	352	283	66
Interest expense	(12,430)	(12,878)	(11,647)
Other income (expense), net	173	678	(384)
Income before provision for			
state and foreign income			
taxes	24,170	19,597	12,951
Provision for state and foreign			
income taxes	1,024	840	637
Net income	$ 23,146	$ 18,757	$12,314
Net income allocated to			
partners:			
General partner	$ 231	$ 188	$ 123
Class A limited partners	$ 13,820	$ 18,569	$ 12,191
Class B limited partners	$ 9,095	—	—
Weighted average number of			
outstanding limited			
partnership interests:			
—Class A interests	11,099,573	11,099,573	11,099,573
—Class B interests	22,127,615	22,199,146	22,199,146
Earnings per limited			
partnership interest:			
—Class A interest	$ 1.25	$ 1.67	$ 1.10
—Class B interest	$ .41	—	—
Pro forma earnings per limited			
partnership interest:			
—Class A interest	$ 1.10	$ 1.10	$ 1.10
—Class B interest	$ .48	$ .29	—

enterprises and folded them into its operation, reducing their overhead and making them more profitable. That was Sun's growth strategy. It's goal, Marshall explained, was to become a super grocery store for wires, fasteners, glass, and other such parts.

When you buy a company, you usually have to pay more than book value. This premium becomes the goodwill, and it has to be accounted for on the balance sheet.

Prior to 1970, companies did not have to penalize earnings to make up for goodwill. Under the old accounting system, when Company X bought Company Y, Company X could carry the full purchase price of Company Y as an asset. One of the consequences was that if Company X paid too much for Company Y, the foolishness of the purchase was hidden from the shareholders, who had no way of knowing if the purchase price for Company Y would ever be recovered.

To solve this problem, the people who make the accounting rules changed the system. Now when Company X buys Company Y, the amount it pays over and above the value of the tangible assets, i.e., the goodwill premium, must be deducted from the earnings of Company X over several years.

This "penalizing" of earnings is a paper transaction, which results in a company's reported earnings being less than its actual earnings. Consequently, companies that make acquisitions appear to be less profitable than they really are, a situation that often results in their stocks being undervalued.

In this instance, Sun Distributors had $57 million in goodwill to write off, and this accounting exercise reduced its reported earnings for the two classes of stock to $1.25 a share—when in fact it earned nearly twice that amount. These phantom earnings that the company has but can't claim as earnings are called the free cash flow.

A healthy free cash flow gives a company the flexibility to change course in good and bad times. This was particularly important in the case of Sun Distributors because the company's debt load was very high—60 percent of total capitalization. The cash flow, I was relieved to discover, was sufficient to cover the interest on the debt four times over.

When the economy was strong, Sun Distributors used its cash flow to expand by buying $41 million worth of businesses. In 1991, Marshall said, the company had responded to the recession by curtailing its acquisitions and devoting its cash flow to reducing its debt. The $110 million it had borrowed at 9½ percent could be retired within two years if Sun used all its excess cash flow for this purpose. Apparently, that is what it has decided to do.

If times get even tougher, Sun can sell some of its acquisitions, such as the auto parts division, to reduce its debt even further.

The temporary moratorium on acquisitions will likely result in Sun's earnings not growing as fast as they did before, but on the other hand, the balance sheet will be strengthened. The move to cut the debt reassured me that the management was facing up to reality, and that the company will survive to make more acquisitions in the future.

Sun Distributors will survive even in a bad economy, but if things pick up, it can become very prosperous. Eventually, when the master limited partnership arrangement expires, the entire enterprise may be sold off. The 11 million Class A shareholders will get their $10 a share, as promised, and the 22 million Class B shareholders will get the rest of the money, which could be as much as $5-$8 a share. If that happens, the Class B shareholders will more than double their investment.

TENERA LIMITED PARTNERS

This was a company with warts. Its greatest virtue was that the stock price had fallen from $9 to $1.25 in the summer of 1991. It was involved in software and consulting—one a high-tech business that I found incomprehensible and therefore untrustworthy, the other too vague for comfort. Its biggest clients were the nuclear power industry and contractors to the federal government.

A couple of phone calls, and I knew why the stock price had collapsed. The company was squabbling with one of its major sources of revenue: the feds. The feds were accusing Tenera of overcharging it for certain services, and had canceled some contracts. Worse than that, a software program, which cost millions to develop and which Tenera hoped to sell to electric utilities around the world, was not paying off.

The company was forced to cut its work force drastically. Some key executives, including the president, Don Davis, had resigned. For those that remained, the atmosphere was far from harmonious. Tenera's competitors in the consulting business were bad-mouthing Tenera to its customers.

In June 1991, the dividend was canceled. The company announced that it would "take a long time" to restore it to its former level of 20 cents a quarter.

I don't mean to tout Tenera too highly. If this company had had even a dime worth of debt, I wouldn't have given it a second's worth of attention. Since it had no debt and no large expenses to pay, I figured it wasn't going out of business in the next day or two. These were the positives: zero debt, no capital spending to speak of (what do consultants need, except for a desk, a calculator to add up their fees, and a telephone?), and a well-regarded nuclear services division that could be sold at a profit in a liquidation.

Tenera had earned between 77 and 81 cents a share in each of the four years prior to 1991; it still had earning power. Maybe it would never reach 80 cents again, but if it earned 40 cents, the stock might be worth $4.

With conditions as desperate as these, I wasn't counting on earnings. I was counting the potential value of the assets as spare parts. I figured a Tenera on the auction block was worth more than $1.50 a share (the price at the time I did this analysis), and with no debts and expenses, the entire amount minus the legal fees would go to the shareholders.

If the company solved some of its problems, the stock would make a big rebound, and if it didn't, the stock would make a small rebound. That, at least, was my expectation.

Tenera had brought in Bob Dahl, a guy I'd met when he worked in the telecommunications industry, to oversee the recovery. Dahl reached me in New York the night before the *Barron's* panel. He suggested that a turnaround of the company's operations was possible within the next 6–12 months. He also said that insiders were holding on to their shares. This convinced me there was still some value in the company.

Stock Symbol	Company	1/13/92 Price
SDP.B	Sun Distributors L.P., Class B	$2.75
TLP	Tenera L.P.	$2.38

FIFTEEN

THE CYCLICALS

What Goes Around Comes Around

When the economy is in the doldrums, the professional money manager begins to think about investing in the cyclicals. The rise and fall of the aluminums, steels, paper producers, auto manufacturers, chemicals, and airlines from boom to recession and back again is a well-known pattern, as reliable as the seasons.

What confuses the issue is the fund manager's perpetual itch to get ahead of the competition by returning to the cyclicals before everybody else does. It seems to me that Wall Street is anticipating the revival of cyclical industries earlier and earlier before the fact, and this makes investing in cyclicals a trickier and trickier proposition.

With most stocks, a low price/earnings ratio is regarded as a good thing, but not with the cyclicals. When the p/e ratios of cyclical companies are very low, it's usually a sign that they are at the end of a prosperous interlude. Unwary investors are holding on to their cyclicals because business is still good and the companies continue to show high earnings, but this will soon change. Smart investors are already selling their shares to avoid the rush.

When a large crowd begins to sell a stock, the price can only go in one direction. When the price drops, the p/e ratio also drops, which to the uninitiated makes a cyclical look more attractive than before. This can be an expensive misconception.

Soon the economy will falter, and the earnings of the cyclical will decline at breathtaking speed. As more investors head for the exits, the stock price will plummet. Buying a cyclical after several years of record earnings and when the p/e ratio has hit a low point is a proven method for losing half your money in a short period of time.

Conversely, a high p/e ratio, which with most stocks its regarded as a bad thing, may be good news for a cyclical. Often, it means that a company is passing through the worst of the doldrums, and soon its business will improve, the earnings will exceed the analysts' expectations, and fund managers will start buying the stock in earnest. Thus, the stock price will go up.

The fact that the cyclical game is a game of anticipation makes it doubly hard to make money in these stocks. The principal danger is that you buy too early, then get discouraged and sell. It's perilous to invest in a cyclical without having a working knowledge of the industry (copper, aluminum, steel, autos, paper, whatever) and its rhythms. If you're a plumber who follows the price of copper pipe, you have a better chance of making money on Phelps Dodge than the M.B.A. who decides to put Phelps Dodge in his portfolio because it "looks cheap."

My own record with cyclicals is moderately good, and whenever there's a recession I pay attention to this group. Since I always think positively, and assume that the economy will improve no matter how many bleak headlines appear in the papers, I'm willing to invest in cyclicals at their nadir. Just when it seems that things can't get any worse with these companies, things begin to get better. The comeback of a depressed cyclical with a strong balance sheet is inevitable, which brings me to Peter's Principle # 19:

> **Unless you're a short seller or a poet looking for a wealthy spouse, it never pays to be pessimistic.**

PHELPS DODGE

We've already discussed how I was foiled in my attempt to get in on the rebound in the housing market by purchasing the home builders' stocks—too many other buyers had beaten me to those. But they hadn't yet anticipated the rebound in the copper market, and it was hard to ignore the bargain that appeared before me in January

1992 in the form of Phelps Dodge. I checked with my plumber, and he confirmed that the price of copper pipe was going up.

Phelps Dodge was a stock I'd recommended in 1991, and it hadn't gone anywhere the entire year. A stock's having gone nowhere is not necessarily a reason to ostracize it, and it may be a reason to buy more. On January 2, 1992, I reviewed the Phelps Dodge story, and it sounded even better than it had a year earlier.

I used to visit Phelps Dodge in New York, but since it relocated to Arizona, we communicate by telephone. I called the company and talked to the chairman, Douglas Yearly.

From earlier flirtations with this company, I'd learned a few facts about copper that convinced me it was a more valuable commodity than, say, aluminum. There's a lot of aluminum in the earth's crust (8 percent, to be exact), and not only is aluminum as common as tumbleweed, it's relatively easy to extract. Copper is scarcer than aluminum to begin with, and it's a vanishing asset. Mines run out of copper or get flooded and are forced to close. It's not like the assembly line for Cabbage Patch dolls, where you can get more Cabbage Patch dolls by adding another shift.

Environmental regulations have forced the closing of many of our nation's smelters, and many companies have given up smelting for good. There's a smelter shortage in the U.S. already, and one is developing worldwide. People who live downwind of smelters can breathe easier because of this trend, and so can the shareholders of Phelps Dodge. Phelps Dodge has plenty of smelters, and not nearly as many competitors as it had before.

Although the demand for copper was slack in the short term, I figured it was bound to pick up. All the developing nations of the world, including the many spin-offs from the old Soviet Union, are dedicated to improving their phone systems. Everybody wants to be a capitalist these days, and it's hard to be a capitalist without a telephone.

A traditional phone system requires miles and miles of copper wire. Unless all these start-up countries opt for a cellular phone in every pocket (a strategy that's unlikely), they are going to be frequent buyers in the copper market. Developing countries are much more copper intensive than mature countries, and the preponderance of the former bodes well for the future of this metal.

Recently, Phelps Dodge stock had followed the typical cyclical pattern. In 1990, before the recession, the company earned $6.50

(adjusted for a recent split), and the stock sold in a range of $23–$36, giving it a low p/e ratio of between 3.5 and 5.5. In 1991, earnings dropped to $3.90 and the stock price retreated from its $39 high back to $26. That it didn't retreat further is evidence that many investors thought highly of this company's long-term prospects. Or perhaps the cyclical players were betting on the next cycle earlier than usual.

The most important question to ask about a cyclical is whether the company's balance sheet is strong enough to survive the next downturn. I found the information on page 30 of the 1990 Phelps Dodge annual report, the most recent I could get my hands on at the time. The company had equity of $1.68 billion and total debt (minus cash) of only $318 million. Clearly, this was no candidate for bankruptcy no matter what the price of copper (well, zero would be a problem). Many weaker competitors will be forced to close their mines and pack up their slag and go home before Phelps Dodge even has to refinance.

Since this is a big company, and since it had diversified into many industries besides copper, I wanted to see how those other businesses were doing. The CEO, Yearly, went down the list: carbon black was OK, he said; magnet wire was OK, truck wheels was OK, and Canyon Resources, the Montana gold mine discovery in which Phelps Dodge has a 72 percent interest, could become a big money-maker.

These subsidiary enterprises earned less than $1 a share in a bad year (1991), and it was not farfetched to assume they could earn as much as $2 in a decent year. Assigning them a modest p/e ratio of 5–8, I concluded they might be worth $10–$16 a share on their own. The gold operations could be worth $5 a share to Phelps Dodge.

I often do this sort of thumbnail appraisal of a company's various divisions, which may represent a sizable hidden asset. This is a useful exercise to perform on any sort of company whose shares you might want to buy. It's not unusual to discover that the parts are worth more than the whole.

It's easy enough to find out if a company has more than one division—the annual report tells you that. It also gives you a break-down of the earnings. If you take the earnings of each division and multiply by a generic p/e ratio (say, 8–10 for a cyclical on average earnings, or 3–4 on peak earnings), you'll get at least a rough idea of how much the division is worth.

TABLE 15-1. CONSOLIDATED BALANCE SHEET—PHELPS DODGE
CORPORATION
(dollars in thousands except per share values)

	December 31, 1990	December 31, 1989
ASSETS		
Current assets:		
Cash and short-term investments, at cost	$ 161,649	12,763
Receivables, less allowance for doubtful accounts (1990—$16,579; 1989—$11,484)	307,656	346,892
Inventories	256,843	238,691
Supplies	95,181	84,283
Prepaid expenses	17,625	8,613
Current assets	838,954	691,242
Investments and long-term receivables	93,148	79,917
Property, plant and equipment, net	1,691,176	1,537,359
Other assets and deferred charges	204,100	196,109
	$2,827,378	2,504,627
LIABILITIES		
Current liabilities:		
Short-term debt	$ 43,455	92,623
Current portion of long-term debt	32,736	33,142
Accounts payable and accrued expenses	362,347	307,085
Income taxes	51,193	46,197
Current liabilities	489,731	479,047
Long-term debt	403,497	431,523
Deferred income taxes	110,006	67,152
Other liabilities and deferred credits	116,235	156,743
	1,119,469	1,134,465
MINORITY INTEREST IN SUBSIDIARIES	24,971	20,066
COMMON SHAREHOLDERS' EQUITY		
Common shares, per value $6.25; 100,000,000 shares authorized; 34,441,346 outstanding* (1989—34,618,723) after deducting 3,152,955 shares (1989—2,975,578) held in treasury	215,258	215,367
Capital in excess of par value	268,729	281,381
Retained earnings	1,269,094	917,848
Cumulative translation adjustments and other	(70,143)	(65,500)
Shareholder equity	1,682,938	1,350,096
	$2,827,378	$2,504,627

*Before recent 2-for-1 split.

Handwritten annotations: DEBT → $479 MILLION; MINUS CASH 161 MILLION; TOTAL DEBT $318 MILLION; Clearly no candidate for bankruptcy

In the Phelps Dodge exercise, if the gold mine was worth $5 a share, the other ancilliary divisions were worth $10–$16 a share, and the stock was selling for $32, you were getting the copper business for very little.

I also looked at capital spending, which is the ruination of so many industrial companies. This didn't appear to be a problem at Phelps Dodge. In 1990 it spent $290 million to upgrade its plants and its equipment, less than half its cash flow.

Page 31 of the 1990 annual report (see Table 15-2) shows a cash flow of $633 million, which exceeded capital spending and dividend payments combined. Even in a bad year, 1991, cash flow exceeded capital spending. It's always a good sign when a company is taking in more money than it spends.

Phelps Dodge's mines and other facilities were in excellent shape. Unlike a computer company that must spend vast sums every year on new product development or to cannibalize old products, Phelps Dodge spends very little to maintain its mines. It's also better off than a steel company that invests a fortune on upgrading its plants, only to be squeezed by foreign competitors who sell steel for less.

No matter what happens to capital spending or its various subsidiaries, the fate of Phelps Dodge is tied to the price of copper. The basic math is as follows. Phelps Dodge produces 1.1 bilion pounds of copper a year (it says so in the annual report), so a penny increase in the price per pound creates an extra $11 million in pretax earnings. With 70 million shares outstanding, the extra $11 million in earnings is worth 10 cents a share after taxes. Ergo, every time the price of copper goes up a penny a pound, the earnings go up 10 cents, and if copper goes up 50 cents a pound, the earnings improve by $5 a share.

If people know what the price of copper will be next year and the year after that, then they automatically become geniuses on the subject of when to buy and sell Phelps Dodge. I claim no such prescience, but I thought copper was cheap in 1990–91 because of the recession, and I imagined it wouldn't be cheap forever, and I was certain that when it got more expensive the shareholders of Phelps Dodge would be the principal beneficiaries. All we have to do is wait and be patient and continue to collect the dividend.

Table 15-2. CONSOLIDATED STATEMENT OF CASH FLOWS—PHELPS DODGE CORPORATION

	1990	1989	1988
OPERATING ACTIVITIES	$ 454,900	267,000	420,200
Net income			
Adjustments to reconcile net income to cash flow			
from operations:			
Depreciation, depletion, and amortization	132,961	133,417	116,862
Deferred income taxes	$50,918	(53,670)	70,323
Undistributed earnings of equity investments	(5,280)	(8,278)	(15,807)
Provision for nonproducing assets and other	—	374,600	50,000
Cash flow from operations	633,499	712,979	641,578
Adjustments to reconcile cash flow from operations to net cash			
provided by operating activities:			
Changes in current assets and liabilities:			
(Increase) decrease in receivables	42,115	76,850	(69,278)
(Increase) decrease in inventories	(24,700)	11,394	(26,706)
(Increase) decrease in supplies	(9,713)	(2,801)	(6,344)
(Increase) decrease in prepaid expanses	(10,565)	1,778	6,986
Increase (decrease) in interest payable	(983)	(2,958)	(918)
Increase (decrease) in other accounts payable	35,016	(38,816)	(6,770)
Increase (decrease) in income taxes	2,702	(11,292)	14,687
Increase (decrease) in other accrued expenses	23,500	24,898	(2,031)
Other adjustments	(48,995)	(27,833)	(8,413)
Net cash provided by operating activities	641,876	744,199	542,791
INVESTING ACTIVITIES			
Capital outlays	(290,406)	(217,407)	(179,357)
Capitalized interest	(1,324)	(1,529)	(6,321)
Investment in subsidiaries	(4,405)	(68,797)	(253,351)
Proceeds from assets sales	3,155	5,131	35,413
Net cash provided by investing activities	(292,980)	(282,602)	(403,616)
FINANCIAL ACTIVITIES			
Increase in debt	19,124	79,830	184,727
Payment of debt	(98,184)	(114,244)	(235,048)
Purchase of common shares	(21,839)	(141,235)	(30,371)
Preferred dividends	—	(4,284)	(15,000)
Common dividends	(103,654)	(454,307)	(29,202)
Other	4,543	13,102	1,959
Net cash used in financing activities	(200,010)	(621,138)	(122,935)
INCREASE (DECREASE) IN CASH AND SHORT-TERM INVESTMENTS	148,886	(159,541)	16,240
CASH AND SHORT-TERM INVESTMENTS AT BEGINNING OF YEAR	12,763	172,304	156,064
CASH AND SHORT-TERM INVESTMENTS AT END OF YEAR	161,649	12,763	172,304

GENERAL MOTORS

The autos, often misidentified as blue chips, are classic cyclicals. Buying an auto stock and putting it away for 25 years is like flying over the Alps—you may get something out of it, but not as much as the hiker who experiences all the ups and downs.

In 1987, I reduced my holdings in Chrysler, Ford, and other auto stocks that had been my biggest positions in the Magellan Fund because I sensed that the great car-buying spree that began in the early 1980s was about to end. But in 1991, a year into the recession, with the auto stocks down 50 percent from their recent highs, and with widespread gloom in auto showrooms and car and truck dealers playing pinochle to pass the time, I decided to give the autos another look.

Until someone invents a reliable Hovercraft for home use, it's a certainty that cars will continue to be America's most beloved personal possession. Sooner or later, we all replace our cars, either because we are tired of the old ones or because the brakes are shot and we can see the road through the rusted floorboards. I've held out as long as I could with my 1977 AMC Concord, but even Old Faithful is beginning to sputter.

When I took a big position in the autos in the early 1980s, annual car and truck sales in the U.S. had declined from 15.4 million vehicles in 1977 to 10.5 million in 1982. It was possible, of course, that sales would fall further, but I knew they couldn't go to zero. In most states, cars have to pass a yearly inspection, which is another reason that people can't keep their clunkers forever. Eventually, these clunkers will be barred from the road.

It's true that a new gimmick may have retarded the rebound of the auto industry from the latest recession: the 60-month auto loan. In the old days of the 36-month auto loan, a car was paid off by the time the owner decided to get rid of it. Usually, there'd be some equity left in the car when it was driven onto the lot for a trade-in. The 60-month paper has changed all that. Many four- and five-year-old cars are now worth less than the outstanding loan balances, and their owners can't afford to trade them in. But eventually, these loans will be retired.

One useful indicator for when to buy auto stocks is used-car prices. When used-car dealers lower their prices, it means they're having trouble selling cars, and a lousy market for them is even lousier for the new-car dealers. But when used-car prices are on the rise, it's a sign of good times ahead for the automakers.

An even more reliable indicator is "units of pent-up demand." I located this telling statistic in a chart that's published in a Chrysler Corporation publication called *Corporate Economist*—another good candidate for summer reading at the beach. (The chart appears here as Table 15.3.)

In the second column we find the actual car and truck sales, arranging by calendar year, with each number representing 1,000 vehicles. The third column, called "Trend," is an estimate of how many cars and trucks *should* have been sold, based on demographics, sales in previous years, the ages of cars on the road, and other considerations. The difference between the two gives us the units of pent-up demand.

In the four years from 1980 to 1983, when the economy was sluggish and people were trying to save money, actual car sales lagged the trend by 7 million vehicles—7 million people who should have bought cars and trucks had delayed their purchases. That told us to expect a boom in auto sales. Sure enough, we had a boom from 1984 to 1989, years in which auto and truck sales exceeded the trend by a combined 7.8 million units.

After four or five years when sales are under the trend, it takes another four or five years of sales above the trend before the car market can catch up to itself. If you didn't know this, you might sell your auto stocks too soon. For instance, after the boom year of 1983, when car sales increased from 10.5 to 12.3 million vehicles, you might have decided to take your profits in Ford or Chrysler stock because the auto boom was over. But if you followed the trend, you could see that there was still a pent-up demand for more than 7 million vehicles, which wasn't exhausted until 1988.

A year to sell auto stocks was 1988, when the pent-up demand from the early 1980s was all used up. The public had bought 74 million new vehicles in five years, and sales were more likely to go down than up. Even though 1989 was a decent year for the economy at large, auto sales fell by 1 million units. Auto stocks declined.

Starting in 1990, we've once again begun to build up a little pent-up demand. We've had two years under trend, and if things continue on their current course we'll build up 5.6 million units of pent-up demand by the end of 1993. This should produce a boom in car sales in 1994–96.

Table 15-3. U.S. AUTO AND TRUCK INDUSTRY SALES, ACTUAL
VERSUS TREND
(in thousand units, by calendar year)

Year	Actual	Trend	Units Above/ (Below) Trend	Units of Pent-up Demand
1960	7,588	7,700	(112)	(112)
1970	10,279	11,900	(1,621)	(2,035)
1980	11,468	12,800	(1,332)	(1,336)
1981	10,794	13,000	(2,206)	(3,542)
1982	10,537	13,200	(2,663)	(6,205)
1983	12,310	13,400	(1,090)	(7,295)
1984	14,483	13,600	883	(6,412)
1985	15,725	13,800	1,925	(4,487)
1986	16,321	14,000	2,321	(2,166)
1987	15,189	14,200	989	(1,177)
1988	15,788	14,400	1,388	211
1989	14,845	14,600	245	456
1990	14,147	14,800	(653)	(197)
1991	12,541	15,000	(2,459)	(2,656)
		Estimates*		
1992	13,312	15,200	(1,888)	(4,544)
1993	14,300	15,400	(1,100)	(5,644)

Source: Chrysler Corporation
*Estimates by Peter Lynch

Even though 1992 sales are above 1991 levels, we're still well under trend,
and it will take four to five good years of auto and truck sales to catch
up.

Timing the auto cycles is only half the battle. The other half is picking the companies that will gain the most on the upturn. If you're right about the industry and wrong about the company, you can lose money just as easily as if you're wrong about the industry.

During the upturn that began in 1982, I concluded (1) that it was a good time to own auto stocks and (2) that Chrysler, Ford, and Volvo had more to gain than General Motors. Since GM was the number-one automaker, you would have thought it would do the best, but it didn't. That's because GM's reputation for excellence far exceeded any desire to live up to it. The company was arrogant, myopic, and resting on its laurels, but other than that it was in great shape.

The filmmaker of *Roger & Me* wasn't the only person who had trouble getting into GM buildings. On one trip I was assigned to an investor relations guy who couldn't find the research-and-development center, which was roughly the size of a big college campus. It took the two of us a couple of hours to figure out where it was. When the investor relations department hasn't read the locator map, you can assume that the rest of the company is just as lost.

GM in the 1980s left a bad impression among buyers of auto stocks. GM stock doubled in 10 years, but the people who bought Chrysler near the 1982 bottom made almost 50 times their money in five years, and those who bought Ford made 17 times their money. By the end of the decade, GM's foibles were no secret. A man on the street could tell you that America's number-one automaker had lost a war to the Japanese.

But in the stock market it rarely pays to take yesterday's news too seriously, or to hold an opinion too long. As GM was declining, the popular view on Wall Street was that this was a powerful company with a profitable future. In 1991, the popular view was that GM was a weak company with a miserable future. Though I was no fan of GM in the past, my hunch was that this latest popular opinion would prove to be as misguided as the last one.

You could almost take the old articles about Chrysler being the stumbling giant of 1982 and switch the name Chrysler to General Motors, and you'd have the same story all over again. The only difference is that GM has a better balance sheet in 1992 than Chrysler did in 1982. The rest is the same: powerful enterprise forgets how to make cars, loses the public's confidence, lays off thousands of workers, heads for the scrap heap of has-been corporations.

It was all this negativity about GM that attracted me to it in 1991. A glance at the third-quarter 1990 report and I knew I was onto something. While most of the attention is focused on GM's flagging car sales in the U.S., it turns out that GM can succeed without selling more cars in the U.S. Its most profitable businesses are its European operations, its financing arm (GMAC), plus Hughes Aircraft, Delco, and Electronic Data Systems (thank you, Ross Perot).

All of these other GM divisions are doing so well that if the company can only break even on the U.S. auto business, it could earn $6–8 a share in 1993. Giving these earnings a p/e ratio of 8, the stock should sell for $48–$64, a big advance from the current price. If GM's auto business improves beyond the break-even point, as it should when the economy revives, the company could earn $10 a share.

The closing of several plants will cost thousands of workers their jobs, but it will also enable GM to cut costs in its least profitable enterprise. The company doesn't need to win the war with Japan and recapture the American car buyer. GM is upset that its market share has shrunk from 40 percent to 30 percent, but that's still bigger than the market share of all the Japanese carmakers combined. Even if GM gets only 25 percent of U.S. car buyers, its auto divisions can once again contribute to earnings by scaling down their manufacturing and reducing their expenses (something they have already started to do).

The very week that I'd arrived at this conclusion, the newspapers reported that several GM cars had won major awards, including the much-disparaged Cadillac, which once again had charmed the critics. The trucks looked good, the mid-sized cars looked good, and the company had plenty of cash. Since GM's reputation could hardly be worse, all the surprises should be happy ones.

Stock Symbol	Company	1/13/92 Price
GM	General Motors	$31.00
PD	Phelps Dodge	$32.50

SIXTEEN

NUKES IN DISTRESS

CMS Energy

Utility stocks were the great growth stocks of the 1950s, but since then their main attraction has been yield. For investors who need income, buying utility stocks has been more profitable in the long run than buying CDs from the bank. With a CD, you get the interest plus your money back. With a utility stock you get the dividend, which is likely to be increased every year, plus a chance at a capital gain.

Even in the recent era, when the demand for electricity has slowed in most parts of the country and utilities are no longer regarded as great growth stocks, there have been some big winners in the group, including Southern Company ($11 to $33 in five years), Oklahoma Gas and Electric ($13 to $40), and Philadelphia Electric ($9 to $26).

For brief periods at Magellan, I had 10 percent of the fund invested in utilities. Usually this happened when interest rates were declining and the economy was in a sputter. In other words, I treated the utilities as interest-rate cyclicals, and tried to time my entrances and my exits accordingly.

But the utilities with which I've done the best have been the troubled ones. At Fidelity, we made a bundle for our shareholders on General Public Utilities after the Three Mile Island disaster, and more bundles on Public Service of New Hampshire bonds, Long Island Lighting, Gulf States Utilities, and the old Middle South Utilities, which has changed its name to Entergy. This brings us to Peter's Principle #20:

Corporations, like people, change their names for one of two reasons: either they've gotten married, or they've been involved in some fiasco that they hope the public will forget.

Each of the troubled utilities mentioned above had problems with nuke plants or the financing of nuke plants that never got built, and the nuke fears depressed the stock prices.

The reason my record with troubled utilities is better than with troubled companies in general is that utilities are regulated by the government. A utility may declare bankruptcy and/or eliminate its dividend, but as long as people need electricity, a way must be found for the utility to continue to function.

The regulatory system determines what prices the utility can charge for the electricity or gas, what profit it's allowed to make, and whether the costs of its mistakes can be passed along to the customer. Since the state government has a vested interest in the survival of the enterprise, the odds are overwhelming that the troubled utility will be given the wherewithal to overcome its problems.

Recently, the work of three analysts at the NatWest Investment Banking Group (Kathleen Lally, John Kellenyi, and Philip Smyth) was brought to my attention. Kellenyi I've known for years. He's an excellent analyst.

These utility watchers have identified what they called "the troubled utility cycle," and they give four examples of companies that have lived through it: Consolidated Edison, which faced a cash crisis after the surge in oil prices during the 1973 embargo; Entergy Corporation, which was saddled with a lavish nuke plant it couldn't afford; Long Island Lighting, which built a nuke plant and then couldn't get a license for it; and General Public Utilities, the owner of Three Mile Island Unit Two, which had a famous accident.

The stocks of all four of these utilities in distress fell so far and so fast that their shareholders also were left in distress, and those who sold in the panic have been even more distressed to see the prices quadruple or quintuple on the rebound. Meanwhile, the buyers of these downtrodden shares are celebrating their good fortune, which proves once again that one person's distress is another's opportunity. You had a long time to profit from each of these four recoveries, which, according to the three analysts, proceeded through four recognizable stages.

In the first stage, disaster strikes. The utility is faced with a sudden loss of earnings, either because some huge cost (the increase in fuel prices in Con Ed's case) cannot be passed along to customers, or because a huge asset (usually the nuke plant) is mothballed and removed from the rate base. The stock suffers accordingly and loses anywhere from 40 percent to 80 percent of its value in a one- to two-year period: Con Ed dropped from $6 to $1.50 in 1974, Entergy from $16.75 to $9.25 in 1983–84, General Public Utilities from $9 to $3.88 in 1979–81, and Long Island Lighting from $17.50 to $3.75 in 1983–84. These drops are horrifying to people who regard utilities as safe and stable investments.

Soon enough, the distressed utility is trading at 20–30 percent of its book value. The stock has taken this drubbing because Wall Street is worried that the damage to the company may be fatal, especially when a multibillion-dollar nuke plant has been shut down. How long it takes to reverse this impression varies from disaster to disaster. With Long Island Lighting, the threat of bankruptcy kept the stock selling at 30 percent of book value for four years.

In the second stage, which our trio of experts calls "crisis management," the utility attempts to respond to the disaster by cutting capital spending and adopting an austerity budget. As part of the austerity, the dividend on the stock is reduced or eliminated. It is beginning to look as if the company will survive its difficulties, but the stock price doesn't reflect the improved prospects.

In the third stage, "financial stabilization," management has succeeded in cutting costs to the point that the utility can operate on the cash it receives from its bill-paying customers. The capital markets may be unwilling to lend it money for any new projects, and the utility is still not earning anything for its shareholders, but survival is no longer in doubt. The stock price has recovered somewhat, and the shares are now selling at 60–70 percent of book value. People who bought the stock in stages one or two have doubled their money.

In stage four, "recovery at last!," the utility once again is capable of earning something for the shareholders, and Wall Street has reason to expect improved earnings and the reinstatement of the dividend. The shares now sell at book value. How things progress from here depends on two factors. (1) the reception from the capital markets, because without capital the utility cannot expand its rate base, and (2) the support, or nonsupport, of the regulators, i.e., how many costs they allow the utility to pass along to the customers in the form of higher rates.

Figures 16-1, 16-2, 16-3, and 16-4 show a stock price history for each of our four examples. As you can see, you didn't have to rush into these troubled utilities to make substantial profits. In each instance, you could have waited until the crisis had abated and the doomsayers were proven wrong, and still you could have doubled, tripled, or quadrupled your money in a relatively short period.

Buy on the omission of the dividend and wait for the good news. Or, buy when the first good news has arrived in the second stage. The problem that some people have with this is that if the stock falls to $4 and then rises to $8, they think they have missed it. A troubled nuke has a long way to go, and you have to forget about the fact that you missed the bottom. There's a need here to apply some psychological Wite-Out.

The difference between a troubled nuke and an opera is that the troubled nuke is more likely to have a happy ending. This suggests a simple way to make a nice living from troubled utilities: buy them when the dividend is omitted and hold on to them until the dividend is restored. This is a strategy with a terrific success ratio.

In the summer of 1991, the experts at NatWest identified five more distressed utilities (Gulf States, Illinois Power, Niagara Mohawk, Pinnacle West, and Public Service Company of New Mexico) in various stages of recovery, all selling below their book values. But I had another idea for a *Barron's* recommendation: CMS Energy.

This used to be the old Consumers Power of Michigan. It changed its name after it built the Midland nuclear plant—something it hoped the shareholders would forget. The stock had been sailing along in the $20s and then sank to $4.50 in less than a year, hitting bottom soon after the dividend was omitted in October 1984.

CMS, né Consumers Power, was the latest 10-bagger in the wrong direction, and the latest utility to have designed and constructed an expensive nuke plant on the foolish presumption that the regulators who approved the project throughout its development would allow it to operate in the end. Like Lucy with the football, state utility commissions across the land got into the habit of supporting nuke plants until their owners were fully committed and it was too late for them to reverse direction. Then, at the last minute, the public agencies would snatch away the projects and watch the utilities fall flat on their backs.

When this happened to Consumers Power, the company was forced to take a hefty write-off of $4 billion to cover the costs of building

CONSOLIDATED EDISON CO. OF NEW YORK, INC. (ED)

Electric & gas service in New York City

FIGURE 16-1

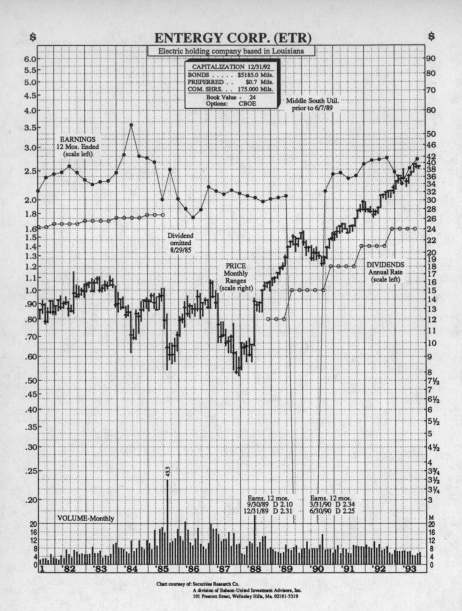

ENTERGY CORP. (ETR)

Electric holding company based in Louisiana

$

CAPITALIZATION 12/31/92
BONDS . . . . . $5185.0 Mils.
PREFERRED . . $0.7 Mils.
COM. SHRS. . . 175.000 Mils.
Book Value - 24
Options: CBOE

Middle South Util.
prior to 6/7/89

EARNINGS
12 Mos. Ended
(scale left)

Dividend
omitted
8/29/85

PRICE
Monthly
Ranges
(scale right)

DIVIDENDS
Annual Rate
(scale left)

Earns. 12 mos.
9/30/89 D 2.10
12/31/89 D 2.31

Earns. 12 mos.
3/31/90 D 2.34
6/30/90 D 2.25

VOLUME-Monthly

1   '82   '83   '84   '85   '86   '87   '88   '89   '90   '91   '92   '93

Chart courtesy of: Securities Research Co.
A division of Babson-United Investment Advisors, Inc.
101 Prescott Street, Wellesley Hills, Ma. 02181-3319

FIGURE 16-2

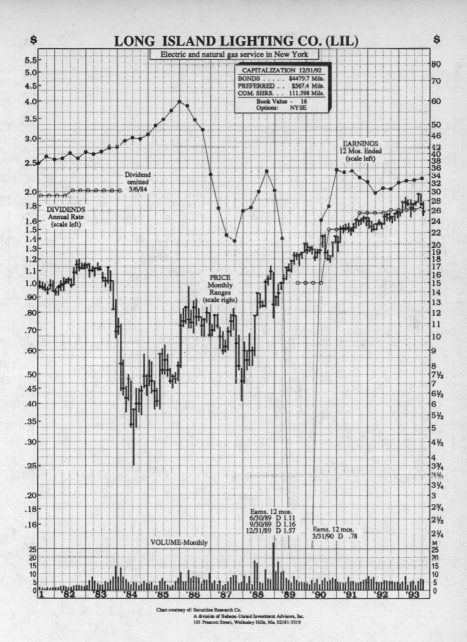

FIGURE 16-3

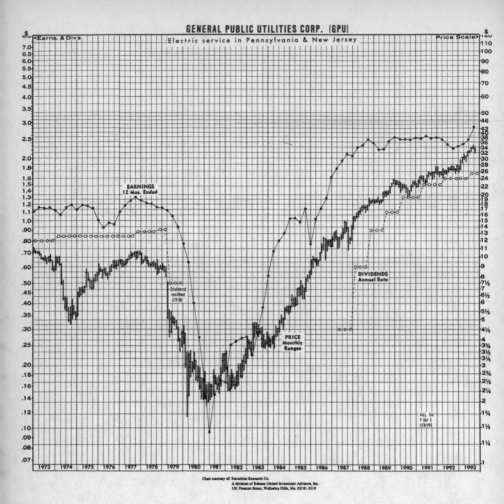

FIGURE 16-4

the nuke plant it wasn't allowed to use. As Wall Street saw it, bankruptcy was not far from the doorstep.

But CMS did not go bankrupt, and by the end of the 1980s it had made the best of a bad situation by converting the unusable nuclear plant to natural gas. This conversion (carried out with the help of Dow Chemical, CMS's biggest customer) was expensive, but not as expensive as watching a $4 billion investment go to waste. The converted plant was opened in March of 1990, at a cost of $1,600 per kilowatt, which was somewhat under budget, and the plant seemed to be working fine. The stock had come all the way back and then some, to $36 a share, for a ninefold gain in five years. But then a couple of unfavorable rate decisions by the Michigan Public Service Commission drove the price down to $17, which is where it was when I stumbled onto it.

The story came to me through Danny Frank, manager of Fidelity's Special Situations Fund, who had brought several of the troubled nukes to Fidelity's attention. Frank had thoroughly investigated the situation at CMS. He indicated that CMS's latest problems, which mostly had to do with an unfriendly commission, did not justify the 50 percent devaluation in the price of the stock.

On January 6, 1992, I talked to CMS's new president, Victor Fryling, whom I'd met years earlier when he worked for the energy/pipeline company Coastal. Fryling mentioned a couple of positive developments. The first was that the Midland plant, converted to gas, was producing electricity at a cost of 6 cents per kilowatt, as compared to the 9.2 cents it normally costs to produce electricity from a new coal plant and the 13.3 cents from a nuke. Midland was a low-cost operation, the kind I like.

The second was that demand for electricity in Michigan was on the rise. It had grown 12 years in a row. Even in the recession of 1991, the region consumed 1 percent more electricity than it did in the prior year. On peak days for electricity use, CMS had only 19.6 percent in extra generating capacity held in reserve, which in utility circles is considered a very thin margin. There were few new plants coming on line in the Midwest to satisfy the growing demand, and it takes 6–12 years to build one from scratch. Even some old ones were being retired. From Economics 101 you learn that when demand grows faster than supply, higher prices result. Higher prices produce more profits.

CMS's balance sheet still had a lot of debt left over from the nuclear fiasco. It sold $1 billion worth of bonds to finance Midland's conversion to gas. (I noted that bondholders must have had faith in these bonds, because the price had increased since the initial offering.) CMS had also sold $500 million worth of senior notes, which I was glad to see were not callable for 10 years. When a company is deeply indebted, you want it to be a debt that doesn't have to be paid in full anytime soon.

CMS had enough cash flow to pay the interest to its lenders, and then some. I assured myself of that by reading the balance sheet. I took the earnings and added those to the depreciation, then divided by the number of shares and came up with a cash flow of $6 a share. Since most of CMS's generating equipment was new, the company was not forced to spend a lot of money on repairs. What was set aside for depreciation could be used for other purposes. The company could (a) buy back its own stock, (b) make acquisitions, or (c) increase the dividend, all of which would eventually benefit the shareholders. My preference was for (a) and (c).

I asked Fryling about CMS's plans for the cash. He said CMS was going to use it to expand the gas plant and to improve the efficiency of the transmission lines, both of which would add to the company's generating capacity. When a utility adds, say, 10 percent to capacity, it automatically adds 10 percent to its earnings, based on the formula that is applied by the regulators who set the rates. It is a wonderful thing for shareholders when a utility builds a new plant (one that gets a license to operate, at least) or takes other steps to increase capacity. When capacity grows, so does the rate base, and so do the earnings.

Fryling and I also discussed the recent oil discovery in Ecuador, on land that CMS owns jointly with Conoco. Production is scheduled to begin in 1993, and if this goes according to plan, CMS will receive $25 million in annual profits by 1995. This $25 million will add 20 cent a share to earnings. Fryling also informed me that the so-called Power Group, a CMS subsidiary that owns several small cogeneration plants and has been losing money of late, could turn a profit by 1993.

CMS had hoped to go to Long Island and help Long Island Lighting convert its Shoreham nuke plant, idled by politics, to natural gas. This collaboration fell apart in 1991. But the greatest ongoing disappointment was with the regulators.

A utility in the final stages of recovery depends on regulators to treat it gently and pass along the costs of its mistakes, but the Michigan commission was uncooperative. It had handed down three unfavorable rate decisions in a row and had refused to let CMS charge its customers the full price of the natural gas burned at the Midland plant.

Apparently, the company had reason to believe that a recent appointee to the commission would be more accommodating, i.e., only mildly hostile. Mildly hostile would be an improvement over the commission's traditional attitude. The commission's own staff had produced a study that favored certain concessions to CMS, and the full commission would soon be voting on these concessions.

If CMS got a reasonable decision from the company's point of view, it would be allowed to earn $2 a share in the upcoming year, as opposed to the $1.30 that Wall Street was expecting, and the earnings could grow steadily thereafter. This possibility was much on my mind when I recommended the stock in *Barron's*.

I also thought CMS was more than just a gamble on Michigan regulatory politics. In the long run, I expected the company to thrive with or without an accommodative public service commission. Its powerful cash flow would enable it to reenter the ranks of the strong utilities, and when that happened it could once again borrow money at lower interest rates.

If all items were resolved in the company's favor, CMS would be allowed to earn $2.20, and if not, it would earn in the neighborhood of $1.50, but either way it would prosper in the long run. If the regulators restricted its earnings, it could plow the cash back into more generating capacity and grow the business internally. With the stock selling at $18, and below book value, I saw a lot of potential reward without much risk.

If you don't like CMS Energy, you can always look into the hapless Public Service Company of New Mexico or the more hapless Tucson Electric. You can be sure that the investor relations person won't be too busy to talk to you.

Stock Symbol	Company	1/13/92 Price
CMS	CMS Energy	$18.50

SEVENTEEN

UNCLE SAM'S GARAGE SALE

Allied Capital II

When Uncle Sam or the Queen of England is having a garage sale, I always try to attend. Not-So-Great Britain is way ahead of us in sponsoring these events, having sold everything from the waterworks to the airlines, but if our own deficit spending continues at the present rate, someday we may have to privatize the national parks, the Kennedy Space Center, and even the White House Rose Garden just to pay the interest on our national debt.

Privatization is a strange concept. You take something that's owned by the public and then sell it back to the public, and from then on, it's private. From a practical standpoint, what's useful to know about this is that whenever the Americans or the British have privatized something by selling shares in it, it's usually been a good deal for the buyers.

The reason is not hard to imagine. In the democratic countries, the buyers of privatized industries are also voters, and governments have enough trouble getting reelected without having to contend with a mass of disgruntled investors who've lost money on the telephone company or the gasworks.

The British learned this lesson in 1983, after two of their earliest privatizations, Britoil and Amersham International, came out overpriced, creating widespread ill will when the prices declined. Since then, the British have structured their offers so it's been unlikely that investors would lose, at least in the early going. British Telecom doubled in price in one day. Three million Brits snapped up the shares. No wonder the Tories are still in office. This leads us to Peter's Principle #21:

Whatever the queen is selling, buy it.

A few years ago, I was introduced to a tempting proposition from a British contingent that showed up in our offices at Fidelity. They introduced each other as Lord So-and-So and Sir So-and-So. They brought along a large bound volume which proved to be a prospectus for a group of British water utilities that were about to be privatized. The prospectus was numbered like the limited edition of a rare print. On the cover were the names and the corporate logos of the new companies—Northumbrian Water, Severn Trent, Yorkshire Water, Welsh Water PLC, etc.

Even though Magellan had already taken part in the bonanzas of British Telecom (the largest public flotation the world had ever seen at the time—$4 billion) and British Airways, I was unprepared for the benefits that were built into these waterworks deals. They were monopolies, just as water utilities everywhere tend to be—it's always nice to own a monopoly. The British government, before setting them free, had absorbed most of the prior debt.

These companies were coming out debt free, with extra capital provided by the government, which had given them a "green dowry" to get them off on the right foot. They agreed to embark on a 10-year program of upgrading the water systems, an effort that would be partially subsidized by the green dowry, with the rest paid for by an increase in water bills.

In our conversation in my office, the water lords told me that water bills in England were so low (100 pounds a year) that even if these prices doubled the customers would not resent it. Even if they did resent it, there was nothing they could do about it except stop using water, which was unlikely. Water demand in England was growing at 1 percent a year.

These new water shares could be bought on the installment plan, just like cars or stereos or rugs. You could put 40 percent down and pay the rest in two easy installments, one due in 12 months and the other in 20 months. The British had offered the same sort of deal, which they called "partially paid shares," on British Telecom. When British Telecom came public at $30, all the buyer had to pay was $6 down. Then, when the share price rose to $36, the buyer who paid $6 could sell and double his money.

The implications of this partial-paid concept I failed to appreciate with British Telecom. I thought the stock price was going up too fast, but when I finally understood the benefits of the partial-paid feature, I could see that the buying frenzy was justified. The same sort of deal was offered with the water companies, as follows.

In addition to allowing you to buy shares on the installment plan, the water companies paid an 8 percent dividend, beginning immediately. For at least a year, you got this 8 percent dividend on the full value of shares you acquired at 40 percent down. That gave you a 20 percent return on your investment in the first 12 months—even if the stock price stayed flat.

The British water shares were understandably quite popular. Before the initial public offering, U.S. fund managers and other institutional investors were given an allotment. For Magellan, I took everything I was allotted, and then bought more shares in the aftermarket, as they began to trade on the London Stock Exchange. A portfolio of all five of the water utilities doubled in value in three years.

The other British companies sold to the public have done just as well or better in the six months to one year after the offerings. This brings us to another what-if fund, the Queen's Garage Sale Fund. Any U.S. investor could have put together a portfolio of the stocks shown in Table 17-1 and gotten the results shown there.

Every time a telephone company has been privatized, in whatever country—the Philippines, Mexico, Spain—the shareholders have reaped once-in-a-lifetime rewards. Politicians around the world are dedicated to improving phone service, and in the developing countries there is such a hunger for phones that these companies are growing at 20–30 percent a year. What you've got here is the growth rate of a small growth company, the size and stability of a blue chip, and the guaranteed success of a monopoly. If you missed AT&T in 1910, you could have made up for it with Spanish and Mexican telephones in the late 1980s.

Magellan shareholders made a lot of money on Mexican telephones. You didn't need to visit the Mexican telephone company to see that a bonanza was coming. The country knew it had to

Table 17-1. QUEEN'S GARAGE SALE FUND

Company Name	Shares Issued On	% Increase One Year Later
British Airways	2/81	103.0
British Gas	12/86	194.0
British Steel	12/88	116.0
British Telecom	11/84	200.0
Northumbrian Water	12/89	75.9
Severn Trent	12/89	54.6
Welsh Water	12/89	76.9
Yorkshire Water	12/89	74.4

Source: DataStream
Based on price of shares sold in U.S. market.

improve the phone service before the rest of the economy could expand. Phones were as important as roads. The country also knew that it couldn't have a good phone system without a well-capitalized, well-managed phone company. And it couldn't attract the capital without allowing shareholders to make a decent profit.

Here's another great what-if portfolio, Telephones of the Emerging Nations:

Table 17-2. TELEPHONES OF EMERGING NATIONS

Company Name	% Increase	Time Period
Compañía de Teléfonos de Chile	210.0	7/90–9/92
Teléfonos de México	774.8	7/90–9/92
Hong Kong Telecommunications Ltd.	72.3	12/88–9/92
Telefónica de España	100.0	6/87–9/92
Philippine Long Distance	565.0	1/90–9/92

Based on prices of shares sold in U.S. market, in dollars

By 1990, sales of privatized companies worldwide had reached $200 billion, with more to come. The French have sold their electric utilities and their trains, Scotland has sold its hydroelectric plants, the Spaniards and the Argentinians have parceled out their oil companies, the Mexicans their airlines. Britain may someday sell its railways and its ports, Japan its bullet trains, Korea its state-run bank, Thailand its airline, Greece a cement company, and Portugal its telephones.

In the U.S. there hasn't been as much privatizing as we've seen abroad, because there isn't as much to privatize here. Our oil companies, phone companies, and electric companies were private to begin with. The biggest recent deal was Conrail, or, more formally, the Consolidated Rail Corporation, which was assembled from the wreckage of Penn Central and five other bankrupt lines in the Northeast. For several years the government ran Conrail at a deficit, until the Reagan administration decided that taking Conrail private was the only way to stop it from seeking more government handouts, which already had exceeded $7 billion.

Some political factions favored selling Conrail to an existing railroad, with Norfolk Southern the most likely buyer, but after much congressional wrangling, a plan to sell it to the public prevailed. In March 1987, Conrail became the largest public offering in U.S. history, $1.6 billion. The government spent a fortune gold-plating this railroad, upgrading the rails and equipment, and pumping in money. The initial price was $10 a share, and as of this writing that same share is worth $46.

At a gathering to celebrate the Conrail deal, President Reagan quipped: "OK, when do we sell the TVA?" Of course, no serious attempt has ever been made to privatize the Tennessee Valley Authority, but if it happened, I'd be standing in line for the prospectus. There was talk, once, of privatizing Amtrak, and also the naval petroleum reserves in California and Wyoming, and I'd stand in line for those prospectuses, too. Maybe someday they'll sell off the National Gallery or the Marine Band or Niagara Falls.

As it was, there were no exciting new privatizations coming to market at the time I was looking for stocks for the *Barron's* panel. The old ones that I follow, such as the Mexican telephone company (the original Taco Bell) and the Spanish telephone company (Flamenco Bell), had made big gains in the prior year and seemed to be getting ahead of themselves. Did this mean there was no way for an investor to profit from government giveaways in 1992? Not as long as we've got a Resolution Trust Corporation.

We've already discussed one way to take advantage of the S&L mess—buying shares in the healthy S&Ls that are acquiring the branches and the deposits of their failed brethren. Another way was to buy stock in a company called Allied Capital II.

Allied Capital is one of the few venture capital firms that is publicly traded. It lends money, mostly to small companies, and in return gets a relatively high rate of interest plus a "kicker" (stock options, warrants, etc.) that gives Allied a stake in the profits if the venture succeeds. This strategy has been so productive that a person who invested $10,000 in Allied Capital I when it came public in 1960 is sitting on a $1.5 million nest egg today.

One tangible result of an Allied Capital start up loan is the air purifier that sits in our bedroom in Marblehead. This amazing piece of equipment removes so much grit from the air that our bedroom has the air quality rating of a genetic engineering lab. I've given one of these units to my mother-in-law and one to my secretary so they, too, can rid their lives of dust. The machine is made by Envirocare, a high-tech firm in which Allied Capital now has a large equity interest to go along with its loan.

Recently, the people from Allied Capital decided to perform an encore. They created a second pool of money ($92 million) by selling shares in Allied Capital II, which now trades on the over-the-counter market. The basic idea was the same as for the first Allied. The company borrows against its pool of money, in this case $92 million, to raise another $92 million. Now it has a pool of $184 million. It uses this $184 million to buy loans that pay, say, 10 percent interest.

If Allied II's own cost of borrowing is, say 8 percent, and it acquires a portfolio of loans that pay 10 percent, it can make a comfortable spread for its shareholders, plus the occasional equity "kicker" as described above. The company has few employees and few expenses.

The key to Allied's success has been the management's ability to get its money back. Unlike bankers, the lenders at Allied have been very picky about who can borrow the money, and very stringent about how much collateral the borrowers must put up. Allied Capital II, I'd heard, was using a portion of its pool of money to buy loans from the Resolution Trust Corporation.

We normally think of the Resolution Trust Corporation as selling condos, golf courses, gold-plated flatware, overpriced artwork, and corporate jets once flown by the owners of the bankrupt S&Ls. But the RTC also sells loans that were made by those wild and crazy guys. Among the many bum loans in these S&L portfolios, there are actually some good ones advanced to reputable borrowers with solid collateral.

Wall Street investment houses and the big banks have bought up many such loans in the multimillion-dollar category, but the loans of $1 million or less have not been so easy for the RTC to unload.

It's here that Allied Capital II had planned to enter the auction.

I called the company to assure myself that the same team that ran the original Allied Capital was also making the decisions at Allied Capital II. It was. Shares in Allied II were selling for $19, with a 6 percent dividend. Investing in Allied II seemed like a simple way to turn the S&L fiasco into something advantageous. Here was a chance to make back some of the taxes we all have to pay to finance the S&L bailout.

Stock Symbol	Company	1/13/92 Price
ALII	Allied Capital Corporation II	$19.00

EIGHTEEN

MY FANNIE MAE DIARY

Every year since 1986, I've recommended Fannie Mae to the *Barron's* panel. It's getting to be boring. I touted it in 1986 as the "best business, literally, in America," noting that Fannie Mae had a quarter of the employees of Fidelity and 10 times the profits. I touted it in 1987 as the "ultimate savings and loan." In 1988, I said it was "a much better company than it was a year ago, and the stock is eight points lower." In 1989, when Alan Abelson asked, "What is your favorite stock?" I answered, "A company that you have heard of before, the Federal National Mortgage Association."

It's no accident that there's a snapshot of Fannie Mae headquarters alongside the family photographs on the memento shelf in my office It warms my heart to think of the place. The stock has been so great they ought to retire the symbol.

During my final three years at Magellan, Fannie Mae was the biggest position in the fund—half a billion dollars' worth. Other Fidelity funds also loaded up on Fannie Mae. Between the stock and the warrants (options to buy more shares at a certain price), Fidelity and its clients made more than $1 billion in profits on Fannie Mae in the 1980s.

I'm submitting this result to the *Guinness Book of World Records*: most money ever made by one mutual-fund group on one stock in the history of finance.

Was Fannie Mae an obvious winner? In hindsight, yes, but a company does not tell you to buy it. There is always something to worry about. There are always respected investors who say that you're wrong. You have to know the story better than they do, and have faith in what you know.

For a stock to do better than expected, the company has to be widely underestimated. Otherwise, it would sell for a higher price to begin with. When the prevailing opinion is more negative than yours, you have to constantly check and recheck the facts, to reassure yourself that you're not being foolishly optimistic.

The story keeps changing, for either better or worse, and you have to follow those changes and act accordingly. With Fannie Mae, Wall Street was ignoring the changes. The old Fannie Mae had made such a powerful impression that people had a hard time seeing the new Fannie Mae emerging in front of their eyes. I saw it, but not right away. Not right away was still soon enough to make a sixfold profit on a $200 million investment. This is my Fannie Mae diary.

1977

I took my first position in this $5 stock. What did I know about the company? It was founded in 1938 as a government-owned enterprise and then was privatized in the 1960s. Its function in life was to provide liquidity in the mortgage market, which it accomplished by buying mortgages from banks and S&Ls. Its motto was "Borrow short and lend long." Fannie Mae borrowed money at cheap rates, used the money to buy long-term mortgages that paid higher fixed rates, and pocketed the difference.

This strategy worked OK in periods when interest rates were going down. Fannie Mae earned a lot of money during such times, because the cost of its borrowing decreased while the proceeds from its portfolio of fixed-rate mortgages stayed constant. When interest rates went up, the cost of borrowing increased, and Fannie Mae lost a lot of money.

I sold the stock a few months after I bought it, for a small profit. I saw that interest rates were going up.

1981

Fannie Mae had a lot in common with the heroine of *The Perils of Pauline*: it was trying to avert the latest calamity. All the long-term mortgages it had bought in the mid-70s were paying from 8 to 10 percent. Meanwhile, short-term rates had skyrocketed to 18–20 percent. You can't get very far by borrowing at 18 to make 9. Investors knew this, which is why the stock, which sold for as much as $9 a share in 1974, fell to a historic low of $2.

This was one of those rare periods when a homeowner could say: "My house is OK, but my mortgage is beautiful." Out the window there might be a slag heap, but people didn't want to move. They were staying put for the sake of their beautiful mortgages. This was bad for the banks, and terrible for Fannie Mae. There were rumors the company would go out of business.

1982

Under my nose, Fannie Mae was about to undergo a major personality change. Some people noticed. Elliot Schneider of Gruntal & Co., an analyst who was known as the world's most dedicated Fannie watcher, predicted to his clients: "Fannie Mae will become the kind of girl you bring home to mother."

The company we all thought we understood as an interest-rate play, losing millions one year, making millions the next, was trying to reinvent itself. A guy named David Maxwell was brought in. Maxwell was a lawyer and former insurance commissioner of Pennsylvania who earlier had started his own mortgage insurance company and made a success of it. He knew the industry.

Maxwell was determined to put a stop to Fannie Mae's wild swings. He wanted to turn the company into a stable, mature enterprise with reliable earnings. This he hoped to accomplish in two ways: (1) by putting an end to borrow short–lend long and (2) by imitating Freddie Mac.

Freddie Mac, formally known as the Federal Home Loan Mortgage Corporation, was also started by the federal government. Its mission was to purchase mortgages exclusively from S&Ls. Freddie Mac became a publicly traded company in 1970. In addition to simply buying mortgages and holding them, Freddie Mac had stumbled onto the newfangled idea of packaging mortgages.

The idea was simple: buy a bunch of mortgages, bundle them together, and sell the bundle to banks, S&Ls, insurance companies, college or charitable endowments, etc.

Fannie Mae copied the Freddie Mac idea and began packaging mortgages in 1982. Let's say you had a mortgage on your house that came from Bank X. Bank X would sell your mortgage to Fannie Mae. Fannie Mae would lump it together with other mortgages to create a "mortgage-backed security." It could then sell the mortgage-backed security to anybody, even back to the banks that had originated the mortgages in the package.

Fannie Mae got a nice fee for doing this. And by selling mortgages that it used to hold in its own portfolio, it passed the interest-rate risk on to new buyers.

This packaging service was very popular in banking circles. Before mortgage-backed securities came along, banks and S&Ls were stuck with owning thousands of little mortgages. It was hard to keep track of them, and it was hard to sell them in a pinch. Now the banks could sell all their little mortgages to Fannie Mae and use the proceeds to make more mortgages, so their money wasn't tied up. If they still wanted to own mortgages, they could buy a few mortgage-backed securities from that same Fannie Mae.

Soon there was a market for the mortgage-backed securities, and they could be traded instantly, like a stock or a bond or a bottle of vodka in Moscow. Mortgages by the thousands, and later by the millions, were converted into packages. This little invention, if you could even call it that, was destined to become a $300-billion-a-year industry, bigger than Big Steel or Big Coal or Big Oil.

But in 1982, I was still looking at Fannie Mae as an interest-rate play. I bought the stock for the second time in my career, as interest rates were falling. In the notes I took after calling the company on November 23, 1982, I wrote: ". . . I figure they'll make $5 a share." That year the stock rebounded in typical Fannie Mae fashion, from $2 to $9. This is what happens with cyclicals: the company loses money in 1982 and the stock increases fourfold, as investors anticipate the next golden age.

1983

When I called in February, the company was doing $1 billion a month in these new mortgage-backed securities. It occurred to me that Fannie Mae was like a bank, but also had major advantages over a bank. Banks had 2–3 percent overhead. Fannie Mae could pay its expenses on a .2 percent overhead. It didn't have a blimp. It didn't give away toaster ovens. It didn't pay Phil Rizzuto to advertise mortgage-backed securities on TV. Its entire payroll was around 1,300 people, spread out in four offices located in four different cities. The Bank of America had as many branches as Fannie Mae had employees.

Thanks to its status as a quasigovernmental agency, Fannie Mae could borrow money more cheaply than any bank, more cheaply than IBM or General Motors or thousands of other companies. It could, for instance, borrow money for 15 years at 8 percent, use the money to buy a 15-year mortgage at 9 percent, and earn a 1 percent spread.

No bank, S&L, or other financial company in America could make a profit on a 1 percent spread. It doesn't sound like much, but a 1 percent spread on $100 billion worth of loans is still $1 billion.

Fannie Mae had begun to chip away at what it called the "block of granite"—the portfolio of long-term mortgages it had acquired in the mid-1970s at unfavorable rates. This was a slow process. The mortgages would roll over and Fannie Mae would replace them with mortgages that paid higher rates of interest. Still it owned $60 billion worth, yielding a collective 9.24 percent, when the average cost of its debt was 11.87 percent.

The company had gotten the attention of Thomas Hearns at Merrill Lynch, Mark Alpert at Bear Stearns, and Thomas Klingenstein at Wertheim. A lot of analysts were saying good things about it. They saw that further declines in interest rates would, as one of them said, "explode the earnings."

After eight straight quarters of losses, Fannie Mae actually posted a profit in 1983. The stock went nowhere.

1984

My commitment to the stock was a whopping .1 percent of Magellan's assets. But even a small position enabled me to keep in touch. I increased it, gingerly, to .37 percent by the end of the year. The stock fell in half again, from $9 to $4, and in typical old Fannie Mae style—interest rates rose and earnings fell. The benefits of mortgage-backed securities were still outweighed by the block of granite.

To avoid this predicament in the future, Fannie Mae had begun to "match" its borrowing to its lending. Instead of borrowing short-term money at the cheapest rates, it was offering 3-, 5-, and 10-year bonds at higher rates. This increased Fannie Mae's cost of money, penalizing earnings in the short term. But in the long run it made the company less vulnerable to the swings in rates that had been its bugaboo in the past.

1985

The potential of these things was beginning to dawn on me. Mortgage-backed securities could be a huge industry—Fannie Mae was now packaging $23 billion of these a year, twice the number in 1983–84. Big pieces from the block of granite were being chipped away. Management now talked about "the old portfolio" and "the new portfolio." There were two different businesses here: packaging mortgages and selling them, and originating mortgages and holding on to them.

A new fear crept in: not interest rates, but Texas. Crazy S&Ls down there had been lending money in the oil-patch boom. People in Houston who'd gotten mortgages with 5 percent down were leaving the keys in the door and walking away from their houses and their mortgages. Fannie Mae owned a lot of these mortgages.

In May, I visited the company in Washington and spoke to David Maxwell. Several important competitors in the mortgage business had dropped out. With fewer competitors buying and selling mortgages, the profit margins on loans had widened. This would boost Fannie Mae's earnings.

I must have been impressed with Fannie Mae's progress. I bought more stock—enough to make Fannie Mae 2 percent of the fund, one of my top 10 holdings.

Beginning in July, I called Paul Paquin at the investor relations department for regular updates. The two numbers that appeared most frequently on my office phone bills were for Fannie Mae and my house in Marblehead.

Here's the key question to ask about a risky yet promising stock: if things go right, how much can I earn? What's the reward side of the equation? I figured that if Fannie Mae could pay for its overhead on the proceeds from mortgage-backed securities and then make 1 percent on its own $100 billion portfolio, it could earn $7 a share. At 1985 prices, that gave the stock a p/e ratio of 1. When a company can earn back the price of its stock in one year, you've found a good deal.

At first, I took pages and pages of notes on my conversations with Fannie Mae, but now I knew the company so well I could jot down the new developments on a single sheet.

Fannie Mae lost 87 cents a share in 1984 but made 52 cents in 1985. The stock rebounded from $4 to $9.

1986

I retreated a bit. Now only 1.8 percent of the fund was invested in Fannie Mae. Wall Street was still worrying about Texas and the keys in the doors. Here in my notes of May 19 was a more important development: Fannie Mae had just sold $10 billion of its block of granite, and only $30 billion of these unfavorable loans remained. For the first time, I told myself: "This stock is a buy on the mortgage-backed securities alone!"

Another new card that turned up: Fannie Mae was tightening its lending standards on new mortgages. This turned out to be a very smart move, because it protected Fannie Mae in the next recession. While banks like Citicorp were making it easier to get mortgages with little documentation—no-doc mortgages, low-doc mortgages, call-the-doc mortgages—Fannie Mae was making it harder. Fannie Mae did not want to repeat the Texas mistake. In that state, it was promoting the no-way-José mortgage.

The blemishes on Fannie Mae were obscuring the beauty of the mortgage-backed securities. This business was sure to grow, as refinancing turned into the national pastime. Even if new houses weren't selling, the mortgage business would grow. Old people would move out of old houses and new people would buy the old houses, and new mortgages would have to be written. Many of these would end up in Fannie Mae's packages, and Fannie Mae would get more fees.

The company had remade itself, and was on the verge of the great explosion that Thomas Klingenstein foresaw in 1983, yet most analysts were now skeptical. Montgomery Securities told its clients that "Fannie Mae is overvalued relative to the average thrift in our coverage." Was this really an average thrift? "The significant recent drop in oil prices," Montgomery continued, "could negatively impact the firm's $18.5 billion in mortgages exposed to the [Southwest] region."

Fannie Mae was chipping away at the block of granite. It sold another $10 billion of its old mortgages that carried interest rates unfavorable to Fannie Mae.

In the last five months of 1986, the stock rose from $8 to $12. The company earned $1.44 for the year.

1987

Between 2 and 2.3 percent of Magellan was invested in Fannie Mae throughout the year. The stock seesawed from $12 to $16, back to $12, back to $16, and then suffered a setback to $8 in the Great Correction of October. Wiggle watchers were befuddled.

I'm getting ahead of myself. In February, I talked to four Fannie Mae executives on a conference call. I learned that foreclosures on houses with Fannie Mae mortgages were still on the rise. Fannie Mae had taken back so many houses in Texas that it had become the biggest real-estate mogul in Texas, literally by default.

Thirty-eight Fannie Mae employees were working in Houston alone to get rid of these houses. The company had to spend millions on foreclosure actions, and millions more to cut the grass and paint the stoops and otherwise maintain the abandoned houses until buyers could be found. At the moment, buyers were scarce.

The housing market in Alaska had also deteriorated. Fortunately for Fannie Mae, the Alaska housing market is very small.

In my mind, these negatives were overshadowed by the amazing success of mortgage-backed securities—$100 billion worth packaged in this single year. Also, Fannie Mae had solved the problem of ups and downs. It no longer qualified as a cyclical. It was beginning to resemble Bristol-Myers or General Electric, a steady grower with predictable earnings. But it was growing much faster than Bristol-Myers. Its earnings had jumped from 83 cents to $1.55.

On October 13, days before the Great Correction, I called the company again. David Maxwell, the CEO, made an interesting statement that confirmed my suppositions: if interest rates were to rise 3 percent, he said, Fannie Mae's earnings would decline by only 50 cents. Never could such a thing have been said about the old Fannie Mae. This was a watershed—the company was telling us that the transformation had succeeded.

Along with the rest of the stocks, Fannie Mae got clobbered on October 19. Investors were panicky and commentators predicted the end of the world. I was comforted by the fact that whereas Fannie Mae's foreclosure rate was still rising, its 90-day delinquencies were falling. Since delinquencies lead to foreclosures, this fall in the delinquency rate suggested that Fannie Mae had already seen the worst.

I reminded myself of the Even Bigger Picture, that stocks in good companies are worth owning. I was convinced Fannie Mae was a good company—what was the worst thing that could happen to it? A recession that turned into a depression? In that situation, interest rates would drop, and Fannie Mae would benefit by refinancing its debt at lower short-term rates. As long as people were paying on their mortgages, Fannie Mae would be the most lucrative business left on the planet.

As the end of the world approached and people stopped paying their mortgages, Fannie Mae would go down with the banking system and all the other systems, but it wouldn't happen overnight. The last thing people would give up on (except in Houston, apparently) would be their houses. I couldn't imagine a better place to be invested in the twilight of civilization than Fannie Mae stock.

Fannie Mae must have agreed with me. In the aftermath of the Great Correction, the company announced it was buying back up to 5 million shares.

1988

There are different shades of buys. There's the "What else I am going to buy?" buy. There's the "Maybe this will work out" buy. There's the "Buy now and sell later" buy. There's the "buy for your mother-in-law" buy. There's the "Buy for your mother-in-law and all the aunts, uncles, and cousins" buy. There's the "Sell the house and put the money into this" buy. There's the "Sell the house, the boat, the cars, and the barbecue and put the money into this" buy. There's the "Sell the house, boat, cars, and barbecue, and insist your mother-in-law, aunts, uncles, and cousins do the same" buy. That's what Fannie Mae was becoming.

I boosted Magellan's holding to 3 percent throughout most of 1988. The company earned $2.14, up from $1.55. Sixty percent of its mortgage portfolio had been acquired under the new, tougher standards.

Fannie Mae's foreclosures had dropped for the first time since 1984. In addition, the government had new accounting rules on the mortgage business. Heretofore, mortgage commitment fees were "booked" as income as soon as Fannie Mae received them. The company might receive $100 million in fees one quarter and $10 million the next. This accounting system caused severe fluctuations in Fannie Mae's quarterly earnings. It was not uncommon for Fannie

Mae to report a "down" quarter, which would scare investors and create a sell-off in the stock.

Under the new rules, commitment fees had to be amortized over the life of each new mortgage loan. Fannie Mae has not suffered a down quarter since these rules went into effect.

1989

I noted that great investor Warren Buffett owned 2.2 million shares. I talked to the company several times. July showed a major improvement in nonperforming assets. There was a small problem with defaults in Colorado, but the Texas problem was going away. Miracle of miracles: house prices were on the rise in Houston.

From the National Delinquency Survey, my latest bedside entertainment, I learned that Fannie Mae's 90-day delinquency rate had dropped again, from 1.1 percent in 1988 to .6 percent in 1989. I also checked the "price of the median house" statistic to reassure myself that home prices weren't collapsing. They weren't. They were rising, as usual.

This was the year I backed up the truck. "Backing up the truck" is a technical Wall Street term for buying as many shares as you can afford. Now 4 percent of Magellan's assets were invested in Fannie Mae, and toward the end of the year I reached my 5 percent limit. It was my largest position by far.

Fannie Mae was now packaging $225 billion worth of new mortgage-backed securities. It would now earn $400 million a year from a packaging business that didn't exist in 1981. Not an S&L in the universe wanted to own a mortgage now. They shipped them all off to Freddie Mac or Fannie Mae.

Finally, Wall Street was catching on to the idea that this company could continue to grow at a 15–20 percent rate. The stock rose from $16 to $42, a two-and-a-half-bagger in one year. As so often happens in the stock market, several years' worth of patience was rewarded in one.

Even at this higher price, Fannie Mae was still undervalued, with a p/e of 10. A negative article on the housing market, called "Crumbling Castles," appeared in *Barron's* in December. The tag line read: "The Recession in Real Estate Has Ominous Implications." The illustration showed a two-story house with a sign in the front yard that pleaded: "For Rent, for Sale, for Anything!"

If it weren't for the housing fear that refused to die, Fannie Mae would have been a $100 stock.

1990

I tried to maintain the 5 percent limit, the maximum allowed by the SEC. Fannie Mae's shares had increased in price to the point that for a short period the holding actually represented 6 percent of the value of the fund. This was OK, as long as the 5 percent limit had been exceeded because the stock price had gone up, and not because I'd bought more shares.

In the summer and fall, I watched with fascination as more weekend worrying sank this stock just when everything in the company was going right. Saddam Hussein had invaded Kuwait, and we had invaded Saddam. The worry this time was that the Gulf War would produce a national depression in real estate, a coast-to-coast version of the Texas calamity. Hundreds of thousands of people would be walking away from their homes and sending the keys to Fannie Mae. Fannie Mae would become the nation's landlord, wasting all its billions on paint, for-sale signs, and lawyers' bills.

Never in all my years of seeing worthy companies get clobbered for no good reason had I seen one that deserved it less. Fannie Mae's delinquency problems were now minuscule, but still it suffered from fear by association. In November 1990, *The Wall Street Journal* published an article entitled "Citicorp Lenders Lament," which described how that bank's loan delinquencies had increased from 2.4 percent to 3.5 percent. This had nothing to do with Fannie Mae, but the price of Fannie Mae stock (along with that of many mortgage-related issues) fell in sympathy.

What a pity for the shareholders who paid attention to the big global picture instead of the goings-on at the company and sold their shares because of the coming depression in housing. Except for the fat-cat houses, there was no coming depression in housing. The National Association of Realtors subsequently reported that in 1990, and again in 1991, the price of an average house increased in value.

If you kept up with the story, you knew that Fannie Mae hadn't written any fat-cat mortgages above $202,000, so it wasn't involved in the trophy-house market. Its average mortgage was $90,000. You knew it had tightened its underwriting standards, and no longer made Texas-style loans on 5 percent down. You knew that the mortgage-backed securities business was still growing at a fast clip.

Fannie Mae stock fell from $42 to $24 in the Saddam Sell-off, and then promptly rose again to $38.

1991

I was gone from Magellan. It was up to my successor, Morris Smith, to keep tabs on Fannie Mae. He did and the stock remained the number-one holding. The price rose again from $38 to $60. The company had record earnings of $1.1 billion.

1992

For the sixth year in a row, I recommended Fannie Mae in *Barron's*. The stock was selling for $69 and earning $6, giving it a p/e ratio of 11, which compared very favorably with the market's p/e of 23.

Once again, the underlying story had improved. Fannie Mae was reducing its interest-rate risk by issuing callable debt. Callable debt gave Fannie Mae the right to buy back its bonds when such a move would be favorable to the company, especially when interest rates fell and it could borrow more cheaply.

It now suffers a short-term penalty for issuing callable debt, since it must pay a higher rate of interest to attract borrowers who otherwise wouldn't want to own callable bonds. But in the long run, this is another way that Fannie Mae can protect its earnings no matter what happens to rates.

Fannie Mae was still a 12–15 percent grower and still undervalued, just as it had been for the past eight years. Some things never change.

Stock Symbol	Company	1/13/92 Price
FNM	Federal National Mortgage Association	$68.75

NINETEEN

TREASURE IN THE BACKYARD

The Colonial Group of Mutual Funds

For several years, I missed one of the best-performing groups on Wall Street, the mutual-fund industry. Like the mall manager who neglected to buy the Gap as the sales results passed under his nose, I neglected to buy Dreyfus, Franklin Resources, Colonial Group, T. Rowe Price, State Street Bank, Alliance Capital Management, and Eaton Vance. I don't know why, really. Perhaps I couldn't see the trees for the forest. The only one I did buy was United Asset Management, a company that had 30–40 fund managers under contract and hired them out to other institutions.

These companies are so-called direct mutual-fund plays, as opposed to, say, Putnam, which is a subsidiary of Marsh-McLennan, or Kemper, which has a fund business but mostly sells insurance. All eight did well in 1988 and 1989, as the fear of the collapse of the mutual-fund industry after the Great Correction of 1987 turned out to have been exaggerated.

That correction gave me the chance to buy these fellow mutual-fund companies, which I had overlooked before, and at low prices. Here is another of my favorite what-if portfolios: if you had divided your money equally among these eight stocks and held them from the beginning of 1988 to the end of 1989, you would have outperformed 99 percent of the funds that these companies promote.

During periods when mutual funds are popular, investing in the companies that sell the funds is likely to be more rewarding than investing in their products. I'm reminded that in the Gold Rush the people who sold picks and shovels did better than the prospectors.

When interest rates are declining, the bond and equity funds tend to attract the most cash, and the companies that specialize in such funds (Eaton Vance and Colonial, for instance) are exceptionally profitable. Dreyfus manages a lot of money-market assets, so when interest rates are going up and people are getting out of the stock market and out of long-term bonds, Dreyfus prospers. Alliance Capital manages money for institutional clients, and also manages mutual funds that are sold to individuals through brokers. It's been a public company since 1988. The stock price took a slight dip in 1990, and then headed straight for the attic.

Given the billions of dollars that recently have been pouring into bonds, stocks, and money-market mutual funds, it should be no surprise that these mutual-fund companies have outperformed the market. If there's any surprise here, it's that nobody has yet launched the Mutual-Fund Company Mutual Fund.

The information about who is getting in and out of which kind of fund is published by the industry, and professionals and amateurs alike have an opportunity to take advantage of it. If you didn't buy these stocks after the last big correction, you could have bought them during the Saddam Sell-off at the end of 1990, which left Eaton Vance with a one-year decline of 30 percent, Dreyfus with a decline of 18.86 percent, and the others with smaller but nonetheless significant declines as well.

Once again, rumors of the collapse of this industry proved to be unfounded. All you had to do to dispel the latest fear was to look at the sales figures for mutual funds in December 1990 and January 1991. Yet in spite of my determination not to revert to my old habits, I was caught napping once again, and failed to recommend a single mutual-fund company to the 1991 *Barron's* panel. The fans of Lynch's predictions (if there are any, besides my wife) missed the rebound in Franklin (a 75 percent gain in 1991), Dreyfus (55 percent), T. Rowe Price (116 percent), United Asset Management (80 percent), Colonial Group (40 percent), and State Street Bank (81.77 percent). Our mythical Mutual-Fund Company Mutual Fund portfolio nearly doubled in value that year.

In my defense, Your Honor, I hope I'm allowed to mention that I did recommend Kemper, an insurance company with a sizable stake in the mutual-fund business via the $50 billion worth of funds it manages. This was not the sole reason I picked Kemper—its insurance business was starting to turn around, and so were its brokerage subsidiaries, including Prescott, Ball, and Turben. Kemper's stock also doubled in value in 1991, so to that extent maybe I'm redeemed.

At the onset of 1992, I reminded myself not to make the same mistake I'd made prior to 1987 and again in 1991. This time, I took a very close look at the fund situation. With interest rates dropping, and $200 billion in certificates of deposit maturing every month, a great tide of capital was emptying out of the banks and rolling into all manner of funds. This, certainly, was bullish for the big seven mentioned above. On the other hand, after huge gains in 1991, most of these stocks seemed overpriced. The one that didn't was Colonial Group.

In spite of the 40 percent appreciation in the stock in 1991, Colonial Group was selling for the same $17 it sold for in 1985, at its initial public offering. Back then, Colonial managed $5–$6 billion worth of mutual funds and earned $1 a share. Now, it managed $9 billion worth of mutual funds and was earning $1.55 a share, plus it had amassed $4 a share in cash and had bought back 7 percent of its stock. So six years after the offering, a much stronger company could be purchased for the same price, and if you subtracted the $4 in cash, you were getting it for $4 less than in 1985. The company had no debt. No Wall Street analyst had uttered a word about Colonial Group in two years.

The technique of finding the undervalued stock within an attractive group is one I've often employed with good results. T. Rowe Price was selling for 20 times earnings, Franklin was selling for 20 times earnings, but Colonial Group was selling for only 10 times earnings. Of course, you had to ask yourself why Colonial was undervalued.

One reason might have been that those earnings had stayed flat for four years. Colonial had nearly doubled its assets under management, but this was only a trickle in the great tide of capital that had moved into funds in general. People had heard of Dreyfus, T. Rowe Price, and Eaton Vance, but Colonial was not a household word.

But did this mean that Colonial deserved to be valued at half the going rate of its competitors? I couldn't see why. The company was making money. It had a habit of raising its dividend and buying back shares. It could use future profits to do more of the same.

I talked to the corporate treasurer, Davey Scoon, on January 3. He said that business had improved, especially in the muni bond funds. Colonial has several of these, so it will benefit from the rising popularity of munis as an escape from higher taxes. It had launched some interesting new funds, such as a utility fund.

I learned long ago that if you make 10 inquiries at 10 different companies, you are going to discover at least 1 unexpected development. Unexpected developments are what make stocks go up and down, and Scoon had an interesting one to relate. The Colonial Group had just been chosen by the State Street Bank to market some new funds that State Street had concocted.

State Street is a commercial bank that does the paperwork, also known as the "back office" work, for most of the mutual-fund industry. This back office function (customer service, recording of purchases and sales, keeping up with who owns what) has been very lucrative for the bank. State Street stock had an 81 percent gain in 1991.

When Scoon mentioned State Street, it reminded me of a mistake I'd made with my mother-in-law. Some years ago, when it appeared that money-market assets were on the decline, I talked my mother-in-law into selling her State Street shares, on the grounds that (1) the company's earnings were likely to drop and (2) she'd doubled her money in the stock already. Since she took this brilliant advice, State Street stock has tripled again, a sad fact that has been hidden in her confusion over State Street's three-for-one stock split. When she looks in the paper, it appears that the stock price has gone nowhere since I gave the sell signal. She often congratulates me for this savvy call, and until now I haven't had the courage to confess the truth.

Stock splits can be a pain in the neck, but one of the good things about them is that they enable the stockpicker to cover up the mistake of having sold too soon, at least from friends or relatives who don't follow the market.

In any event, State Street's experience in the back office with other people's mutual funds led it to consider starting its own mutual funds, to get in on the front end of this bonanza. But State Street did not want to anger its clients by competing against them directly, which is why it decided to camouflage the State Street funds by hiring the Colonial Group to market them. This extra bit of business will benefit Colonial.

Stock Symbol	Company	1/13/92 Price
COGRA	Colonial Group	$17.38

TWENTY

THE RESTAURANT STOCKS

Putting Your Money Where Your Mouth Is

In 1992 I didn't recommend any restaurant stocks, but I should have. Every year, it seems, a new crop appears at the airports or the shopping malls, or off the exits of the turnpikes. Since the 1960s, when fast food became an accessory to the automobile and people learned to eat their lunches, then breakfasts, and finally dinners on the road, restaurant chains have become great growth companies, with new ones forever taking over where the old ones left off.

The potential for restaurants was proven to me in 1966, early in my career as a Fidelity analyst, when one of the first companies brought to my attention was Kentucky Fried Chicken. Kentucky Fried Chicken was created out of desperation after a superhighway diverted traffic from Colonel Sanders's country restaurant. Facing bankruptcy due to a shortage of customers, this enterprising 66-year-old took to the road in his battered Cadillac, offering his chicken recipe to better-situated restaurants in exchange for royalties. He wore a dark suit, not the white planter's costume that later became his trademark.

KFC stock went on sale in 1965. Before that, Dunkin' Donuts had come public in Massachusetts (it's had 32 years of continuous up earnings since), and Howard Johnson, the pioneer of the turnpike eatery, had traded on the New York Stock Exchange since 1961. Bob Evans Farms, famous in the Midwest, followed in 1963, and by the mid-60s, McDonald's and Shoney's also made their stock-market debuts. Hundreds of thousands of customers who could see that these places were very profitable had a chance to profit from the observation.

At the time, Wall Street would have scoffed at the idea that a bunch of donut shops and hamburger joints could compete with the famous Nifty Fifty stocks, mostly technology issues that proved to be highly overrated, while Shoney's became a 168-bagger (rising from 22 cents a share, adjusted for splits, to a high of $36⅞), Bob Evans Farms an 83-bagger, and McDonald's a 400-bagger. Howard Johnson was a 40-bagger by the time it was taken private, and Kentucky Fried Chicken a 27½ bagger when it was acquired by PepsiCo.

If you invested $10,000 in these five issues, putting your money where your mouth was, by the end of the 1980s you would have become a millionaire at least two times over, and you would have become a millionaire four times over had you put the entire $10,000 into McDonald's alone. McDonald's has been one of the most rewarding stock-market performers in modern history, due to its refusal to rest on its laurels and its constant restructuring of its menu with new McDishes, as well as its practice of exporting its golden arches.

Hamburger joints, cafeterias (Luby's, Morrison's), family steak houses (Ponderosa, Bonanza), all-purpose eateries (Denny's, Shoney's), ice cream places, yogurt places, domestic food restaurants, international food restaurants, coffee bars, pizza parlors, smorgasbords, and buffets have each produced one or more gigantic winners in the stock market, under the noses of an entire nation of investors. We all know which places are popular and well maintained, which are disheveled and passé, which have reached the saturation point and which have room to grow.

If you missed the restaurants in the 1960s, when the baby boomers were getting their first drivers' licenses and turning their cars into portable lunch counters, you could have made up for it in the 1970s by buying International Dairy Queen, Wendy's, Luby's, Taco Bell, Pizza Hut, and Jerrico when Long John Silver appeared on the scene. You would have done especially well had you invested after the bear market of 1972, when solid franchises were selling for a pittance. Taco Bell, which had never had a disappointing quarter, dropped to $1 a share, promptly rebounded to $40, and then was acquired by PepsiCo, which likes to own food companies because they help sell Pepsi's soft drinks.

In the 1980s you might have discovered Cracker Barrel, with its popular gift shop and delicious seafood and biscuits; or Chili's, which came public in 1984 and I foolishly ignored; or Sbarro (1985), Ryan's Family Steak Houses (1982), and Uno Restaurants (1987). Chi-Chi's was another rewarding investment—eventually it was bought out.

Every region of the country has been the incubator for one or more of these small-town successes that went on to capture the stomachs and wallets of the country: Luby's, Ryan's, and Chili's in the Southwest, McDonald's in the Midwest, Chi-Chi's and International Dairy Queen in Minneapolis, Sbarro in New York, Dunkin' Donuts in New England, Shoney's and Cracker Barrel in the Deep South, Sizzler and Taco Bell in the Far West.

A restaurant chain, like a retailer, has 15–20 years of fast growth ahead of it as it expands. This is supposed to be a cutthroat business, but the fledgling restaurant company is protected from competition in a way that an electronics company or a shoe company is not. If there's a new fish-and-chips chain in California and a better one in New York, what's the impact of the New York chain on the California chain? Zero.

It takes a long time for a restaurant company to work its way across the country, and meanwhile there's no competition from abroad. Denny's or Pizza Hut never has to worry about low-cost Korean imports.

What continues to separate the triumphs from the flops among the restaurant chains is capable management, adequate financing, and a methodical approach to expansion. Slow but steady may not win the Indianapolis 500, but it wins this kind of race.

The tale of two hamburger franchises, Chili's and Fuddrucker's, is instructive. Both started in Texas (Chili's in Dallas, Fuddrucker's in San Antonio). Both featured the gourmet burger. Both created pleasant and distinctive surroundings, although Chili's had table service and Fuddrucker's was cafeteria style. One became famous and lost a fortune, while the other achieved both fame and fortune.

Why? One reason was that Chili's diversified its menu as hamburger went out of style, while Fuddrucker's stuck with the burgers. But the key difference is that Fuddrucker's expanded too rapidly. When a company tries to open more than 100 new units a year, it's likely to run into problems. In its rush to glory it can pick the wrong sites or the wrong managers, pay too much for the real estate, and fail to properly train the employees.

Fuddrucker's fell into this trap and went the way of Flakey Jake's,

Winners, and TGI Friday's, all of which moved too fast and suffered for it. Chili's, on the other hand, has maintained a sensible pace of adding 30–35 new units a year. Revenues, sales, and net income have grown steadily under the experienced eye of Norman Brinker, founder of this chain as well as Steak & Ale and Bennigan's. Chili's expects to reach a ceiling of 400–450 restaurants in 1996–98, which it hopes will produce $1 billion in sales.

There are several ways a restaurant chain can increase its earnings. It can add more restaurants, as Chili's is doing, or it can improve its existing operations, as Wendy's has done. Some restaurants make money with high turnover at the tables and low-priced meals (Cracker Barrel, Shoney's, and McDonald's fit this category), while others have low turnover and higher-priced meals (Outback Steakhouse and Chart House are recent examples). Some make their biggest profits on food sales, and some have gift shops (Cracker Barrel). Some have high profit margins because their food is made from inexpensive ingredients (Spaghetti Warehouse), others because their operating costs are low.

For a restaurant company to break even, the sales have to equal the amount of capital invested in the operation. You follow a restaurant story the same way you follow a retailer. The key elements are growth rate, debt, and same-store sales. You'd like to see the same-store sales increasing every quarter. The growth rate should not be too fast—above 100 new outlets a year, the company is in a potential danger zone. Debt should be low to nonexistent, if possible.

Montgomery Securities in California keeps regular tabs on the entire restaurant group and produces excellent reports. Its latest analysis is that hamburger joints such as McDonald's and Wendy's are suffering from overexposure (the top five chains have 24,000 locations in the U.S.), and that the baby boomer generation is turning away from fast food. The momentum has shifted to niche restaurants such as Au Bon Pain and Spaghetti Warehouse, and medium-priced family restaurants that offer a varied menu.

If you had bought the top eight stocks on Montgomery Securities' recommended restaurant list at the beginning of 1991, you would have doubled your money by December. These winners were as follows:

Bertucci's
Cracker Barrel
Brinker International (Chili's)

Spaghetti Warehouse
Shoney's
Rally's
Applebee's
Outback Steakhouse

Several of these stocks may be overpriced as of this writing, with p/e ratios of 30 or higher, but it's worth keeping in touch. The restaurant group as a whole is growing at only 4 percent a year (soon this will be another nongrowth industry), but the superior operators with strong balance sheets will prosper in the future, as they always have in the past. As long as Americans continue to eat 50 percent of their meals outside the home, there will be new 20-baggers showing up in the food courts at the malls and in our neighborhoods, and the observant diner will be able to spot them.

Au Bon Pain is one I've spotted—where else? In the Burlington Mall. It started in my own neighborhood, Boston, in 1977 and went public in 1991 at $10 a share. I can't pronounce it correctly, but it's a great concept. You may have seen an Au Bon Pain in an airport or at a food court. It's a croissant and coffee shop that managed to combine French sensibility with U.S. efficiency.

Here you can get a plain croissant for breakfast, or a ham-and-cheese-filled croissant for lunch, or a chocolate-filled croissant for dessert, all in less than three minutes. The bread is made at one central location and is sent uncooked to the outlets, where it rises and is shoved in the ovens so it comes out hot and fresh baked.

Lately, Au Bon Pain has introduced fresh orange juice and fruit salad, and it's about to launch the state-of-the-art bagel. If it's a choice between investing in the state-of-the-art computer chip and the state-of-the-art bagel, I'll take the bagel any time.

By early 1992, the stock had doubled in price and carried a p/e ratio of 40 (based on expected 1992 earnings), which is why I decided not to recommend it. But nine months later, the price had fallen to $14, or less than 20 times 1993 earnings. Any time you can find a 25 percent grower selling for 20 times earnings, it's a buy. If the price dropped any further, I'd back up the truck. This company is doing well in a recession and can grow for a long time without running into itself. It has a lot of potential overseas as well.

TWENTY-ONE

THE SIX-MONTH CHECKUP

A healthy portfolio requires a regular checkup—perhaps every six months or so. Even with the blue chips, the big names, the top companies in the *Fortune* 500, the buy-and-forget strategy can be unproductive and downright dangerous. Figures 21-1, 21-2, and 21-3 illustrate the point. Investors who bought and forgot IBM, Sears, and Eastman Kodak are sorry that they did.

The six-month checkup is not simply a matter of looking up the stock price in the newspaper, an exercise that often passes for Wall Street research. As a stockpicker, you can't assume anything. You've got to follow the stories. You are trying to get answers to two basic questions: (1) is the stock still attractively priced relative to earnings, and (2) what is happening in the company to make the earnings go up?

Here you can reach one of three conclusions: (1) the story has gotten better, in which case you might want to increase your investment, (2) the story has gotten worse, in which case you can decrease your investment, or (3) the story's unchanged, in which case you can either stick with your investment or put the money into another company with more exciting prospects.

With this in mind, in July 1992 I did a six-month checkup on the 21 selections I made in *Barron's* in January. As a group, these 21 had performed extremely well in a so-so market. The "portfolio" had increased in value by 19.2 percent, while the S&P 500 had returned only 1.64 percent. (I've adjusted all these numbers for the various stock splits, special dividends, etc., that were declared in this six-month period.)

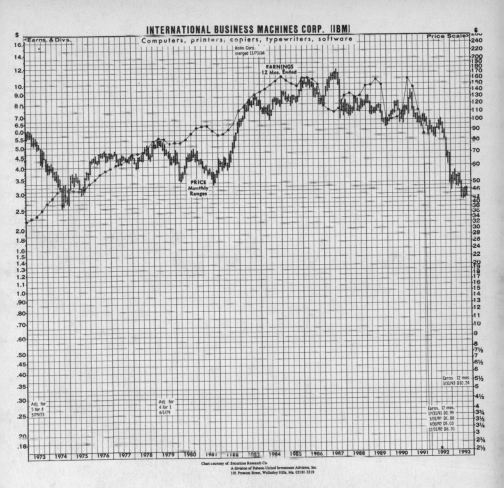

FIGURE 21-1

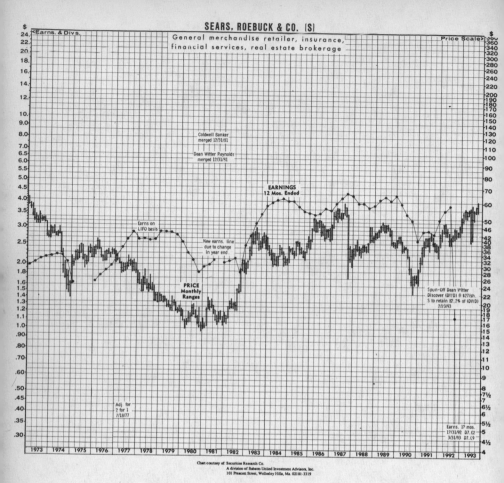

FIGURE 21-2

EASTMAN KODAK CO. (EK)

Photographic products, chemicals, plastics, fibres

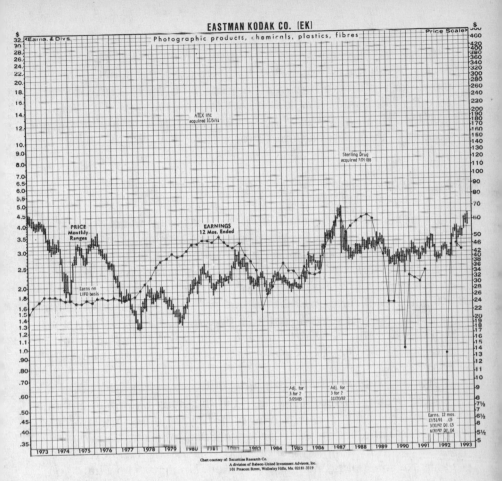

FIGURE 21-3

I read the latest quarterly reports from all 21 companies, and I called most of them. Some stories had gone flat, while others were more exciting than before, and in a few cases my research led me to other companies that I liked better than the ones I'd recommended. That's how it is with stocks. It's a fluid situation in which nothing is absolutely certain. I proceeded as follows:

THE BODY SHOP

Back in January, I determined that the Body Shop was a wonderful company, but overpriced relative to current earnings. I was looking for a drop in price as a chance to buy more. It didn't take long to get one—by July the stock had fallen 12.3 percent, from 325 pence to 263 pence. The Body Shop was now selling for 20 times the estimated 1993 earnings. I don't mind paying 20 times for earnings in a company that's growing at a 25 percent annual rate. As of this writing, the entire New York Stock Exchange was selling at 20 times earnings, for companies that on average were growing at a 8–10 percent rate.

The Body Shop is a British stock. British stocks had taken a terrible beating in recent months, and the Body Shop had gotten some bad publicity. A chieftain from the Kayapó Indian tribe, which the Body Shop had hired to produce Brazil nut hair conditioner, was arrested in London and charged with raping the Portuguese nanny for some of his numerous children. No matter how hard you try to imagine the next event that will make trouble for a company, it's usually something you haven't thought of.

Checking the price history of this stock, I noticed it had suffered two major setbacks, one in 1987 and the other in 1990, both in spite of the fact that the company was perking along with no sign of a letup. I attribute these exaggerated sell-offs to the fact that British shareholders are not as familiar with small growth companies as we are, and therefore abandon them more readily in a market crisis. Also, since the Body Shop is a global venture, British investors may equate it with several notable failures at expanding abroad, e.g., Marks & Spencer.

Even if you bought shares in the Body Shop after the 1990 setback, you had to be prepared for further declines, when you might consider buying more. But the fundamentals still had to be favorable, which

Table 21-1. STOCKS SELECTED FOR 1992 *BARRON'S* ROUNDTABLE:
SIX-MONTH CHECKUP

Company	1/13/92 Price	Six-Month Return (through 7/13/92)
Allied Capital Corporation II	$19.00	6.00%
Body Shop	325p	−12.31
CMS Energy	$18.50	− 4.11
Colonial Group	$17.38	18.27
Eagle Financial	$10.97*	38.23
Federal National Mortgage Association	$68.75	− 6.34
First Essex Bancorp	$ 2.13	70.59
General Host	$ 7.75	10.39
General Motors	$31.00	37.26
Germantown Savings	$14.50	59.31
Glacier Bancorp	$10.12*	40.91
Lawrence Savings Bank	$ 1.00	36.78
People's Savings Financial	$11.00	26.00
Phelps Dodge	$32.50	48.96
Pier 1 Imports	$ 8.00	3.31
Sovereign Bancorp	$ 4.59*	64.50
Sun Distributors L.P., Class B	$ 2.75	6.95
Sun Television & Appliances	$ 9.25*	−10.74
Sunbelt Nursery	$ 6.25	−30.00
Supercuts	$11.33	0.73
Tenera L.P.	$ 2.38	0.00
Lynch Portfolio		19.27%
S&P 500		1.64%
Dow Jones Industrials (DJIA)		6.29%
NASDAQ		− 7.68%
Value Line		− 2.13%

*Because these prices have been adjusted for splits through 9/30/93, some are different from prices given earlier in the book.

Table 21-2.

	Stock Performance Update (as of 7/13/92)	Story	Action
Allied Capital Corporation II	up slightly	unchanged	buy
Body Shop	down slightly	slightly worse	hold/buy
CMS Energy	down slightly	fuzzy	wait
Colonial Group	up	better	buy
Eagle Financial	up sharply	unchanged	hold
Federal National Mortgage Association	down slightly	unchanged	buy
First Essex Bancorp	up sharply	better	hold/buy
General Host	up slightly	unchanged	hold/buy
General Motors	up sharply	slightly worse	switch to Chrysler
Germantown Savings	up sharply	slightly better	hold
Glacier Bancorp	up sharply	unchanged	hold
Lawrence Savings Bank	up sharply	slightly worse	hold
People's Savings Financial	up	unchanged	hold
Phelps Dodge	up sharply	unchanged	hold
Pier 1 Imports	up slightly	unchanged	buy
Sovereign Bancorp	up sharply	slightly better	hold
Sun Distributors L.P., Class B	up slightly	unchanged	buy
Sun Television & Appliances	down	better	strong buy
Sunbelt Nursery	down sharply	worse	hold/buy
Supercuts	flat	better	buy
Tenera L.P.	flat	slightly better	buy

was the point of the checkup. I called the company. Jeremy Kett, chief financial officer, told me that same-store sales and earnings had both increased in 1991, a considerable achievement given the fact that the Body Shop's four major markets are England, Australia, Canada, and the U.S.—all countries struggling with recession.

Another promising card had turned over. The company was using some of its cash to buy up suppliers of various potions and lotions. This would cut the cost of the merchandise down the line, and improve the profit margin. This was the technique that helped Shaw Industries become the low-cost carpet maker.

I talked to Cathy Stephenson, my old friend from the Fidelity library who owns the Body Shop at the Burlington Mall plus the one in Harvard Square. She reported a 6 percent gain in sales over the previous year's results at Burlington and said it was too early to tell about Harvard Square. Her customers were flocking to several new products, including Complete Color for eyes, cheeks, and lips; tinted face moisturizer with sunscreen; pumice foot scrub; and mango body butter, which she couldn't seem to keep on the shelf—"Who knows what they're doing with it?"

The market for lotions, potions, and bath oil is still vast, with plenty of room to grow. The Body Shop was sticking to its expansion plan—40 new outlets in the U.S. in 1993, 50 more in 1994, 50 per year in Europe, an equal number in the Far East. I placed the company in the attractive mid-life phase—the second decade of 30 years of growth.

PIER 1 IMPORTS

Pier 1 Imports had made a nice run, from $8 to $9.50, then promptly reverted. This is an example of Wall Street's being deaf to good news. The analysts had pegged Pier 1's first-quarter earnings at 18–20 cents, Pier 1 actually earned 17 cents, and the stock got clobbered. The company was expected to earn 70 cents for the year, and this in a wallet-hugging environment.

Pier 1 had strengthened its balance sheet by selling $75 million worth of convertible debentures and using the proceeds to retire debt. Long-term debt, which already had been reduced, was pared down even further.

Pier 1 had cut debt, reduced inventory, and continued to expand. Its major competitors, the department stores, were getting out of the home furnishings business. The longer this recession lasted, the more competitors would drop by the wayside. When the recovery comes, Pier 1 may have a virtual monopoly on wicker side tables, Scandinavian place settings, and Oriental room dividers.

It didn't take much wishful thinking to foresee Pier 1 earning 80 cents a share from its own stores, plus an additional 10–15 cents from a revived and dried-off Sunbelt Nursery, a company in which

Pier 1 continues to hold a substantial stake. That's a buck a share, which, given a reasonable p/e ratio of 14, makes Pier 1 a $14 stock.

GENERAL HOST, SUNBELT NURSERY

General Host is another stock that rose up and then drifted back to just above where I'd recommended it. Nimble sellers had gotten a 30 percent gain, while long-term investors saw paper profits dwindle from $2 a share to 50 cents.

A disappointing card had turned over. In April, the company issued $65 million worth of a new convertible preferred stock with an 8 percent yield. This was exactly what Pier 1 had done, except that General Host had to pay a higher interest rate due to its shakier financial condition.

Shareholders in convertible stock or debentures have the right to trade these in for shares in the common stock at a fixed price sometime in the future. This creates more shares of common, which dilutes the earnings for the existing shareholders of the common. Earlier, General Host had bought back some of its common shares, which was a positive move, and now it had reversed itself by issuing the convertible, which was a negative move.

Whereas Pier 1 had used the proceeds from its convertible sale to pay off debt, thus reducing interest expense, General Host was using its proceeds to further renovate its Frank's Nursery stores. This was a chancier proposition, with no immediate benefit.

Meanwhile, sales at the Frank's nurseries were sluggish to moribund, as the revival in the housing market had begun to fizzle. Back in January, when the stock was selling for $7.75, the company was expected to earn 60 cents for the year, but now it was an $8 stock in a company that was expected to earn 45 cents.

Still, General Host had a strong cash flow, its dividend had been raised for the 14th year in a row, the stock was selling for less than book value, and the expansion was proceeding according to plan. From punching up GH on my Quotron, I learned that Mario Gabelli had bought a million shares for his value-oriented fund. I counted this stock as a hold.

Sunbelt, my other recommendation from the nursery, had lost money since January. More rain in the Southwest, where Sunbelt is located, had dampened people's enthusiasm for working in the garden. What had been an $8.50 stock at its initial public offering in 1991 was now a $4.50 stock, and this for a capable company with $1.50 a share in cash. If you bought Sunbelt now, you were getting all the garden outlets for $3, and someday, when the rains abate and people rediscover flowers, they will have a sunnier disposition toward Sunbelt shares as well.

What keeps me from backing up the truck and buying more Sunbelt is Calloway's. You may recall that Calloway's was regarded as the class of the industry, which I hadn't recommended the first time around because Sunbelt was cheaper. But while checking up on Sunbelt, I discovered that Calloway's stock also had fallen in half in the rain.

To find out more, I called Calloway's to talk to Dan Reynolds, the investment relations person. He told me there were 20 employees in the administrative office, all of them sharing the same 3,000 feet of floor space. I could hear them the background. Obviously, there is no communications gap in this company—to get the management's attention, all you have to do is stand up and yell.

Calloway's has 13 nurseries, plus 50 cents per share in cash, and is expected to earn 50 cents in 1993. This gives the stock a p/e ratio of 10. Calloway's has no followers on Wall Street, and the company is buying back its own shares.

When the best company in an industry is selling at a bargain price, it often pays to buy that one, as opposed to investing in a lesser competitor that may be selling at a lower price. I'd rather have owned Toys "R" Us than Child World, Home Depot than Builder's Square, or Nucor than Bethlehem Steel. I still like Sunbelt, but at this point I think I like Calloway's slightly better.

SUPERCUTS

After a strong run and a three-for-two stock split, Supercuts, too, has reverted to its January price. Two lousy cards have turned over. The first is the fact that Ed Faber, the expert from Computerland who knew how to roll out a franchise, has left the company. The word is that Faber wants to devote himself to managing his own Supercuts salon. This explanation is not entirely convincing.

The second lousy card is something I noticed in the proxy statement. I must have overlooked it earlier. A group called Carlton

Investments owns 2.2 million shares of Supercuts stock. It turns out that Carlton is part of Drexel Burnham Lambert, the bankrupt Wall Street firm. Drexel's creditors will surely demand Carlton's liquidation, which means that along with everything else, the 2.2 million shares of Supercuts will be sold. This will cause the price to fall. In fact, the price may already have fallen on fears of this "overhang," which is what Wall Street calls a big block of shares that's about to be dumped on the market.

The company itself is having a good year. Supercuts was named "Official Hair Salon Services Supplier for the Olympics," so maybe the same woman who snipped off my sideburns got to shave the swimmers' heads. The all-important same-store sales are up 6.9 percent in the first quarter of 1992. Several new Supercuts have opened in upstate New York, where the mayor of Rochester got a free ceremonial haircut.

As long as same-store sales improve and the company succeeds in new markets, I'll add to my position, although I'm beginning to worry that the company may expand too fast. Between 80 and 100 new franchises are planned for 1993.

I've already seen several promising franchises, from Color Tile to Fuddrucker's to Bildner's, ruined by overeager corporate conquistadores. "If you have a choice between reaching your goal in fifteen years or in five years, fifteen is better," I advised the CEO of Supercuts in July.

THE SEVEN S&LS

So far, the best performers of my 21 *Barron's* picks are the S&Ls. This is no accident. Take the industry that's surrounded with the most doom and gloom, and if the fundamentals are positive, you'll find some big winners. With interest rates falling, it's been a happy year for financial institutions in general. They're making huge earnings thanks to the spreads between the interest rates they charge for mortgage loans and the rates they pay on savings accounts and CDs.

Since I recommended it, Germantown Savings is up 59 percent, Sovereign has declared two 10 percent stock dividends and also is up 64.5 percent, Eagle Financial has advanced from $11 to $16, Glacier Bancorp has climbed over 40 percent, and People's Savings Financial is up 26 percent.

Of my two long-shot S&Ls, Lawrence is up 37 percent and First Essex is up 70 percent, proving that the riskiest stocks often carry the greatest rewards. I called CEO Leonard Wilson at First Essex to see how things are going. This is the man who earlier described his predicament as "bottom fishing with a six-hundred-foot line," but by late spring he had reduced the length of the line to 60 feet.

Wilson reported improvements on several fronts: foreclosed properties are selling, nonperforming loans are down, and the mortgage market is picking up. Not only has First Essex managed to break even in the first quarter, it actually dared to make a new construction loan. Though I normally dislike construction loans, the fact that First Essex feels optimistic enough to make one after having been driven close to the poorhouse means that somebody thinks this region has a future.

Wilson is considerably cheered by the news that Shawmut Bank, his biggest competitor in the area, also has recovered enough to escape the financial intensive care unit. First Essex still has a book value of $7, and the stock is selling for $3⅝. If the real-estate market continues to improve, First Essex could eventually earn $1 a share. Then the stock will be worth $7–$10.

Lawrence Savings, the other S&L with warts, I contacted in April and again in June. In April, the CEO, Paul Miller, reported that seven pages of nonperforming loans had been reduced to one and that new mortgage business was strong. He sounded optimistic. In June, he sounded discouraged.

At this point, Lawrence still had $55 million in commercial real estate loans outstanding, and its net worth was down to $21 million. If half of these commercial loans go sour, Lawrence will be wiped out.

This is the biggest difference between Lawrence and First Essex. First Essex had $46 million in net worth and $56 million in commercial loans outstanding, so if half of its commercial loans default, First Essex may manage to survive. Lawrence is in a more precarious position. If the recession gets worse and there is another wave of defaults, Lawrence will disappear.

First Federal of Michigan

Six months later, I counted six of the seven S&Ls I'd picked in *Barron's* as holds, mostly because they'd already gone up in price.

Also, a better buying opportunity had entered the picture: First Federal of Michigan (FFOM).

FFOM was brought to my attention by Dave Ellison, Fidelity's S&L analyst, during a plane ride to New York we shared back in January. It was too late to do the homework then, so I put the idea aside. I'm glad I did, because while all these other S&Ls had increased in value, FFOM hadn't budged.

If all stocks went up at the same rate, there would be nothing left to buy and stockpickers everywhere would be out of business. Fortunately, this is not the case. There is always a laggard to fall back on once you've sold a stock that has gotten ahead of itself. As of July 1992, FFOM was just such a stock.

This is a $9 billion Jimmy Stewart thrift that has avoided commercial lending and has minimal operating costs. It is being held back by two negative factors: the money it borrowed from the Federal Home Loan Bank (FHLB), and some unfavorable interest rate futures contracts.

Most S&Ls have benefited from the falling interest rates in recent years, but not FFOM. That's because FFOM financed its operations in part with loans from FHLB, and these loans carry a fixed rate. FFOM must continue to pay FHLB 8–10 percent through 1994, when all this high-priced paper comes due. Meanwhile, its own borrowers are refinancing their mortgages at lower and lower rates. This has put the squeeze on FFOM.

When you own mortgages that pay you 8–10 per cent, and you've borrowed money at the same level of interest, you won't make much of a profit. This is a painful lesson that FFOM has had to learn. Its operations in general are profitable, but the FHLB "block of granite" has been holding down the earnings.

This unfortunate situation will reverse itself once the FHLB debt is retired and the interest rate futures contracts expire. Then FFOM's earnings will explode. The resolution of these two problems has the potential of adding more than $2 a share to earnings in 1994–96. On current earnings of $2 a share, this is a $12 stock, so imagine what will happen if the company earns $4.

Moreover, FFOM has a book value of more than $26 a share. Back in 1989, it was a touch-and-go operation with an equity-to-assets ratio of only 3.81. Since then, it has crossed the magic threshold of 5. It reinstated the dividend in early 1992 and then proceeded to raise it. Its nonperforming loans are less than 1 percent of assets.

If short-term rates continue to decline, the stock might well fall below $10, but investors who know the story will be prepared to buy it on the way down. There's no coverage from the major brokerage houses.

COLONIAL GROUP

An article published in *The Wall Street Journal* on June 30 reminded me that billions of dollars were pouring into the bond funds. The Colonial Group specializes in bond funds, particularly the tax-exempt and limited maturity U.S. government funds, which enjoy widespread popularity these days. Only 9 percent of the money it manages is invested in stock funds. If we have a bear market, as many people now predict, investors who are scared out of stocks will retreat into bond funds, and Colonial Group will become even more profitable than it already is.

Davey Scoon, the treasurer, tells me that sales of Colonial Group funds are up 58 percent in the recent quarter. It now manages $9.5 billion worth of assets, as opposed to the $8.1 billion it managed a year earlier. There is $4 a share in cash, with the stock now selling for around $20. Subtracting the cash, this becomes a $16 stock in a company that is expected to earn at least $1.80 in 1992. To add to the good news, the company has announced a $10 million stock buyback.

CMS ENERGY

Stock in this Michigan utility bobbed up into the $20s on rumors that the public service commission would accept a rate compromise that was somewhat favorable to the company. After the commission rejected the compromise, the stock sank back to $16 then rose slightly to $17.75. And with no agreement currently in sight, Moody's has lowered its rating on CMS bonds to speculative levels.

This is always the issue with distressed utilities on the rebound— how much latitude will the governing bodies allow? Absent an equitable ruling from the state commission, CMS will take a write-off against earnings to pay for some of the costs it can't pass along to customers. The stock might fall to $10. Unless you're prepared in advance to respond to such a drop by buying more shares, it's best not to own CMS during this uncertain stage.

In the long run, I'm convinced CMS will do well. The company is making plenty of money, and its excess cash flow eventually will lead to higher earnings. Energy demand is growing in the Midwest, and few if any new plants are being built to meet it. With reduced supply and increased demand, you know what will happen to electricity prices.

SUN TELEVISION & APPLIANCES

As with several other stocks on our list, the price of Sun TV moved higher at first, and then settled back to below where I recommended it. I called Bob Oyster, the CEO, on June 5. He reminded me that Sun TV has only $4 million in total debt. This is a very strong company, and its weaker competitors continue to disappear. Since January, one competitor has closed all his stores in the Ohio area, and another has gone completely out of business.

Sun TV is making money in spite of the recession. It might have made more except that cold weather in the spring and early summer hurt air conditioner sales. People who are freezing do not buy air conditioners. But they are still buying refrigerators and television sets, and Sun TV is sticking to its plan to open four to six new stores in 1993.

Mr. Oyster noted that Sun TV has the wherewithal to pay for several years' worth of expansion without selling more stock or taking on more debt.

THE MASTER LIMITED PARTNERSHIPS: SUN DISTRIBUTORS, TENERA

Lou Cissone, Sun's vice-president of finance, went down the list of the various divisions. His report sounded so pessimistic that I was surprised the company as a whole had a profitable first quarter. The big issue is still the debt, $22 million of which is due in February 1993. Sun has been preparing for this payment the same way you and I would—cutting costs and repressing the instinct to go shopping. Sun continued to refrain from making any new acquisitions. This was too bad, according to Cissone, because many companies in Sun's line of business—glass, hydraulics, and auto parts—could be bought at bargain prices

The story here, as you may recall, is that the Class A shareholders get back $10 a share in 1997, whereas the Class B shareholders get the remaining assets. If the economy improves, I figure that the Class B shares could be worth $5–$8 apiece; in the current market they continue to sell for $3.

Meanwhile, I remind myself that if the economy gets worse, Sun can easily sell off any number of its previously acquired divisions to raise the cash to cover its debt payments. These valuable franchises give the company some disaster protection.

Tenera, the nuclear consulting firm in distress, is another victim of good news. The company announced two new contracts, one with Martin Marietta and one with Commonwealth Edison, the largest operator of nuclear power plants in the U.S. This proved that Tenera's consulting business is still viable—otherwise, why would Martin Marietta and Commonwealth Edison be wasting time with these people? Then the company announced it was close to a settlement of a class action suit, which is going to cost less than some investors had feared, and on top of that it broke even in the first quarter. The stock responded by going nowhere.

I remember what attracted me to Tenera in the first place—the company had no debt and a valuable consulting business, even though the software division was in shambles, and the stock was $2. If Tenera can make just $40 million in annual revenues, which seems more likely now than it did in January, the company could earn 40 cents a share. This is a long shot for which the story is getting better and the price has stayed the same. That puts it on the buy list.

Cedar Fair

I can't review one or two master limited partnerships without checking in on a few of the others that I have owned and recommended in the past. The high yields and the tax advantages make this a very attractive group. This time, I found two more to elevate to the buy list: Cedar Fair and Unimar.

Cedar Fair runs the Cedar Point amusement park on the shores of Lake Erie. My family and I go there to ride the roller coasters in early August. This is my favorite summer research.

Cedar Fair has just made an important announcement: it is acquiring Dorney Park, a big amusement palace outside of Allentown, and another place to do summer research. This company hasn't adopted the stock symbol FUN for nothing.

What stopped me from recommending Cedar Fair at the beginning of 1992 was that I couldn't see how the company was going to boost its earnings. The Dorney Park acquisition is the answer. Cedar Fair will take over Dorney Park, add new rides, use the proven Cedar Fair techniques to attract more customers, and cut costs.

Whereas 4–5 million people live within driving distance of Cedar Point on Lake Erie, 20 million can reach Dorney Park in less than three hours.

The Cedar Fair people aren't exactly acquisition happy—this is the second they've made in 20 years. The math looks very favorable. The purchase price for Dorney is $48 million. Since Dorney earned nearly $4 million in the prior year, the p/e of the acquisition is 12.

Cedar Fair is not paying all cash. It is paying $27 million in cash, financed by debt, and the balance in a million Cedar Fair shares, to be given to the owners of Dorney Park.

Here's how I analyze the deal. Cedar Fair was earning $1.80 a share prior to the purchase. With a million new shares on the books, it will have to come up with an extra $1.8 million in earnings to maintain the status quo. It will also have to pay $1.7 million in interest on the $27 million it borrowed to make the acquisition.

Where will Cedar Fair get this $3.5 million in extra earnings plus interest payments? From Dorney Park's estimated $4 million annual earnings. On the face of it, this deal adds to Cedar Fair's earnings.

So what happened when the Dorney Park sale was announced? Cedar Fair's stock didn't budge from $19 for weeks. You don't have to be an insider to get in on this deal. You can read about it in the newspapers, take your time analyzing the situation, and still buy Cedar Fair stock at a predeal price.

Unimar

Unimar has no employees. The payroll is nonexistent. This is a holding company with a simple job: collecting the proceeds from the sale of liquid natural gas that comes from Indonesia. These proceeds are distributed quarterly to shareholders as a big dividend, which recently has been running at a nice 20 percent a year.

In the third quarter of 1999, the contract that Unimar has with Indonesia oil and gas producers will dissolve, and the stock will be worthless. This is a race against time—how much gas can be extracted and sold, and how many dividends will be paid, for the remaining six and a half years before the contract runs out.

As I write this, Unimar stock is selling for $6. If by 1999 the shareholder receives $6 worth of dividends, then Unimar has not been much of an investment. If he or she receives $10 worth of dividends, it will be a decent investment, and at $12 in dividends Unimar begins to get exciting.

The size of the dividend depends on two factors: how much natural gas Unimar can extract from the Indonesian fields (recently, the company has expanded the output, which adds to the attractiveness of this stock) and at what price it can sell the gas. If oil and gas prices go up, Unimar's payout goes up: if prices decline, so does the payout.

Unimar offers investors a chance to profit from a future increase in oil prices, and receive a handsome dividend along the way. This beats buying oil and gas futures, which is an expensive and more dangerous game.

FANNIE MAE

Another bobble in the stock price gives investors the umpteenth chance to pick up shares in this remarkable company at a discount. The stock has fallen to the mid-$50s because legislation favorable to Fannie Mae has stalled in Congress.

Meanwhile, the company has enjoyed a good first quarter and a good second quarter and the mortgage-backed securities portfolio has grown to $413 billion. In the midst of a housing recession, Fannie Mae's loan delinquencies are a minuscule six tenths of 1 percent, half the level of five years earlier. The company will earn $6 in 1992 and $6.75 in 1993; it is maintaining its double-digit growth rate, and still was selling at a p/e of 10.

I called Janet Point, a corporate spokesperson, on June 23, 1992, to get the scoop on this stalled legislation. She assures me it's a nonevent. A bill that defines the roles of Fannie Mae, Freddie Mac, etc., is almost sure to get through Congress, but whether it does or it doesn't is of little consequence to Fannie Mae, which can get along perfectly well without it.

ALLIED CAPITAL II

These are the people who make venture capital loans in return for a stake in the companies that borrow the money. What attracted me to Allied Capital II was its plan to acquire some of the better loans that originally were made by failed S&Ls. These loans were being auctioned off by Resolution Trust, often at a discount.

Since I recommended Allied Capital II, an entirely new Allied fund, Allied Capital Commercial, has been launched to purchase different types of loans. There are now five funds in the Allied family. This proliferation has gotten me interested in Allied Capital Advisors, a separate company that gets the management fees from the other Allied ventures. Allied Capital Advisors is also publicly traded, and this is where the executives who have created the five funds will reap their rewards.

THE CYCLICALS: PHELPS DODGE AND GENERAL MOTORS

You can't hold on to a cyclical stock the way you hold on to a retailer in the midst of expansion. Phelps Dodge was up 50 percent in six months. It is one of the biggest winners of my 21 selections, but I fear that all the easy money has already been made. It was extremely cheap at the beginning of 1992, based on 1992 earnings, but its future prosperity depends on what happens to copper prices in 1993.

I talked to Doug Yearly, the CEO, who noted that as the price of the stock rose, the Wall Street analysts increased their earnings estimates for the company. This is an example of tailoring the means to fit the ends. Since nobody can predict whether copper prices will go higher or lower, it might as well be soothsayers who are making the estimates. I wouldn't be buying Phelps Dodge at this price. I'd rather be putting my money into Pier 1, Sun TV, or First Federal of Michigan.

General Motors advanced 37 percent from the January price, then began giving up part of the gains. With car sales still several million under trend, I foresee some good years ahead for the autos. Demand ought to be high, and the lower dollar and the problems in Japan will help the U.S. automakers win back a larger share of the market.

I like GM and Ford, but my most recent inquiries have convinced me to put Chrysler back on the top of my list. I'm doing this in spite of the fact that Chrysler's stock already doubled in price in 1992, outperforming the other two automakers. I am surprised by this result.

Rejecting a stock because the price has doubled, tripled, or even quadrupled in the recent past can be a big mistake. Whether a million investors made or lost money on Chrysler last month has no bearing on what will happen next month. I try to treat each potential investment as if it had no history—the "be here now" approach. Whatever occurred earlier is irrelevant. The important thing is whether the stock is cheap or expensive today at $21–$22, based on its earnings potential of $5 to $7 a share.

On that score, the latest news from Chrysler was exciting. While this company has been skating on the edge of bankruptcy, it has managed to amass $3.6 billion in cash, enough to pay off its long-term debt of $3.7 billion. The Chrysler financial crisis is now overrated. With the company in better shape than before, its finance subsidiary, Chrysler Financial, will be able to borrow money at decent rates. This will improve Chrysler's earnings.

The revamped Jeep Cherokee is so popular that Chrysler has no trouble selling it without the rebate. The company makes several thousand dollars on each Jeep and also on each minivan. These two products alone bring in $4 billion a year in a difficult car market.

The T300 full-sized pickup, which car buffs are calling the "off-the-road BMW," gives Chrysler its first strong challenge in the truck market, where Ford and GM have made their biggest profits. Chrysler never had a full-sized truck before. Its mediocre small-car lines, the Sundance and Shadow, are being phased out. It has introduced the first really new basic car design in a decade, the LH system.

The LH cars—Eagle Vision, Chrysler Concorde, and Plymouth Intrepid—are all priced high enough to return a decent profit. If they turn out to be as popular as the Saturn or the Taurus have been, they will have a huge impact on Chrysler's earnings.

If anything holds Chrysler back, it's the millions of shares the company has had to sell in recent years to raise cash. In 1986, there were 217 million shares outstanding; now there are 340 million. But if Chrysler lives up to its promise, the higher earnings in 1993–95 will be more than enough to offset the burden of extra shares.

I was back on "Wall Street Week with Louis Rukeyser" in September. This was the 10th anniversary of my initial appearance on that show, and another chance to recommend a new passel of stocks. I did several weeks of homework, just as I do for *Barron's,* and was ready to share the results with Lou's millions of viewers.

On "Wall Street Week" you have no idea what they're going to ask, and you have a limited time to respond. If they'd let me, I could go on for an entire half hour with my latest picks, the same way grandparents go on about their grandchildren. As it was, I spent so much time struggling to pronounce Au Bon Pain that I didn't get to mention Fannie Mae, or First Federal of Michigan, or several other of my favorite S&Ls.

I managed to get in a good word about Ford and also Chrysler, a stock I recommended the first time I was on "Wall Street Week"—against the advice of several colleagues. I guess we've come full circle.

25 GOLDEN RULES

Before I turn off my word processor, I can't resist this last chance to summarize the most important lessons I've learned from two decades of investing, many of which have been discussed in this book and elsewhere. This is my version of the St. Agnes good-bye chorus:

• Investing is fun, exciting, and dangerous if you don't do any work.

• Your investor's edge is not something you get from Wall Street experts. It's something you already have. You can outperform the experts if you use your edge by investing in companies or industries you already understand.

• Over the past three decades, the stock market has come to be dominated by a herd of professional investors. Contrary to popular belief, this makes it easier for the amateur investor. You can beat the market by ignoring the herd.

• Behind every stock is a company. Find out what it's doing.

• Often, there is no correlation between the success of a company's operations and the success of its stock over a few months or even a few years. In the long term, there is a 100 percent correlation between the success of the company and the success of its stock. This disparity is the key to making money; it pays to be patient, and to own successful companies.

• You have to know what you own, and why you own it. "This baby is a cinch to go up!" doesn't count.

• Long shots almost always miss the mark.

• Owning stocks is like having children—don't get involved with more than you can handle. The part-time stockpicker probably has time to follow 8–12 companies, and to buy and sell shares as conditions warrant. There don't have to be more than 5 companies in the portfolio at any one time.

• If you can't find any companies that you think are attractive, put your money in the bank until you discover some.

• Never invest in a company without understanding its finances. The biggest losses in stocks come from companies with poor balance sheets. Always look at the balance sheet to see if a company is solvent before you risk your money on it.

• Avoid hot stocks in hot industries. Great companies in cold, nongrowth industries are consistent big winners.

• With small companies, you're better off to wait until they turn a profit before you invest.

• If you're thinking about investing in a troubled industry, buy the companies with staying power. Also, wait for the industry to show signs of revival. Buggy whips and radio tubes were troubled industries that never came back.

• If you invest $1,000 in a stock, all you can lose is $1,000, but you stand to gain $10,000 or even $50,000 over time if you're patient. The average person can concentrate on a few good companies, while the fund manager is forced to diversify. By owning too many stocks, you lose this advantage of concentration. It only takes a handful of big winners to make a lifetime of investing worthwhile.

• In every industry and every region of the country, the observant amateur can find great growth companies long before the professionals have discovered them.

• A stock-market decline is as routine as a January blizzard in Colorado. If you're prepared, it can't hurt you. A decline is a great opportunity to pick up the bargains left behind by investors who are fleeing the storm in panic.

• Everyone has the brainpower to make money in stocks. Not everyone has the stomach. If you are susceptible to selling everything in a panic, you ought to avoid stocks and stock mutual funds altogether.

• There is always something to worry about. Avoid weekend thinking and ignore the latest dire predictions of the newscasters. Sell a stock because the company's fundamentals deteriorate, not because the sky is falling.

• Nobody can predict interest rates, the future direction of the economy, or the stock market. Dismiss all such forecasts and concentrate on what's actually happening to the companies in which you've invested.

• If you study 10 companies, you'll find 1 for which the story is better than expected. If you study 50, you'll find 5. There are always pleasant surprises to be found in the stock market—companies whose achievements are being overlooked on Wall Street.

• If you don't study any companies, you have the same success buying stocks as you do in a poker game if you bet without looking at your cards.

• Time is on your side when you own shares of superior companies. You can afford to be patient—even if you missed Wal-Mart in the first five years, it was a great stock to own in the next five years. Time is against you when you own options.

• If you have the stomach for stocks, but neither the time nor the inclination to do the homework, invest in equity mutual funds. Here, it's a good idea to diversify. You should own a few different kinds of funds, with managers who pursue different styles of investing: growth, value, small companies, large companies, etc. Investing in six of the same kind of fund is not diversification.

The capital-gains tax penalizes investors who do too much switching from one mutual fund to another. If you've invested in one fund or several funds that have done well, don't abandon them capriciously. Stick with them.

• Among the major stock markets of the world, the U.S. market ranks eighth in total return over the past decade. You can take advantage of the faster-growing economies by investing some portion of your assets in an overseas fund with a good record.

• In the long run, a portfolio of well-chosen stocks and/or equity mutual funds will always outperform a portfolio of bonds or a money-market account. In the long run, a portfolio of poorly chosen stocks won't outperform the money left under the mattress.

POSTSCRIPT

Stockpicking is a dynamic exercise, and a lot has happened since I made my selections for the 1992 *Barron's* Roundtable, as described in the foregoing text. For starters, I participated in the 1993 *Barron's* Roundtable by selecting a new group of stocks, including eight repeaters from the 1992 Roundtable. By the time you read this, I will already have done my research for 1994.

My routine is always the same. I search for companies that are undervalued, and I usually find them in sectors or industries that are out of favor. For two years running, I found no bargains among the blue-chip growth stocks, a group that includes Merck, Abbott Labs, Wal-Mart, and Procter & Gamble. The poor performance of these popular issues is proof that the chart-reading technique described on page 142 actually works.

By looking at the long-term charts of these companies in 1991–92, you would have seen that their stock prices had strayed far beyond their earnings, a danger signal that told us to back off for a while from the Mercks, Wal-Marts, and similar growth companies that were the star performers of the late 1980s, but lately have faltered.

Whenever a popular stock suffers a big drop in price, especially a stock that is widely held by pension funds and mutual funds, Wall Street has to make up a reason for the decline that gets the fund managers off the hook for owning it. Recently we've heard that the drug company stocks declined because Wall Street was nervous about the Clinton health plan, and Coca-Cola declined because investors were worried about the effect of a stronger dollar on Coca-Cola's earnings, and Home Depot declined because of sluggishness in the housing market. The real reason these stocks declined is that they had gotten terrifically overpriced relative to current earnings.

What usually happens to an overpriced blue-chip growth stock is that the stock price will fall or move sideways for a couple of years as the corporate earnings continue to grow as usual, and eventually the price and the earnings will come back into balance. When that occurs, the price line and the earnings line will converge on the chart, as they did for Abbott Labs in late 1993. (See the illustration on page 144.) Perhaps the blue-chip growth sector has had its correction, and some of these stocks can be recommended in 1994–95.

In my experience, the price of a stock, the "p" in the p/e equation, cannot run too far ahead of the earnings, the "e" in the equation, without something having to give.

While some of the larger growth stocks were bid up too high and then stumbled, many bargains could still be found among the smaller growth stocks. The New Horizons indicator described on pages 66–67 has continued to show the smaller stocks at the bottom of their price range relative to the S&P 500. (See the chart on page 66.) As long as the small companies remain cheap compared to their larger counterparts, there's a good chance they will outperform the larger companies, at least until the New Horizons indicator turns north.

Another interesting development in 1993 was that the natural gas business had revived to the point that energy and energy service companies could do well. These sorts of enterprises had been in the doldrums for as long as I could remember, but years of cost-cutting and consolidating and shutting down the drilling rigs had produced a promising situation for the survivors.

The risk/reward ratio was excellent in these companies. Many a natural gas stock had been thrashed so thoroughly that they could hardly be beaten down much further, and the odds were favorable that some of them would rise and shine. So I recommended five energy companies in 1993: two service companies and three producers.

Based on the pent-up demand indicator described on pages 241–242, I also thought that the auto industry would sell more cars and trucks than a lot of people were predicting. After a down cycle in autos, it normally takes five to six years of an up cycle before the pent-up demand is satisfied, and we were entering only the third year of the latest up cycle. With that in mind, I recommended three automakers plus Harman International, which supplies car stereo equipment to the automakers.

In my discussions with various analysts and also with executives

Table PS-1. LYNCH'S 1993 *BARRON'S* PORTFOLIO

Ticker	Company Name	Total Return 1/11/93– 12/31/93	Price 1/11/93	Price 12/31/93
ABBK	Abington Savings Bank	27.78%	$ 9.00	$11.50
AMX	AMAX, Inc. (through 11/15/93)	47.71	16.88	****
AHC	Amerada Hess Corporation	3.78	44.00	45.13
APA	Apache Corporation	33.12	17.75	23.38
AS	Armco, Inc.	−5.77	6.50	6.13
—	Body Shop	37.20	164p	225p
BP	British Petroleum PLC–ADR	46.81	44.88	64.00
BST	British Steel PLC–ADR	97.81	9.50	18.50
C	Chrysler Corporation	49.00	36.25	53.25
CCI	Citicorp	71.51	21.50	36.88
CMS	CMS Energy Corporation	39.30	18.50	25.13
CSA	Coast Savings Financial, Inc.	34.12	10.63	14.25
DBRSY	De Beers Consolidated Mines–ADR	84.64	13.75	24.25
DME	Dime Savings Bank of New York	20.37	6.75	8.13
FDX	Federal Express Corporation	27.99	55.38	70.88
FNM	Federal National Mortgage Association	3.66	77.50	78.50
FFOM	Firstfed Michigan Corporation	62.24	16.08	25.50
FOFF	50-Off Stores, Inc.	−42.71	12.00	6.88
F	Ford Motor Company	47.37	45.13	64.50
GH	General Host Corporation	−18.38	9.00	7.00
GM	General Motors Corporation	63.26	34.25	54.88
GLM	Global Marine, Inc.	65.00	2.50	4.13
GGUY	Good Guys, Inc.	18.18	11.00	13.00
HWG	Hallwood Group, Inc.	−8.89	5.63	5.13
HAR	Harman International Industries	94.92	14.75	28.75
AHM	H. F. Ahmanson & Co.	11.07	18.50	19.63
HPBC	Home Port Bancorp, Inc.	66.46	7.38	11.75
IAD	Inland Steel Industries, Inc.	51.43	21.88	33.13
MAXC	Maxco, Inc.	106.06	4.13	8.50
MSEL	Merisel, Inc.	67.05	11.00	18.38
NSBK	North Side Savings Bank, Bronx, NY	39.67	13.33	18.50
NSSB	Norwich Financial Corporation	62.44	5.75	9.00
PXRE	Phoenix RE Corporation	80.16	15.25	27.25
RLM	Reynolds Metals Company	−13.65	53.88	45.38
SERF	Service Fracturing Company	16.96	3.31	3.88
SBN	Sunbelt Nursery GRP/DE	−40.21	5.75	3.44
SDP.B	Sun Distributors, L.P.	25.26	3.50	4.25
CUTS	Supercuts, Inc.	2.62	14.50	14.88
TLP	Tenera, L.P.	4.72	1.31	1.38
	Lynch's 1993 Portfolio Total Return	35.39%		
	S&P 500 Stock Index	11.23		
	NASDAQ Composite Index	13.83		
	Value Line Composite Index New	18.31		

*AMAX total return reflects the 11/15/93 merger/spin-off in which 1 share of AMAX became convertible into: .5 shares ALUMAX, .5 shares Cyprus AMAX, and .245 shares of AMAX Gold.

of various companies that buy and sell steel, I learned that steel prices were starting to firm. Moreover, the U.S. steelmakers were expecting the government to take action to protect them against the "dumping" of cheap steel by foreign producers in our markets. (As it turns out, they didn't get the protection they wanted.) I was also hearing that several of the old and inefficient steel plants in Europe, which for decades were run with massive government-subsidized losses in order to give tens of thousands of workers unproductive jobs, would be closed. Privatization would accelerate this process even further. This would be bullish for steel prices worldwide. I ended up recommending three steel companies and two other metal companies as well.

So my 1993 *Barron's* lineup was heavy on the cyclicals, although I didn't start out with the idea of buying cyclicals because that's what you're supposed to buy in the early stages of an economic recovery. It just happened that in the companies and industries I investigated, the biggest bargains were in cyclicals, and that's where earnings were on the move.

The seven S&Ls I recommended in 1992 all moved up. In 1993, I recommended eight new ones. I continue to be amazed at the performance of this entire group—doubles, triples, quadruples in dozens of issues that have come public since 1991, and hardly a dog in the bunch.

Many of the S&Ls have been doing well for several years, so this is not a situation in which you have to get in and get out. And there are still great opportunities as I'm writing this. If there's another part of the market where so many solid franchises are selling for less than book value and have good earnings growth, with the likelihood that sooner or later they'll be bought out by larger banks or S&Ls at a premium, I haven't discovered it.

The conventional worry on Wall Street is that the S&L party will come to an abrupt end as soon as the economy gets moving and interest rates begin to rise, thus wiping out the profits that S&Ls are making on the current and favorable interest rate "spread." I disagree. A very speedy economy with double-digit inflation could hurt the S&Ls, but an economy that lopes along at a reasonable pace would not.

In fact, the S&Ls will benefit from a steady economic improvement, because in a better real-estate market they can unload their foreclosed real estate more quickly and at higher prices, and they will suffer fewer defaults and delinquencies and thus fewer new foreclosures. This will strengthen their balance sheets and boost their earnings, because they won't have to set aside as much money to cover their loan losses. Also, as the economy improves, these thrifts can increase their lending to creditworthy borrowers, which in turn will add to their earning power.

Finally, I began to take an interest in California companies in 1993. This was because California was in a deep recession and the press reports were so negative you would have thought the entire state was going out of business. New England, my own home region, was in precisely the same predicament in 1990, and the headlines were just as gloomy, but if you managed to ignore the headlines and buy shares in depressed New England companies, particularly banks and S&Ls but also a few retailers, you've been well rewarded to date.

Taking the optimistic view that California would somehow survive its recession the way we New Englanders have survived ours (so far, we've done it with no job growth!), I put three California companies on my 1993 recommended list: Coast Savings Financial, Inc.; H. F. Ahmanson & Co., the nation's largest thrift holding company; and the Good Guys, Inc., a retail chain that sells TVs, stereos, and related electronic devices. I also recommended Fannie Mae, my long-term favorite company, which owns and packages mortgages. Its stock price was depressed because 25 percent of its mortgages are written on California real estate.

THE 24-MONTH CHECKUP

To the six-month checkup of the Lynch portfolio that appears on pages 284–304, we can now add the 24-month checkup. With so much attention given to the ups and downs of stock prices, it's easy to forget that owning a stock is owning a piece of a company. You wouldn't own a rental building without checking every once in a while to see that the units are well maintained and the place isn't falling apart, and likewise, when you own a piece of a company you must stay in tune and watch for new developments.

After doing my lastest round of homework on the companies described in the text, I can report the following:

Allied Capital Corporation II has been a short-term disappointment, as reflected in the stock price. Through no fault of the company, what I hoped would happen in 24 months is going to take much longer. The company had all its equity ready to invest in loans, but it hasn't been able to put all its money to work. Part of its plan was to buy loans from the Resolution Trust Corporation out of the portfolios of S&Ls that were taken over by the government. The idea was to invest in creditworthy borrowers, who were paying 10–11 percent interest.

The unforeseen problem was that a lot of other investors, including banks and the so-called vulture funds, were also trying to buy these loans. Allied couldn't get the ones it wanted, and it wasn't about to lower its standards and purchase the riskier variety. So it sat on its cash, getting 3 percent in the money market. This was not a productive situation for shareholders, who were paying Allied Capital an annual 2 percent management fee.

Allied Capital II is gradually buying loans, but at a slower pace than anyone expected. Meanwhile, the best investment has been the company that manages the Allied funds, Allied Corporation, whose share price has doubled in a year.

Speaking of management companies, *Colonial Group* had a gain of 69.7 percent in 24 months. Once again, when billions of dollars are pouring into mutual funds, as they have in recent years, it pays to invest in the folks who own and operate the mutual funds.

My passion for the nursery companies (*General Host, Sunbelt,* and Calloway's) was a big mistake. I deluded myself about the entire matter. I was so impressed with the fact that consumers were buying plants, rakes, shovels, mulch, etc., in record numbers and that gardening would be to the 90s what cooking was to the 80s that I overlooked the fierce competition among the gardening stores. It's as fierce in plants and flowers as it is in the airlines.

Much of the traffic has gone to the discount centers at K mart, Home Depot, etc., which sell a minor assortment of greenery and huge quantities of fertilizer, mulch, pesticides, and gardening tools that otherwise might be sold by Sunbelt or General Host. I underestimated the impact of the discounters and also the perseverance of the moms and pops in small gardening centers, who are toughing it out and lowering their prices to compete with the discounters. The chain store nurseries are being squeezed at both ends. The extreme weather that we've had—deluges, droughts, etc.—hasn't done them much good either.

Calloway's, a company that made a favorable impression on me when the stock was selling at $8, sold for $3.00 at the end of 1993, and what looked like a growth opportunity a few months ago is now a potential turnaround. It's also a potential asset play, with $1.30 in cash, no debt, and 17 buildings in the Dallas area.

I thought of Sunbelt as a possible takeover candidate, and sure enough, it was taken over by General Host. Alas, the stock was selling for $6.25 when I recommended it, and the buyout price was $5. This was a Pyrrhic victory.

If you still believe in Sunbelt, you can continue to own a piece of it by buying shares of General Host. This hasn't been such a hot prospect either. The sales at its Frank's Nursery & Crafts outlets have been disappointing. Overall, 1993 was a terrible year for Frank's. We've had record heat waves across the country, causing a lot of people to stay indoors and avoid the garden.

General Host may turn around and prosper in the future, but as in the case of Allied Capital, it's going to take longer than I expected.

Pier 1 Imports is also part of the nursery story—it owned a majority interest in Sunbelt before Sunbelt was bought out by General Host. Pier 1 has struggled with the sluggish economy, but it continues to gain market share from the neighborhood furniture stores. I'd say the company is definitely on target.

The immediate future of *CMS Energy* was riding on a judicious settlement of its rate case with the Michigan Public Service Commission, and I had no clue what the outcome would be. I understood the company well enough to know that at $18.50 a share, the stock was a decent buy even if the company got a lousy settlement. So the risk/reward ratio was favorable.

In March 1993, the Michigan PSC made its ruling, which wasn't terrific from the CMS point of view, but was favorable enough to cause the stock price to advance to the mid-$20s. At this level, it became a hold.

Phelps Dodge had a prosperous 1992 because of cost-cutting and because copper prices went up. A softer copper market in 1993 caused the company, and the stock, to stall. If you own shares in a mining company, you'd better keep tabs on the market for whatever is coming out of the mine.

Body Shop is a case where the company did not perform well in 1992, but the fundamentals improved in 1993. When I recommended the stock, it was selling for 325 British pence, and I suggested that investors take a small position that could be increased if the price went down. Did it ever. In February 1993, it hit a low of 140 pence! I never imagined it would fall that far, but one can never predict how far a price may fall. If you own enough stocks, one of them is bound to suffer a similar decline.

When that happens, it's time to review the story. If the story is still good, then you're happy the stock price fell 50 percent, because you can buy more at a bargain level. So the important issue was not that Body Shop had fallen, but why it had fallen.

I called the company and got caught up on the story. Body Shop still had no debt and was continuing to expand into new markets. This was all positive. On the other hand, the company was hurt by the terrible sales in Britain, its home market. Apparently, the British recession had caused people to cut back on soaps and shampoos, an unfortunate development for the crowds in the underground. Or maybe they were buying normal shampoo and not spending 4 pounds on seaweed-and-birch shampoo or Rhassoul mud shampoo from the Body Shop.

Three of the four countries with the most Body Shops, Canada, Britain, and Australia, were all in recessions. And in the U.S., several competitors had appeared with their own lotion-and-potion stores. But the Body Shop will get most of its future growth from other countries, such as France and Japan, where its stores have opened without competition. I see this as a global enterprise in the second decade of a three-decade story. If anything, the story has gotten better than it was when I started following it in 1992. I've checked with my friend the ex-librarian, and she's so delighted with her Body Shop franchises that she's bought one more. I recommended Body Shop again in January 1993 at less than half the price I first bought it at in 1992.

At *Sun Distributors*, a major development occurred four years ahead of schedule. In September 1993, the company announced that it was considering a plan to sell off its various divisions. Investors expected that such a sale might occur, but not until 1997, the last year Sun Distributors will enjoy the tax advantages of being a master limited partnership.

After the company is sold, the owners of Sun's Class A stock will get $10 apiece for their shares, and the owners of the Class B stock will get whatever is left from the proceeds of the sales. I recommended Class B in *Barron's* in 1992 and 1993.

Sun Distributors had been working to maximize the value of the B shares by reducing debt and reducing costs. Several months before the company announced that it was putting itself up for potential sale, it completed a deal to refinance its long-term debt. Because the company's debt problem was a potential overhang, this was exciting news, and you could have read about it in the annual report. Moreover, its annual earnings had increased steadily, even during the recession, and it continued to bring in $1 per share per year in free cash flow. Theoretically, this meant $1 per year was added to the intrinsic value of each share of Class B.

This was another case of the company doing well and the share price going nowhere. Class B had been selling in the $2.50–$3 range for more than two years, and then it jumped to $4.40 in September 1993, the month when the possible sale was announced. The stock market can test your patience, but if you believe in a company, you hold on until your patience is rewarded.

The Class B shares might have fetched $8 a share or even more if the company had stayed intact until 1997. I feel the same way about the potential sale as I felt about Taco Bell being acquired by PepsiCo in the late 1970s. Taco Bell shareholders made a quick profit, but the ongoing enterprise had the potential to be 10 times as rewarding.

Tenera, my limited partnership in recovery, has not fully recovered. If it weren't for the debt-free balance sheet, Tenera would have been a goner long ago. Before you invest in a company that's clinging to life, make sure it has the cash to pay the medical bills.

The stock price rose and then fell, and as of this writing the price is about half of what it was when I recommended the stock in January 1992, and about the same as it was in January 1993 when I recommended the stock again. The company has a new COO and $2 million in the bank, which it has used to buy back some of its own shares. It has attracted new clients for its utility management services, and its problem projects are reduced from six to two. The contract dispute with the government is not yet resolved, but the company has set aside enough money to cover itself if it loses. A win would be a bonus.

The way I see it, if the company never recovers, the liquidation value is $1 per share, and if it does recover, the stock goes to $4.

Two other master limited partnerships I continue to follow but didn't recommend in 1992 are worth mentioning. *Cedar Fair,* the

Table PS-2. **LYNCH'S** 1992 *BARRON'S* PORTFOLIO: 24-MONTH UPDATE

Ticker	Company	Total Return 1/13/92– 12/31/93	Price* 1/13/92	Price 12/31/93
ALTI	Allied Capital Corporation II	−14.11%	$19.00	$14.25
—	Body Shop	−30.77	325p	225p
COGRA	Colonial Group—Class A	69.70	17.38	28.00
CMS	CMS Energy Corporation	43.30	18.50	25.13
EAG	Eagle Financial Corporation*	101.81	10.97	20.50
FNM	Federal National Mortgage Association	19.34	68.75	78.50
FESX	First Essex Bancorp, Inc.	222.68	2.13	6.75
GH	General Host Corporation	−1.32	7.75	7.00
GM	General Motors Corporation	87.45	31.00	54.88
GSBK	Germantown Savings	287.15	14.50	54.75
GBCI	Glacier Bancorp, Inc.*	117.37	10.12	21.00
LSBX	Lawrence Savings Bank	225.00	1.00	3.25
PBNB	People's Savings Financial Corporation	85.42	11.00	18.75
PD	Phelps Dodge Corporation*	60.97	32.50	48.75
PIR	Pier 1 Imports, Inc.—DEL	23.53	8.00	9.75
SVRN	Sovereign Bancorp, Inc.*	250.90	3.83	13.13
SBN	Sunbelt Nursery Group/DE	−44.99	6.25	3.44
SDP.B	Sun Distributors, L.P.	65.87	2.75	4.25
SNTV	Sun Television & Appliances, Inc.*	130.48	9.25	21.25
CUTS	Supercuts, Inc.*	31.26	11.33	14.88
TLP	Tenera, L.P.	−42.11	2.38	1.38
	Lynch's 1992 Portfolio Total Return	**80.43**		
	S&P 500 Stock Index	19.19		
	NASDAQ Composite Index	25.77		
	Value Line Composite Index New	33.07		

*Split adjusted.

amusement park company, has continued to thrive after its acquisition of the Dorney Park amusement complex near Philadelphia, which I visited with my family in 1993. It has one of the highest splash rides in the world. More to the point, the stock has a 6 percent yield with certain tax advantages until 1997, and the company continues to grow by adding new rides and making acquisitions. It could become an acquisition target itself. I can think of a lot of buyers out there, particularly the entertainment giants, which might want their own amusement parks with Bart Simpson rides or Arsenio Hall of Fame rides or whatever. Disney has already bought a hockey team and named it the Mighty Ducks, so imagine how well it might do if it bought an amusement it knew something about. It could turn Dorney Park into Buena Vista World.

EQK Green Acres, the partnership that owns the shopping center on Long Island, completed a refinancing of most of the debt that was hanging over the company. Two other bits of positive news were reported in 1993: (1) Home Depot's acquisition of a piece of EQK property, which helped reduce debt; and (2) the purchase by the principal shareholder and CEO of 56,000 additional shares for himself, as noted in a quarterly message to shareholders.

The stock price of EQK rose after the announcement of the refinancing, but not right away. This is another example of how investors don't need inside information to profit from good news. Even after good news is made public, Wall Street can be slow to react.

EQK also has announced that it may convert to a real-estate investment trust (REIT). This will strengthen the balance sheet and enable the company to borrow money at lower rates. In the conversion, the company would have to compensate its major partner, the Equitable, by giving it shares in the new REIT. But the new structure would allow EQK to use its financial clout to buy additional shopping centers, the way Cedar Fair has bought other amusement parks.

Supercuts has made a startling announcement: It will open 200 additional outlets in New York, to be owned by the company in a joint venture with another partner. The company is borrowing money to pay for this expansion, and this will penalize its 1993–94 earnings. Whereas analysts expected Supercuts to earn 80 cents in 1994, it is likely to earn less.

For the longer term, the new stores will accelerate the growth rate of the company. The stock continues at a p/e ratio that's below the market multiple. In today's market, investors are paying a lot more for companies that are growing more slowly and aren't industry leaders, which is what Supercuts has become. Customers continue to line up for the Supercuts shampoo and trim. The all-important same-store sales increased 4–5 percent over the past year, without any increase in prices.

A recent quarterly report includes a coupon good for a $3 discount on a haircut, which may be another reason to own the stock, but after my shearing in Boston, I'm declining the offer.

Sun Television & Appliances, the Ohio retailer, has had a memorable year. In 1993, same-store sales were up 15.2 percent and the company had opened 11 new stores in the past two years. After its triumph in local markets, Sun TV is on the march to Pittsburgh, Cleveland, and Rochester and soon it will enter Buffalo and Syracuse. By deploying its forces from one end of the Great Lakes to the other, Sun TV makes it more difficult for competitors to establish themselves in between. The company is growing at 20 percent and selling at less than 20 times 1994 earnings, and the stock price has more than doubled in 24 months. If the price gets hit in a stock-market correction, I'd be inclined to buy more.

General Motors has been the least-admired of the Big Three, but it may be the best performer over the next few years. Although I recommended all three automakers at the beginning of 1993, and Chrysler has had a great year to date, a reason to like GM is that it sells a lot of cars overseas. GM will benefit when Europe comes out of its recession.

Before the end of the current upswing in car buying in the U.S. (there's still a pent-up demand, as described on pages 241–242), GM also has a decent shot at turning a profit on its domestic car business. With a 30 percent share of the market, it ought to be able to make a profit—Ford makes money with 20 percent and Chrysler with 10. GM has already turned the corner on trucks, and its non-automotive divisions are doing well, so even if the company only manages to break even on cars in the U.S., it could earn $10 or more per share.

This is a different sort of turnaround from, say, IBM's. For IBM to recover, it has to make money in the U.S. computer market, but GM can recover without making money in the U.S. auto market.

Fannie Mae is still underappreciated on Wall Street, and undervalued as well. This company is as close to a sure winner as you'll find. It has a growing share of a booming business. At the end of 1993, the stock price was only slightly higher for the year, despite the company's three strong quarters.

Fannie Mae has only 3,000 employees and it makes $2 billion in profits. Few businesses are more predictable or measurable. Wall Street is always looking for predictable, consistent growers—what's the matter with this one?

The lastest worry about Fannie Mae is that low interest rates will clobber the earnings as millions of homeowners refinance their mortgages. A few years ago, people were worried about high interest rates. Fannie Mae doesn't care what the interest rates are. Because much of its debt is "callable," when interest rates decline Fannie Mae can reduce the cost of its borrowing. The savings on the debt will offset the losses in revenue from the refinanced mortgages. The profits are locked in.

A second worry is that Fannie Mae will be undone by the recession in California, because 25 percent of the mortgages it owns or guarantees are on California real estate. Fannie Mae did get hurt by the Texas recession a few years ago, but that's old news. It has tightened its underwriting standards. The average Fannie Mae mortgage is for $100,000 or less, and in California its mortgages have a loan-to-value ratio of 68 percent, the highest of any lender in the state. Its loan delinquency rate has fallen for seven years in a row, even during the national recession, and currently stands at .6 percent, a historic low. This is not inside information. Fannie Mae mails it out to any shareholder who asks for it.

A third worry is that Fannie Mae is related to Sallie Mae, the company that handles student loans. Sallie Mae got blasted by President Clinton and by Congress, both of whom said the government could do a better job. This is a doubtful assertion, given the record of the post office, but no matter. The politicians were determined to set up a government competitor to Sallie Mae, and they are getting their wish.

Nevertheless, Fannie Mae has nothing to do with Sallie Mae. Last year, Congress passed a bill redefining government-sponsored corporations, and Fannie Mae was left intact. Earnings were up nearly 15 percent in 1993 and projected to be up another 10–15 percent in 1994. Give Fannie Mae a normal valuation in today's market, and it's a $120 stock.

I've already brought you up-to date on the S&Ls—*Eagle, Glacier, First Essex, Germantown, Lawrence, People's Savings Financial,* and *Sovereign.* About the wisdom of investing in mutual savings banks as they come public, I couldn't be more emphatic.

There are 1,372 mutual savings banks and thrifts that may yet convert to public ownership. If there is one in your neighborhood, open a savings account there. If you have $50,000 and deposit $1,000 in 50 different thrifts that aren't yet public, you will improve your chances for participating in a conversion. As the number of lending institutions continues to be reduced by takeovers and buyouts, it's a good bet that all the mutual savings banks and S&Ls will eventually convert.

NEWS FLASH!

As we put this edition to bed, the government's Office of Thrift Supervision has slapped a moratorium on savings bank conversions. The problem is that some officers and directors have been taking advantage of these deals by giving themselves options to buy shares at reduced prices. A few have gotten shares for free. The government wants to stop this profiteering by insiders. Hearings are underway in Congress, and the whole process is being reviewed.

I'm all for that. Meanwhile, only two percent of the depositors nationwide have taken advantage of their opportunity to buy shares at the favorable initial prices. So 98 percent have turned their backs on these superb deals at their own local thrifts in their own neighborhoods. My guess is that once the rules are changed so that insiders can't reward themselves with freebies, the conversions will be allowed to proceed. This is one case where it will pay to keep up with current events.

INDEX